Unplayed Melodies

The publisher gratefully acknowledges the generous
contribution to this book provided by the Music Endowment
Fund of the University of California Press Associates
and by Brown University.

Unplayed Melodies

Javanese Gamelan and the Genesis of Music Theory

MARC PERLMAN

University of California Press

BERKELEY   LOS ANGELES   LONDON

Unless otherwise noted in captions, all music examples
are by the author.

University of California Press
Berkeley and Los Angeles, California

University of California Press, Ltd.
London, England

Library of Congress Cataloging-in-Publication Data

Perlman, Marc.
    Unplayed melodies : Javanese gamelan and the genesis of music
theory / Marc Perlman.
      p. cm.
    Includes bibliographical references (p.) and index.
    ISBN 0-520-23956-3 (cloth : alk. paper)
     1. Music—Indonesia—Java—History and criticism.   2. Gamelan
music—Indonesia—Java—History and criticism.   3. Melody.
    I. Title.
    ML345.J3 P46   2004
    781.2'4'095982—dc21   2003006432

Manufactured in the United States of America
13 12 11 10 09 08 07 06 05 04
10 9 8 7 6 5 4 3 2 1

To my teachers, whose thoughts inspired this book:
Suhardi (R. L. Wignya Bremara, 1937–2000)
Sumarsam
Supanggah

Contents

Illustrations

TABLE

Acknowledgments

The questions I address in this book have preoccupied me for twenty-five years. The search for answers brought me to Java, and if I have made any progress toward solving these puzzles, it is due to the generosity of my friends and teachers there. First and foremost, then, I owe thanks to the Javanese musicians who welcomed me into their world, and especially the three musicians whose ideas of unplayed melody so fascinated me: Sumarsam, Supanggah, and Suhardi—three remarkable men it has been my great good fortune to know. Though they are too numerous to list here, I am grateful to all of the musicians mentioned in this book for generously sharing their knowledge with me during my research in Java. And I'm grateful to I. M. Harjito for his ongoing generosity. If this work falls short of their expectations—if anything in it displeases—I ask their pardon: *nyuwun pangapunten sadaya kalepatan kula*.

When I began this research I was trying to integrate the insights of cultural studies and postcolonial studies into ethnomusicology. I did not plan to apply cognitive anthropology to Javanese music, and I certainly did not envision comparing the historical course of Javanese musical theorizing with that of European art music. Several people inspired this shift of focus, and it is a pleasure to acknowledge them here.

Carol Krumhansl showed me by her example how to think like a cognitive psychologist. An invitation by Lawrence Zbikowski to the "Music, Culture, Mind" conference at the University of Chicago gave me the opportunity to try out my ideas about intra-domain analogical thinking with a group of kindred spirits. It was at that conference that I met the cognitive musicologist David Huron, whose combination of personal warmth, intellectual brilliance, and *joie de vivre* makes him the best possible advertisement for cognitive musicology—and, indeed, for the academic life in general. Around the same time, the philosopher Monique Roelofs convinced me that one can appreciate the insights of cultural studies without being swallowed up by relativism. And throughout it all, David E. Cohen showed me how the history of music theory, when approached with rigorous scholarship and imaginative sympathy, can find the unexpected at the heart of the familiar.

This book relies on material first reported in my dissertation, and I offer renewed thanks to the people I acknowledged there: especially my advisers, Mark Slobin and Roger Solie, and Harold S. Powers, who has inspired me for over thirty years. My dissertation research in Java was conducted under the auspices of the Lembaga Ilmu Pengetahuan Indonesia and the Sekolah Tinggi Seni Indonesia, and I thank them again for their sponsorship.

Two people nurtured this book in its earliest stages: Robert Labaree, who combines vigorous, acute intellect and passionate enthusiasm, and Margaret Sarkissian, who allowed me to subject her to my earliest draft chapters. The final form owes a great deal to my editor, Mary Francis of the University of California Press. The book you are holding is considerably more user-friendly and approachable (not to mention affordable) than the book I originally wanted to write. That book—provisionally titled *Making Sense in Javanese Music*—will, I hope, appear at some future time; but that the present book exists at all—something rather than nothing—is because of Mary.

A book with so many musical examples in two separate notation systems is a challenge for any publisher, and I'm grateful to Laura Harger and Elizabeth Ditmars for the care and extraordinary attention to detail with which they guided my manuscript into print. And thanks to Heike Gleiss for the photograph of Suhardi that appears on the cover—it means a lot to me.

The writing of this book was supported by a semester's sabbatic leave at Brown University and by a fellowship at the Stanford Humanities Center. My colleagues at both institutions gave me invaluable intellectual stimulation, moral support, and practical advice. Many people read portions of the manuscript, and it is a pleasure to thank them here: James Baker, Cynthia Benton-Groner, Anna Maria Busse Berger, Karol Berger, Scott Burnham, Thomas Christensen, David E. Cohen, Richard Cohn, Stephen Hinton, Cristle Collins Judd, Louise Meintjes, Steven Sloman, Claudia Strauss, Sumarsam, R. Anderson Sutton, Michael Tenzer, Wayne Vitale, and Larry Zbikowski. Michael Tenzer and Andy Sutton in particular have been extraordinarily supportive throughout the writing of this book; I couldn't have done it without them.

In writing this book, as in all things, I drew strength from the support of my family. And for keeping me on track, I thank my metaethics consultant, Agnieszka Jaworska.

Conventions of Transcription and Orthography

All musical examples are notated using one variant of the Central Javanese cipher notation known as the *Kepatihan* system. The tones of *sléndro* are represented by the numerals 1, 2, 3, 5, and 6. The tones of *pélog* are represented by the numerals 1 through 7. A period appearing in place of a numeral indicates that the previously played tone is sustained. For example, the period in the phrase 6 .532 represents a continuation of the tone 6. A period has the same durational value as a numeral. A numeral without a dot above or below it represents a tone of the central octave. A dot above the numeral indicates a tone of the high octave; a dot below, a tone of the low octave.

The notation of metrically fixed parts is end-weighted: the last notated tone of a group of tones has the most metric importance (example 1). Spaces between groups of notes are for legibility and do not affect the durational values of the notes.

Strokes on the structural instruments are indicated by superior letters: T for *kethuk;* P for *kempul;* N for *kenong;* G for *gong.* Since *gong*-strokes always coincide with a *kenong*-stroke, the former can also be written as NG. When the *kenong* "slips"—that is, when it plays a pitch that forecasts the future course of the melody *(plèsèdan)*—the N is followed by an arrow and an encircled numeral indicating the pitch of the *kenong*-stroke (example 1).

Each instrument or voice carries a single melodic line except for the *gendèr barung,* which is played with two hands, each of which typically has an independent part. The tones available in the *sléndro* tuning system and their distribution between the player's hands are illustrated in examples 2a and 2b.

EXAMPLE 1. A sample *balungan* passage in *Kepatihan* cipher notation.

N ↘ ⑤

2356 3532
 ↑   ↑

Points of major metric importance

EXAMPLE 2. Key to notation for the *gendèr barung*.

2a. Tones of a typical *sléndro gendèr barung*, from low to high (left to right):

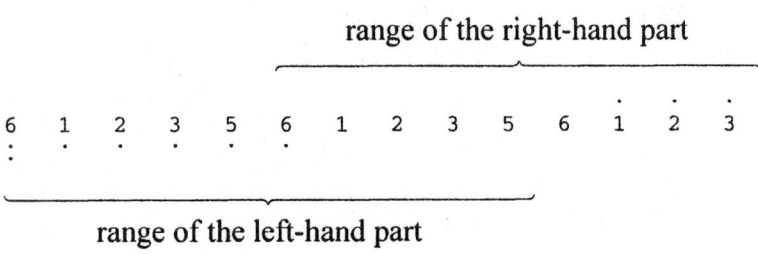

range of the right-hand part

6   1   2   3   5   6   1   2   3   5   6   1   2   3

range of the left-hand part

2b. Disposition of the hands in notation:

[notation for the right hand]
------- ------- ------- -------
[notation for the left hand]

2c. Location of the metrical stress points:

3 2 3 6 . 5 6 5 2 3 5 3 5 6 5 3
------- ------- ------- -------
6 5 6 . 5 6 1 5 6 6 653 5 56356
    ↑   ↑   ↑   ↑

The *gendèr* parts notated herein are metrically bound, hence their notation is end-weighted. The broken line separating the notation of the left and right hands is divided into groups such that the rightmost beat of each group is the metrically important one.

In example 2c the arrows point to the metrically important beats. The rightmost arrow shows the location of the cadential tone *(sèlèh)* of this pattern, played by the left hand (in this case, 6).

In vocal music, texts are provided only when they are specific to a particular melody. The disposition of syllables is indicated by underscores: notes connected by underlining are sung to a single syllable.

STAFF NOTATION

After much soul-searching, I decided to include in this book trans-notations of the cipher examples in the Western staff. Since such trans-notations must be very approximate and can be misleading, I reached this decision with some reluctance. In the end, however, I decided that the potential gains outweighed the disadvantages, for the following reasons.

It has long been acknowledged that Western notation is not an ideal ethnomusicological tool. It is especially unsuited to Javanese music. The pitch materials of the gamelan cannot be represented easily on the staff; furthermore, the staff conveys a presumption of pitch standardization incompatible with the variability of Javanese intonation. In metric terms, the Western representation of downbeats as points of origin rather than points of arrival (beginnings rather than ends of metric units) is inhospitable to Javanese music as well.

Nevertheless, to shun the Western staff entirely in favor of Javanese ciphers is to fetishize notation. Notation is a communicative tool, one that like language requires a good deal of practice if its use is to become automatic and effortless. Because of the cross-cultural implications of this research, I wanted to make its results at least potentially accessible to those without Javanese musical training. Addressing such an audience in Javanese cipher notation would be as sensible as directing a speech in Javanese at monolingual Anglophone listeners. Therefore, at the risk of misrepresenting the music and annoying its adepts, I have introduced these very rough approximations. True, readers who have never heard Javanese music will not be able to use this notation to mentally construct accurate aural images of the sounds. In my defense I submit that this is an unrealistic goal; no form of notation (separated from its associated musical practices and habits) has

TABLE 1. Conventional Western Pitch Equivalents of the Tones of Javanese *Sléndro* and *Pélog* Used in This Book

	Sléndro			*Pélog*	
Pitch Name	Cipher Notation	Western Equivalent	Pitch Name	Cipher Notation	Western Equivalent
barang	1	c–	panunggul	1	c♯
gulu	2	d	gulu	2	d
dhadha	3	e+	dhadha	3	e
			pélog	4	f×
lima	5	g	lima	5	g♯
nem	6	a	nem	6	a
			barang	7	b

this power. I hope only that the staff notations will render the musical examples recognizable: I do not expect my readers to be able to sight-sing the conventional phrase type *ayu kuning* with perfect Javanese intonation and style, but with the aid of the staff notation I hope they can identify it when they hear it—or at least tell it apart from the phrase type *puthut gelut*.

I have therefore not tried to find exact Western pitch equivalents for the Javanese scales (table 1). For example, all of the intervals of *sléndro* are larger than major seconds but smaller than minor thirds. However, I have somewhat arbitrarily modified only two of the Western equivalents to pitches of the *sléndro* scale: thus I represent *dhadha* (3) as e+ and *barang* (1) as c–, while representing the other tones as unmodified d, g, and a. This has the unfortunate effect of making the interval between 3 and 1 look like a minor sixth, whereas the interval between 2 and 6 *(d* and *a)* looks like a perfect fifth—though in fact they are both considered to be the same interval *(kempyung).*

Similarly, I have not tried to reproduce the end-weighted nature of cipher notation in the staff equivalents. Metric stress is indicated as in Western music, with the downbeat of the measure falling immediately to the right of the barline. (Thus the transnotations start with a downbeat not represented in the cipher notation. I have often provided the tones that fall on this initial downbeat, even though they are not given in the cipher notation.)

In the notation of vocal music, I indicate texts only when the association of text and melodic line is fixed. Since in most cases the choice of text is left up to the singers, I generally indicate only the disposition of syllables by means of slurs.

ORTHOGRAPHIC CONVENTIONS

The orthography used in this study is that officially adopted by the Indonesian government since 1972, with certain added diacritical marks for Javanese. For both Javanese and Indonesian, consonants are pronounced as in English, except that *g* is always hard, *d* and *t* are dentals, and *c* is pronounced as *ch* (e.g., "church"). *Ng* represents a velar nasal, the sound of *n* in English "think" or of *ng* in "thing." In Javanese, *dh* and *th* represent palatal *d* and *t*, respectively. (Hence *th* sounds something like an ordinary English *t*, not the *th* sound in "pathetic.")

In both Javanese and Indonesian, the vowels *o, u,* and *i* are pure ("Italian"). In Javanese, *e* without diacritics represents a schwa (the sound of the initial and final vowels in "America"); *é* is pronounced as the *a* in "flame"; *è* is pronounced as in "bet." *A* in Indonesian is always pure. In Javanese its sound varies according to its position: in unclosed final and penultimate syllables it is pronounced like the *aw* in "saw." Some writers approximate its sound by using *o* instead; hence we find variants like *Sri Wibowo* and *Sri Wibawa.*

Some proper names are spelled according to earlier transliteration practice, in which *j* represents modern *y, dj* represents *j, tj* represents *c,* and *oe* represents *u.* In cases where a word appears with variant spellings (e.g., *céngkok, cèngkok*), I have followed W. J. S. Poerwadarminta, *Baoesastra Djawa* (Groningen: J. B. Wolters, 1932).

IN-TEXT REFERENCES

References to published materials follow the standard author-date system. References to interview materials are indicated by a date in the form: day (Arabic numeral), month (Roman numeral), year; for example, (24.xi.85). Since I did not usually record my interviews, most quotations from my teachers are taken from my field notes. When my teachers recounted anecdotes of their personal experiences, I have reproduced them using the third-person pronoun.

Sources for the musical examples are usually given in the captions. When *balungan* notation is not attributed, it is taken from Mloyowidodo (1976).

Introduction

Karawitan, the music of the Central Javanese *gamelan* ensemble, is a highly sophisticated tradition of multipart music. As many as eleven distinct melodic lines create a rich orchestral texture, one that owes nothing to Western principles of harmony or counterpoint. Ethnomusicologists call this texture "heterophonic," meaning that it presents different versions of a single melody simultaneously. This is a very imprecise term, but it does capture an important truth: Javanese musicians usually consider the many melodic lines of a gamelan composition to revolve around one central melody. Paradoxically, however, it is not obvious what that melody is. Javanese musicians themselves disagree over it; some have suggested that there is no *audible* melodic basis but only an *implicit* one, a central melody neither played nor heard. In this book I show how they arrived at this conclusion and argue that these notions of an unplayed, "inner" or "essential" melody can teach us much, not only about Javanese gamelan, but about musical thinking in general.

For decades Javanese pedagogical and notational practice seemed to assume that the center of gravity of a gamelan composition, and the improviser's guideline, is a melody known as the "skeleton" or "framework" *(balungan)*, played in a slow, even rhythm on a set of seven-keyed instruments called *saron*. This assumption became received wisdom within ethnomusicology as well. But in the 1970s a number of Javanese musicians called this premise into question. Some declared that the "framework" was not the melody played on the *saron*. Indeed, some musicians went further, arguing that the actual melodic basis was not the "framework" at all, but an unplayed, inaudible, or "inner" melody.

This idea deserves our attention, for two reasons. First, it is quite unusual when viewed in a global perspective. True, we do have some reports of unplayed melodies in other traditions of multipart music. For example, there is the so-called silent theme tradition in jazz composition (Tirro 1967). In various music cultures, the guiding part in an ensemble can temporarily drop out while the musicians maintain it in their imaginations.[1] But there is nothing especially mysterious about these sorts of unplayed melody: they are melodies that can be, and often are, played, but are simply left unstated in some contexts. Javanese implicit melody is not of this type, however; it is more abstract and is never actually sounded.[2] Furthermore, musicians conceive of it in different ways. Relatively few musicians speak explicitly of it, and while the ones who do so are highly respected, there is no consensus among them on its nature.

This combination of insistence and elusiveness—the shared sense that an unplayed melody exists, combined with the difficulty of saying exactly what it is—this, too, is unusual, and challenges our understanding. These implicit-melody concepts come from the heart of the Central Javanese tradition; they are not the idiosyncratic musings of marginal, eccentric dilettantes but were formulated by three of the most thoughtful, highly respected musicians. They emerged to some degree independently of one another: two of the musicians were entirely unaware of the work of the third. Under these circumstances, the resemblances between these concepts suggest the existence of a common melodic world that they all describe, a world shared among Javanese but hidden to outsiders.

Yet we cannot use them as a clear window through which to view an otherwise occluded musical reality. For they are not representatives of a timeless, homogeneous, undifferentiated body of "Javanese musical thought." It is not only that the formulations studied here are historically recent (they are not yet four decades old), and not only that they differ significantly from one another. Each concept of implicit melody is in some way incomplete or problematic; each one has its areas of indeterminacy, moments when the shape of the postulated melody becomes impossible to specify.

This indefiniteness, along with the limited multiplicity of unplayed melodies, their disparity within unanimity, makes their study doubly rewarding. By comparing Javanese views of Javanese melody we can seek insights both specific and general: we can learn much about the nature of gamelan music but also about the nature of musical cognition—in particular, how musicians think creatively about their music. It is precisely the plurality of implicit-melody concepts that is so valuable; we need to pay close attention to these variants rather than withdraw to a level of general description at which the details of variation blur into a single vague outline. This conceptual diversity is neither a veil concealing the "reality" of Javanese music nor testimony to its fluid and ultimately ungraspable multivocality. These concepts differ in specific, systematic ways, and the patterning of these differences can illuminate important aspects of the music. There is something about the melodic texture of Javanese music that makes the postulation of an unplayed melody plausible but makes its nature impossible to specify precisely. This in-betweenness or neither-norness of the music is, I suggest, its partial patterning, the coexistence within it of regularity and irregularity, of order and contradiction.

Learning to play Javanese music involves learning conventions governing the proper relationships between the melodic parts. Some parts are considered to "guide" or "lead" *(nuntun)* the others, and musicians who know the conventions of interpart relations can hear and follow such guidance. But this guidance is not uniformly offered or completely reliable: in some parts of some compositions it is very explicit, in others it is obscure, and occasionally it is entirely absent. The idea of melodic guidance is not illusory, but neither does it explain everything. I suggest that Javanese concepts of unplayed melody serve to regularize this almost-but-not-quite-regular notion of melodic guidance.

My first aim in this book, then, is to use the multiplicity of Javanese concepts of unplayed melody to shed light on *karawitan*. But to do so I need to consider those concepts not as pure reflections of musical reality, but as products of thought, the results of deliberate meditation, the creative insights of particular individuals in specific socio-historical situations. Hence my second goal: to use the implicit-melody concepts to enlarge our understanding of the nature of musicians' thinking about their own music, and to focus our attention on the *creative* aspect of this thinking—an aspect that has received relatively little attention in the past.

MUSICIANS' THINKING AND MUSICAL SCHOLARSHIP

In this regard Javanese music can contribute to a longstanding tradition of reflection about musicians' conceptualizations of their music. These conceptualizations have attracted the interest of scholars in more than one musical discipline, but there has been little general discussion of their nature and a surprising range of attitudes toward them.[3] On one hand, obeying the anthropological "injunction to see things from the native's point of view" (Geertz 1983:56), we have wanted to use "native" thought as a shield to prevent the imposition of ethnocentric notions on a musical practice for which they are inappropriate. Ethnomusicologists, borrowing a term from anthropology, often refer to this understanding-from-the-inside as "emic" understanding; but this concern is shared by some theorists of Western music as well. Music analysts disturbed by the anachronistic application of latter-day analytical methods to earlier repertories have called for historically informed analysis (Hatch and Bernstein 1993:5).[4]

On the other hand, we have also inherited a certain suspicion of "native" theories. All theories are partial representations of music, since all theorists pass "the raw material of practice through a filter of theoretical presuppositions" or confine them in the "straitjacket [of an] intellectually respectable system" (Wright 1978:2, 25). No theorist can resist "the urge to idealize musical practice in ways congruent with one's world view" (Burnham 1993:77). Music theory is never a direct insight into musical reality but is always culturally mediated (Christensen 1993:305): "A music theory, like any kind of theory, is a construction, not an induction. It represents an interpretive grid superimposed upon musical material that determines the analytic questions to be posed, and the language and arguments deemed sufficient to answer them." This grid may consist of prestigious nonmusical bodies of knowledge; it may be beholden to ancient or even foreign ideas, transmitted or adopted uncritically because of the high social status of their sources. For all these reasons, music theory can be "a curious animal with a life of its own" (Reck 1983:I, xii–xiii), quite distant from the realities of practice (Hood 1971:226).

Some of this diversity of attitude is probably due to the ambiguity of the notion of "the native musician's point of view." It can refer to the processes of perception or production that operate out of the musicians' awareness, or the tacit rules of stylistic appropriateness that musicians become conscious of only when they are violated. It can mean the basic categories they use, the taken-for-granted concepts they apply. Or it can mean the results of reflection: verbalized, consciously elaborated analyses or explanations, whether offhand comments in answer to a student's question, lore transmitted for generations through oral tradition, classification systems written down in treatises, or rules taught in the curricula of educational institutions.

The changing ethnomusicological understandings of the "native" musician's point of view are clearly visible in the history of the research tradition known as ethnotheory.[5] Starting in the 1970s, inspired in part by the anthropological subfield of ethnoscience, some ethnomusicologists made the musician's conceptualization central to their work.[6] Echoing the anthropological ambition to describe a culture "from the inside out rather than from the outside in" (Tyler 1969:20), they hoped to describe musicians' cognitive systems, to capture the "tacit rules" that governed their musical behavior (Feld 1974:211–12). But in practice this anthropological interest in unconscious cognitive systems often gave way to the study of musicians' conscious conceptualizations, perhaps because researchers wanted to correct Western academic assumptions that musicians in nonliterate societies could not possibly reflect on their music. Hugo Zemp ended his famous study of the music theory of the 'Are'are by suggesting that "musical theory is not the privilege of the 'art music' of the so-called 'high civilizations' of Europe and Asia" (1979:34–35). Similarly, Feld observed that Zemp's research, and his own on the music theory of the Kaluli, made it impossible to continue to regard music theory as "a special accomplishment of the West that allows 'us' to analyze 'them'" (1981:44).

At that time, ethnotheory's concept of the "native musician's point of view" seemed to assume a greater degree of homogeneity and integration of culture than actually exists. It posited a timeless cognitive system shared among musicians, one that structured both the sound patterns of the music and the verbalized concepts of the performers. When Feld (1981:45) described music theory as "a conceptual system of cultural principles that scaffold cognition, production, and interpretation of patterned sound in a social setting," he posited an ideal cultural unity of thought and action. His principles *by definition* were common to the sounds produced and the "native" understandings of those sounds, since they were responsible for both their "production" and "interpretation." Hence his music theory was guaranteed to be consubstantial with the sounds it describes and explains.

Furthermore, early ethnotheory research largely focused on concepts assumed to represent a cultural consensus, ignoring issues of intracultural variability, historical change, and individual intellectual creativity. For example, Rice's study of what he called "Bulgarian musical thought" (1980) was based on "the isolated comments of a few individuals" (1994:334 n. 5), but he submerged their individualities in his picture of a shared cognitive system.

The weakness of ethnotheory at this stage was not its intention to understand music from the cultural insider's point of view—to get at the musician's knowledge—but rather its overly homogenized concepts of culture and of knowledge. First, in assuming that there could be something such as *the* native's point of view, it understated the internal heterogeneity of experience within any society. Today, aware that "musical knowledge and understanding is rarely, if ever, uniformly distributed in society" (Rice 1994:334 n. 5), ethnomusicologists pay closer attention to individual differences in musical conceptualization (cf. Koskoff 1982; Porter and Racy

1988) and to the coexistence of different kinds of expertise, with their own patterns of distribution, among the community of musicians (Brinner 1995b:74–109).

Ethnotheory's second oversimplification was its assumption that musical knowledge is a single type of thing, thereby underestimating the internal heterogeneity of cognitive processes. John Baily was one of the first to complicate this picture by pointing out how musicians' concepts can function in two ways: while some have a "dynamic role in the control of ongoing musical performance," others are "representational" models, which "describe what the musician already knows but which [have] little or no direct role in performance" (1988:114). Since then, ethnomusicologists have gone on to recognize the existence of several distinct types of musical knowledge, active and passive, verbal and nonverbal, automatic and deliberate (Rice 1994:66, 98–103; Brinner 1995b:32–39).

But this new attention to the differentiation of musical knowledge and its uneven distribution in society still leaves certain questions unasked. It does not address the historicity of musical thinking; it does not show us musicians' conceptualizations changing over time; and it does not show us the factors responsible for change. We do have a few case studies from which we can begin to inventory the agents of historical transformation; Rice (1994), for example, describes the effects of the nation-state's changing ideologies, as well as new modes of transmission (cf. also Brinner 1995b: 157–59). Other studies document foreign influences: Marcus (1989), for example, shows how many changes in Arab music theory were the result of its encounters with ancient Greek music theory and modern European theory. Harold Powers's study of innovation in North Indian music theory suggests both external influence and the recovery of past thought as catalysts for change. V. N. Bhatkhande (1860–1936)—a Brahmin and English-language-educated lawyer—devised a new classification of rāgas, designed to be more rational and objective than the traditional one, grouping all rāgas into ten seven-tone scale types. The idea of classifying rāgas by their scales—a familiar practice in South Indian, but not North Indian, music— seems to have been suggested by a seventeenth-century treatise Bhatkhande encountered during a trip to South India in 1904 (Powers 1992c:11–12).

Most recently, ethnomusicologists are starting to combine the study of conceptual change with the awareness of individual variability. Monson (1998), for example, describes the formulation of George Russell's Lydian Chromatic Concept as a theory and pedagogy of jazz improvisation, exploring its relation to his interest in spirituality, and its legitimating function, to help establish jazz as an intellectually respectable art music.

In this book I too focus on the creativity of individual conceptualizations, the creativity of three Javanese musicians who, working under particular circumstances, arrived at new ideas about their music. Like Monson I wish to relate each musician's ideas to his or her personal interests or social environment. But because I consider more than one individual, I cannot remain content with a particularizing view. I also try to discern the general processes of creativity that give rise to this variety of new ideas.

Thus I am as interested in the *how* as the *what* of implicit-melody concepts. I focus on process as well as product; hence I deliberately avoid speaking of "musical thought" but prefer to talk of musicians' *thinking*. Treating their conceptualizations as creative activity has several advantages, drawing our attention to aspects of Javanese music we might otherwise overlook—but also opening up possibilities for cross-cultural study that a static view would foreclose.

STUDYING MUSICIANS' THINKING AS COGNITIVE PROCESS

Studying Javanese music in terms of cognitive processes can draw our attention to the great deal of time and energy musicians may put into the quiet effort to make sense of their music. Although Central Java (unlike India, China, or Europe) does not have a long tradition of written music theory, some of my teachers—who had at most an elementary-school education—astonished me with their extraordinary analytic virtuosity. Their idiosyncratic, unstandardized vocabulary was not based on an institutionalized system of instruction but on personal insights. Thus one of my reasons for exploring Javanese musical thinking was to pay tribute to the creative intelligence displayed by my teachers in their performing, their teaching, and their theorizing.

A focus on cognitive process can also bring us close to the experiential texture of musicians' thinking. In particular it reminds us how opaque a music can seem to its own master practitioners. Javanese music is a place of mystery even for its adepts; as one of my teachers put it, "There's much that is mysterious" about *karawitan* (Joko Sungkono 9.xi.84). In cognitive terms there is nothing mysterious about this mysteriousness. Musical knowledge, like all human knowledge, is not a homogeneous body of exhaustively cross-referenced cognitions but is quite disparate and incompletely interconnected; it is, so to speak, partially disarticulated. We become mysteries to ourselves when our different kinds of knowledge are dissociated from each other. This is why Javanese musicians struggled to theorize the music they knew so intimately; like the Kabyle who tried to explain the rituals of their society to Bourdieu, they were "striving to recover a meaning that was both their own and alien to them" (1990a:3).

By studying musical thinking as a creative activity, we can bring out its dynamic and contextual nature. We can focus on the individual agency of individual musicians without ignoring the external factors conditioning their activity and making it possible. By considering musical thinking as situated action, we can relate the apparently abstract, disembodied realm of musical structure to music's social, cultural, and historical matrix. The ideas of implicit melody examined here were formulated in a postcolonial context, and two of them were framed in direct or indirect response to Western ethno-musicological theories of gamelan. To understand them we need to understand the unique historical conjuncture that is twentieth-century Java: the cultural value of indirection and allusiveness in traditional Javanese society, and the dynamics of Self and Other within situations of radical power imbalance that have been analyzed in postcolonial theory.

But insofar as musical thinking marshals general human cognitive resources, its study also leads beyond the scrutiny of a single culture to opportunities for cross-cultural and comparative exploration. I argue that Javanese musicians arrived at their concepts of implicit melody by analogical thinking, a cognitive process of creativity in many societies and many cultural domains. Seeing the cognitive strategies of creative thinking at work in Java may help us notice their presence in other musical arenas. Indeed, by helping us understand how musicians come to think in new ways about their music, it may even fill a lacuna in the historiography of Western music theory, the relative lack of attention to "the dynamics of *discovery* in music theory" (Bent 1992:9).

These are all worthy reasons to study Javanese musical thinking, but they were not the reasons that originally motivated me. I became fascinated by musicians' conceptualizations because I was introduced to Javanese music and Javanese thinking about music at the same time. I first learned to play gamelan music at Wesleyan University, from Sumarsam, a particularly thoughtful young musician. He graciously and patiently tried to answer all my questions. As I soon realized, however, he was also seeking answers to some of his own questions.

Sumarsam had worked closely with Martopangrawit, a highly respected senior performer and theorist at the state conservatory in Solo, Central Java. He promptly made himself at home in the world of scholarship. He had already coauthored one published article, and continued to write. I was one of the students he asked for editorial help, and I spent many hours discussing his drafts with him. In retrospect, the experience of watching Sumarsam make sense of his music may have taught me to think of *karawitan* less as an established fact, a body of received practice and principle, than as an invitation to discovery.

I went on to study in Java at a fortunate historical moment. The attempt to systematically make musical knowledge explicit is relatively young in Central Java. When I arrived in Solo in 1981, the history of this effort was little more than a century old and most of its significant developments were still within living memory. Its single most important practitioner, Martopangrawit, was still active, and he graciously agreed to talk with me on a weekly basis.

I was equally fortunate to meet Suhardi, the leader of the musicians at the studio of Radio Republik Indonesia in the nearby city of Yogyakarta. Suhardi was not a theorist, but he was a formidable thinker. He never wrote down his insights, but he loved to teach. It is not a rhetorical exaggeration to say that he overwhelmed me with his analytical skills. Every Friday I took a two-hour bus ride to Yogyakarta to spend the afternoon with him. He would talk about the music and demonstrate musical examples nonstop for hours. I would emerge from his house after dark and catch a bus back to Solo, and for the entire trip I would sit, physically drained but with brain buzzing and thoughts whirling as I tried to assimilate it all.

I thus had a rare opportunity to observe how the most accomplished Javanese musicians found ways to think about their music, and how they thought *creatively* about it. I have written this book about the ways Javanese musicians think as a contribution to ethnomusicology, and to musical scholarship in general; but I was drawn to the subject because I came under the spell of these charismatic performers and teachers, who made musical thinking irresistibly compelling.

PLAN OF THE BOOK

After an initial chapter providing my theoretical vocabulary (chapter 1), I present a brief introduction to the Javanese gamelan and its melodic organization (chapter 2), followed by a detailed account of the relations between the parts (chapter 3), and of the *balungan* and the general question of melodic guidance (chapter 4). These chapters establish the background for the examination of Javanese musical thinking in the rest of the book. I first describe the social and historical context in which musicians theorized their music (chapter 5), and then present the three implicit-melody concepts of

Suhardi, Sumarsam, and Supanggah, bringing out both their similarities and differences (chapter 6). In chapter 7 I investigate the musical, cultural, historical, and cognitive factors responsible for those similarities and differences. Finally, I turn to an unrelated musical tradition—Western art music—to see if the processes of creative thinking active in the formulation of the Javanese implicit-melody concepts can be found elsewhere.

The style of *karawitan* described herein is the style developed by the two royal courts of the city of Solo (Surakarta), as practiced by the court musicians and their students and as taught at the two state conservatories in that city. The information on which this study is based was gathered through a preliminary period of study in the United States (1973–80, at Wesleyan University; the American Society for Eastern Arts Summer School at Seattle, Washington; and the Center for World Music, Berkeley, California); archival research (at Cornell University; the Radya Pustaka Museum, Surakarta; Reksa Pustaka Library, Surakarta; Sono Budojo Museum, Yogyakarta; National Library, Jakarta); and participant observation in Indonesia (1981, 1984–87, 1990), mostly in Solo but also in Yogyakarta and Jakarta. My years of formal field research were supplemented by brief informal visits (1994, 1997, 1998). Since I began teaching at Brown University in 1995, I have continued to learn from two of my teachers at nearby Wesleyan University, Sumarsam and Harjito, and also at Brown, where Harjito teaches Sekar Setaman, the Brown University gamelan ensemble.

   I was particularly fortunate to have had seven years in which to prepare myself for fieldwork. Thanks to my teachers in the United States (Sumarsam, K. R. T. Wasitodiningrat, I. M. Harjito, Soekanto Sastrodarsono, Turahjo Hardjomartono, R. Soetrisno, Martati, S. Maridi, and S. Ngaliman), I was able to learn enough about Javanese music, dance, and *wayang* to carry on informed conversations with the *empu* (masters) of the Javanese arts as soon as I arrived in Indonesia. My teachers there included most of the major senior figures in the Surakarta music scene, many of the most prominent musicians of the middle generation, and several talented younger musicians. I studied with, or was helped by, over thirty musicians, young and old; their ages spanned four decades. R. Ng. Martopangrawit (1914–1986) and S. Mloyowidodo (1911–1997) were, at the time, the last major representatives of the music of the senior royal court under Paku Buwana X (1893–1939). Turahjo and Wahyopangrawit represent the succeeding generation. Harjito is one of the most respected musicians to emerge from the first generation to be trained in the higher music conservatory, the Indonesian College of Art (STSI; formerly the Indonesian Music Academy, ASKI); Darsono and Joko

Sungkono left STSI early and sought professional careers outside its walls. Supanggah, one of the most astonishingly versatile and creative members of the same generation, is also a prolific composer with an international reputation; as of this writing he is the director of STSI. His scope and originality as a theorist are not fully dealt with in these pages; I hope to do more justice to his ideas on another occasion.[7]

1 Cognitive Preliminaries

The Nature of Musical Knowledge
and the Processes of Creative Thinking

In this book I tell the stories of three Javanese musicians who found new ways to think about their music by postulating an unplayed melody. This abstract entity, they felt, was the key to a more profound mastery and understanding of their music's dense melodic texture. To follow these stories in full we will need to learn many details of Javanese musical practice and many cultural and historical facts about twentieth-century Java, but there is one aspect of these stories that invites attention from a broader viewpoint, a viewpoint I present in this chapter.

The musician's quest for insight through the positing of abstract musical entities is not unique to Java. We find it in other music cultures as well: in Western art music, perhaps the best-known example of this is the radical abstraction of the Schenkerian *Ursatz*, the two-voice contrapuntal sketch that represents the deepest level of underlying voice-leading in a tonal composition; but even such familiar concepts as that of "triad" and "chord root" are abstract, though to a far lesser degree. Musically, these concepts are all very different from the Javanese implicit-melody concepts, and from one another. But though they differ in content, I suggest that they were produced by similar cognitive processes.

I wish to describe the formulation of Javanese implicit-melody concepts with a vocabulary that might be applicable as well to other cases of innovative musical thinking. I regard the Javanese case as one example of a general phenomenon, the fashioning of abstract musical ideas. In this chapter I consider this larger phenomenon, asking how musicians can arrive at such ideas; to answer this question I draw on some of the basic concepts of cognitive psychology and cognitive anthropology.

The abstract ideas we will encounter in this book function as simple models musicians devise to understand the complexities of their experience. They

13

inhabit an ideal order of things, an ideal realm of regularity that musicians posit to help them navigate in and explain the wild, sprawling particularity of their own musical practices. In psychological terms, this is an entirely general strategy, not a uniquely musical one. In everyday life, in the arts, in science, and in philosophy, the mind deals with our complex, variegated world of particulars by typifying and generalizing, constructing a realm of simplicity and uniformity.

This cognitive strategy of positing an ideal order of things behind the spotty, desultory regularities on the surface of experience is so ubiquitous that we do not have a name for it. In philosophy Derrida calls it *"the* metaphysical exigency"*: "the enterprise of returning 'strategically,' ideally, to an origin or to a 'priority' held to be simple, intact, normal, pure, standard, self-identical, in order *then* to think in terms of derivation, complication, deterioration, accident, etc." (1977:93). For want of a more precise or evocative term, I will borrow Derrida's language to refer to it herein.

I am interested in the ways musicians furnish this ideal realm with abstractions, with new, previously unimagined entities such as unplayed melodies. I suggest that *analogy* is an important cognitive strategy musicians use for this purpose, and in this chapter I will describe some of the varieties of analogical thinking, and situate them among other vehicles of creative thinking: conceptual combination, extension, differentiation, and metaphor.

Unplayed melody in Javanese music is not singular, but manifold; there are at least three kinds of implicit-melody concepts. Analogical thinking can account for this variety, since diverse and even conflicting theoretical ideas can be produced through this one cognitive process. As we shall see in chapter 6, analogy allows Javanese musicians to posit different sorts of implicit melody by using different kinds of actual melody as their conceptual models.

But this is only one dimension of cognitive diversity; there are others we must recognize as well in order to understand Javanese ideas of unplayed melody. For the abstract entities generated through analogical thinking can serve different purposes. The origin or "priority" located in the ideal realm of regularity can be interpreted as an *ontological* priority—a source or cause—but it can also be treated as a *practical* priority (a rule of thumb for the student, or a mnemonic aid for the performer).

We posit abstractions to bring order to our experiences, to organize the endless particularities of life into general patterns. But this drive to connect and integrate, this "effort after meaning" (Bartlett 1932:227), has no preordained role within our overall cognitive economy. It finds order and regularity wherever it can, making comparisons, noticing similarities, indifferent to the uses to which they may be put. The abstract entities it generates can function within theoretical explanations, but they can also serve simply as handy pedagogical tools.

Hence analogies can serve different purposes because the processes that produce them and use them can work independently. The multifunctionality of analogical thinking is one example of what Bradd Shore calls the mind's "polyphonic structure" (1996:313), and what I (to avoid confusion between literal and metaphorical musical terminology) will refer to as cognitive disarticulation.

Just as the "effort after meaning" is intrinsic to human cognition, so is disarticulation. The disparate, decentralized nature of knowledge is the context of the mind's pursuit of order; it is the space musicians fill when they think new thoughts about their music. It explains why so many musical "rules" have exceptions; it explains why musicians can be mysteries to themselves—why they are often able to do something but can't explain how they do it.

Before we survey the processes of creative thought, then, we should first learn something about the coexistence of generalization and disarticulation. For this purpose I borrow or adapt certain key concepts from cognitive psychology and cognitive anthropology: classical versus nonclassical categories, and implicit versus explicit knowledge. I introduce these in a nontechnical way, without presuming familiarity with any particular musical tradition insofar as this is possible. I rely on nonmusical examples, supplemented by musical ones taken from traditions likely to be familiar to American readers—particularly Western art music and jazz.[1]

CULTURAL SCHEMAS AS SIMPLIFIED WORLDS

Musical experience would be impossible without generalization. No matter how concrete, how unmediated our relation to music feels, if we can hear the same melodic contour at different pitch-levels (what Western musicians call a sequence), or if we can tell the difference between the verse and chorus of a 1950s rock song, we are perceiving the uniqueness of the sounds in terms of general patterns. In this respect music is like every other aspect of human life. Generic knowledge, the abstract representation of regularities, is crucial to our ability to interpret current experience and shapes our expectations of the future (D'Andrade 1995:122).

Psychologists sometimes use notions of *schemas* or *models* to describe the dependence of perception, memory, and cognition on generic knowledge (Strauss and Quinn 1997:161–67).[2] A schema or model is a typification, an idealization, a simplified world (Sweetser 1987:44) that abstracts away from the manifold complexities of the real world. Schemas testify to the mind's need to find easily graspable dimensions of order, a need to smooth out the rough edges of experience—sometimes to the point of oversimplifying or stereotyping. The mind is biased toward "cognitive structures . . . that fall short of perfect matching of the environment in the direction of too great simplicity or symmetry" (Campbell 1988:467). But despite the disadvantages of oversimplification, cultural schemas are necessary because they fulfill this need for order. By stitching together our experiences into significant shapes, they make our lives possible. Drawing connections between our diverse perceptions and thoughts, they exemplify the "effort after meaning" fundamental to all cognitive processes (Shore 1996:319).

The generality of cultural schemas accounts for the tendency toward integration long noted by scholars of culture, the tendency to bring different domains of experience into alignment. Insofar as the life of a community projects the sense of a coherent whole, that sense is due to the connections between these schemas: "The many cross-mappings among different cultural models guarantee a flow of meaning between discrete domains" (Shore 1996:117). We can describe this as the analogical transfer of a schema from one domain to others, or as the instantiation of very abstract, "foundational" schemas in several different domains (Shore 1996:53, 366). For example, the American interest in self-reliance finds expression in several ways: in the terms of political debate, in the hobbies people choose and the movies they watch (Strauss and Quinn 1997:118–20). Similarly, the valuation of individuality and autonomy is reflected in the way Americans describe their musical tastes and informs their vocabulary of musical approbation. For example, classical music critics reinforce the values of individualism when they deplore the faceless interpretations of "carbon-copy conservatory grads" and praise the performer who has an "immediately recognizable personality" (Schwarz 1993). Fans of popular music likewise say they respect performers who have a distinctive, individual sound (Crafts, Cavicchi, and Keil 1993:116) or who play to please themselves, not to court an audience (p. 83). These listeners may also claim to have distinctive musical tastes that individualize them and set them apart from other people (pp. 70, 72, 83).[3]

The sense of cultural consistency produced by the spread of schemas across domains was captured by earlier scholars in ideas like *Zeitgeist*, worldviews, cultural themes, core values, or *episteme* (Foucault). In ethnomusicology, it has inspired many attempts to find in musical relationships a mirror of social relationships (Blacking 1971:108). Perhaps the best-known example in Western music is the interpretation of the orchestra conductor as a heroic figure who does in music "what many in our time have tried to do in the field of social and political action: to resolve conflicts once and for all through the exercise of unlimited power" (Small 1998:86).

DISARTICULATED KNOWLEDGE

The sharing of common schemas across domains accounts for the "semantic coherence" of cultural life (Shore 1996:117). But global schemas do not organize everything, neither in society nor in any single mind. Cultural knowledge as a whole is not perfectly integrated or self-consistent; cultural models are not uniformly distributed within a society, and a variety of disparate models may coexist within even a small community. Similarly for the individual mind. If we could take a bird's-eye view of the cognitive contents of any mind, it would not look like a single, symmetrical, perfectly cut gemstone, but more like a shapeless mass of rock with nuggets of crystal embedded throughout. Schemas represent pockets of generality and order within that mass: they organize it, but in piecemeal fashion. Much of what people know and feel is unintegrated, lying in different compartments of the self, so to speak, where even mutually contradictory beliefs or values can persist. The disjointedness of schemas at the global level is one example of what Lawler calls the disparateness of knowledge (1981). I will refer to this sort of knowledge, distributed among disconnected or loosely connected cognitive islands of coherence, as disarticulated knowledge.

This fragmentation of cultural knowledge has been widely acknowledged over the past decades. The postmodern critique of the notion of culture as a timeless, bounded, cohesive entity has renewed our awareness of intracultural contestation, just as poststructuralist theory has emphasized how contradiction fissures the self. Integration is a moral ideal for us, and so it is difficult to talk about inconsistency in other than negative terms. But cognitively speaking, consistency is an expensive good, and there are sound psychological reasons to produce it on an as-needed basis; we do not, in general, stockpile it. Bourdieu writes of the "principle of the economy of logic, whereby no more logic is mobilized than is required by the needs of practice" (1977:110). We are fairly good at achieving local consistency; global consistency is much harder, and often serves no practical purpose. While we sometimes try to think globally, it requires an effort, for we live our lives locally. "For the most part we are only as consistent as we need to be to get things done" (Strauss and Quinn 1997:230).[4]

THE HETEROGENEITY OF COGNITIVE SYSTEMS

Disarticulation sets limits to generalization, roping off arenas of local consistency in all cultural domains: in language, regular verbs sit next to irregular verbs; in music, rules mingle with exceptions. But disarticulation is characteristic not only of the mind's contents, but of its systems and processes as well. Human cognition deploys a disparate collection of tools and resources. The mind acts less as a single, perfectly self-consistent, masterful agent than as a more-or-less coordinated ensemble, a team of specialists. Some psychologists compare the mind to a bundle of independent, interacting modules, mobilizing different kinds of concepts (Medin, Lynch, and Solomon 2000), drawing on different kinds of memory (Schacter 1996), employing different kinds of reasoning (Sloman 1996), or using different cognitive processes for different domains of experience (Hirschfeld and Gelman 1994). The members of the team cooperate smoothly, but they maintain their own styles of working. This becomes occasionally visible in dissociations, when the different kinds of memory or reasoning operate independently or produce disparate results.

This cognitive heterogeneity accounts for much of the opacity of human culture, and explains why music can be mysterious to its own expert practitioners. There are many ways of describing this heterogeneity, and psychologists do not all agree on the best way to distinguish different types of learning, memory, reasoning, or knowledge. For my purposes, it will be enough to isolate two dimensions of disparateness; for convenience I will refer to them as the distinction between classical and nonclassical concepts and the distinction between implicit and explicit knowledge.

Classical versus Nonclassical Categories

Cognitive psychologists recognize many different criteria for differentiating kinds of concepts or categories, but for our purposes we can distinguish two broad types. The first, sometimes called "Aristotelian," is rule-based; we can call it "classical." The second type, including what has been called "probabilistic," "exemplar-based," and "family-resemblance" categories, we can call "nonclassical."[5] Both types are vehicles of generalization—both gather up particulars and group them together—but they generalize in different ways.

"Classical," rule-based categories are those demarcated by a set of defining features, usually a relatively short list of necessary and/or sufficient conditions. A bachelor is an unmarried adult male human: here we have four necessary conditions that taken together are sufficient for the category "bachelor" to obtain. A major triad is a set of three tones consisting of the pitches a major third and perfect fifth above a root pitch. Rule-based concepts are useful because they draw strict boundaries; either a thing satisfies the rule—in which case it is included in the extension of the concept—or else it does not. There is no in-between, no ambiguity or room for doubt. And once a thing satisfies the rule, it has no further hoops to jump through: it is accepted into the category on the same basis as all the other category members. There are no grades of membership in the category; all major triads are equally major and equally triadic.

"Nonclassical," probabilistic, or family-resemblance categories do not behave this way. They cannot be defined by a short list of necessary and sufficient conditions. Wittgenstein famously pointed out how the category "game" cannot be defined simply. No matter what necessary conditions we postulate (say, "all games are competitive") we can find counterexamples of games that lack those features (for example, solitaire). Games resemble one another, not because they all share one or two common features, but because of a network of crisscrossing features (1958:32, §67). We say they share a *family resemblance.*

"Nonclassical" categories also demonstrate what psychologists call *graded structure.* Some members of a category are considered better examples than others. A robin is a better example of a bird than is a penguin. An apple is a better example of a fruit than is a watermelon. As a result, the further away we get from the "good" examples of a category, the harder it is for people to decide if the concept applies at all. Is a pumpkin a fruit? People disagree, and can change their minds about the issue. Thus such categories have *fuzzy boundaries.* Membership in such categories is not an all-or-nothing matter, but a question of more or less.

Most of the categories we use in daily life are like this: we cannot define them with necessary and sufficient conditions, and they have graded structure and fuzzy boundaries. We use nonclassical concepts to describe the natural world, but they can also be found in human cultural practices. "Bird" is a nonclassical category, since besides the prototypical robin or sparrow the concept also includes the marginal kiwi, penguin, and ostrich; the birds form a diverse family marked by crisscrossing traits. But irregular verbs, too, form a nonclassical category. Some English verbs form the past tense by change of vowel (sing/sang), and for others the past tense form doesn't change at all (cut/cut). But there are no rules that predict which kind of verb is which, and there are borderline cases: verbs treated as regular by some people, irregular by others (Pinker 1999:275–76).

Everyday Structuralism

The notion of the nonclassical category may in itself be a fruitful one to use in studying music. Zbikowski (2002), for example, finds nonclassical categories in his analysis of several Western compositions. But I am not here interested in myself *applying* such categories to understand musical entities or practices, but in the categories and strategies musicians use to think about those entities or practices. I am interested in how classical and nonclassical categories function in a music culture. And I am especially interested in the coexistence of these two types of concepts.

It seems that both types have important functions in human life. Nonclassical categories provide a convenient way to conceptualize the fuzzy webs of criss-crossing resemblances produced in nature and culture by historical change (Pinker 1999:282–83). Classical concepts may be necessary to explain the regularities of the natural world, but more important for my present purposes, we also find them useful in social life. We artificially sharpen distinctions, impose strict rules, and codify behavior when we have a special interest in regulating social coordination (Bourdieu 1990b:76–86).

Understanding the social uses of schemas means looking beyond the intrapersonal psychological realm that has occupied us to this point. For schemas also lead public lives in the extrapersonal realm, as external forms, public representations, what Bradd Shore calls "instituted models" (1996:50). We can think of them as embodiments of intrapsychic cultural schemas, objectifications in words (proverbs, myths), in material culture, or action (rituals, games).[6]

At the formal, official level, a society's instituted models often seem to draw sharply defined boundaries like "classical" concepts, though in practice they function "nonclassically." For example, Americans know that human maturation is a gradual process and that a youth does not become an adult in a single day; yet the government draws a line in the sands of time and permits people to vote or drink alcohol on the day they officially reach a certain age. Shore coined the term "native structuralism" to describe a society's imposition of a digital conceptual grid over the smooth gradations of social experience. Insofar as we represent our lived-out world in terms of simple categories, we become our own structuralists (cf. 1996:280).

Shore's idea of "native structuralism" is helpful, and I wish to develop and extend it in this book. Since my use of it may differ somewhat from his, I will speak not of "native," but of "everyday structuralism." This is first of all to emphasize that this phenomenon is not peculiar to third-world cultures or oral traditions. It is not found only in small-scale societies or those supposedly regulated by rigid customs. "Collective representations" in all human cultures make black-and-white distinctions.

The "polyphonic" structure of the mind thus expresses itself in human culture through the coexistence of classical and nonclassical concepts. In every society, when the formal, explicit, public, classical regulations of social life are put into practice, they are surrounded by flexible, fuzzy, nonclassical discretionary prerogatives. We shall see musical examples of this in the following pages; but first I must describe a second aspect of the mind's "polyphonic" structure, the coexistence of implicit and explicit knowledge.

Implicit and Explicit Knowledge

Paul Berliner tells a story about jazz teacher Barry Harris, listening to his students trying to improvise in bebop style:

> Four students demonstrated their phrases. After each, Harris smiled warmly and nodded in approval. At a fifth student's performance, however, he shook his head and remarked, "No, you wouldn't do that in this music." Stung by the rebuke, the student defended himself: . . . "But, give me one good reason why you wouldn't," the student protested. "The only reason I can give you," Harris replied, "is that I have been listening to this music for over forty years now, and my ears tell me that that phrase would be wrong to play." (1994:249)

Knowledge of musical style is one of many kinds of musical knowledge that, like linguistic knowledge of grammar or usage, is usually acquired and exercised without explicit formulation. Even in a music culture with a highly developed pedagogy, it is for the most part tacit—mute—knowledge, slowly absorbed through experience (Meyer 1989:10). Since we do not learn it through verbalized explanations or analysis, we are usually unable to put it into words. Our ears tell us when something sounds right or wrong, but supply no rationale for their verdict.

Few of us may have the deep creative immersion in a musical style necessary to speak with Harris's degree of authority, but we can all experience a comparable feeling of inarticulate assurance when it comes to our native language. During my fieldwork years in Indonesia people often asked me to help them with their English. I could correct their mistakes; I could tell them when they were wrong, but I couldn't explain why. My ears told me that it's wrong to say, "I have ever been to Jakarta," but I couldn't explain when to use "ever" and when not to. At first I would try to formulate general rules ("Use 'ever' only in questions"), only to stumble eventually against counterexamples ("That's the biggest drum I have ever seen").

How is it that we can have such inarticulate knowledge? Psychologists and anthropologists distinguish between "knowledge which is implicit, unverbalized, rapid, and automatic" and "knowledge which is explicit, verbalized, slow, and deliberate" (D'Andrade 1995:180). The differences between these two can be roughly characterized in terms of how they are learned and used. We acquire some of our cultural knowledge and skills through explicit tuition, but most we absorb by watching and imitating, in a process we may call "learning without teaching" (Atran and Sperber 1991; Rice 1994:64) or "guided discovery" (D'Andrade 1981:186–87). Knowledge transmitted in this way "from practice to practice" (Bourdieu 1977:87), obtained by example rather than precept, is more likely to remain tacit and unverbalized.[7]

Mute knowledge plays a large role in any music culture. It is built up relatively slowly, but can be summoned up to guide perception or action quickly and automatically. By contrast, when we learn a rule through explicit verbal instruction, we can understand the rule immediately but may be unable to put it in practice fluently. Indeed, we may have problems if the verbal rule conflicts with a schema we have already internalized (D'Andrade 1995:145). A Western singer, accustomed to twelve-tone equal temperament, when learning to sing Javanese music may know that she needs to "make the interval between the tones *nem* and *barang* a little wider than a major second," but this explicit instruction will probably not help her much at first—her internalized schema of Western intonation will take over as soon as she opens her mouth to sing.

The Interaction of Implicit and Explicit

Explicit knowledge plays a larger role in some music cultures than in others, but it is probably never entirely absent. Cultural transmission typically depends on both types of learning, explicit learning-by-precept and implicit learning-by-example closely intertwined (D'Andrade 1995:145). Even in music cultures where learners are expected to "pick up" the basics on their own, they often receive advanced tips in verbal form. We should thus pause to consider the various uses of explicit rules and their relations to implicit knowledge.

Often we combine a fully internalized, automatic skill with explicit pointers or reminders (Collins 1990:87–88). But when implicit and explicit knowledge coexist, they are not necessarily mutually consistent. Sometimes the explicit rules we give beginners do not in fact describe the skill we wish them to acquire, but only a sort of first approximation to it; Collins calls these "coaching rules" (1990:84–85). Teachers may present such a rule to the student, and even provide examples consistent with it, without realizing that their own performance does not perfectly fit the rule and may even conflict with it: that is, their implicit and explicit knowledge of the skill can be dissociated.

I encountered such a "coaching rule" in my first months' study of Javanese music. When Sumarsam gave me my first lessons on the *gendèr barung* metallophone, he showed me how to hold the mallets and how to damp the keys: when playing conjunctly, I was to damp the key previously played with the extremities of the hand at the moment I struck the neighboring key. For example, the right hand, holding the mallet between index and middle fingers, when moving to the right (ascending) would damp the previous tone with the edge of the thumb. When playing disjunctly, the hand could not stretch far enough to both strike a key and damp the previously struck key simultaneously; in such cases I was to damp *after* striking. With much practice I became proficient at this damping technique.

A few months later I attended the American Society for Eastern Arts Summer School, where I met some of the *gendèr* students of K. R. T. Wasitodiningrat ("Pak Cokro"). One of them, after watching me play, asked me why I sometimes damped "on the beat." I explained that I had been taught always to damp "on the beat" unless a melodic skip in the part made it physically impossible to do so. Pak Cokro's student told me to watch Pak Cokro play and I would see that he *never* damped "on the beat," but always slightly after. I found this to be true. The constant overlapping of tones, though just for a fraction of a second, gave a sustained quality to the melodic lines when Pak Cokro played. I wondered if Sumarsam played differently.

Returning to Wesleyan, I watched Sumarsam carefully the next time I saw him play *gendèr*. Sure enough, he too damped "after the beat." Naturally I asked him why he had taught me a damping technique that he himself did not use. To my surprise he insisted that he *did* damp "on the beat," simultaneously with the following stroke, as he had taught me. I protested that I had just seen him doing the opposite. Since we were sitting in front of a *gendèr*, he picked up a mallet in his right hand and played a few notes. To my relief he damped after the beat. I looked back at Sumarsam's face: he was staring at his hand as if it had a life of its own.

Making Implicit Knowledge Explicit

The next day Sumarsam told me that he had figured out why he had given me inaccurate damping instructions. He had learned *gendèr* technique by listening to and watching other players from an early age, but he learned how to *teach gendèr* in the conservatory. He taught me by using the pedagogy of his teachers there. He passed on their damping instructions, not realizing that he himself didn't follow them. Sumarsam's divergent implicit and explicit understandings of damping technique had thus coexisted for years in a disarticulated state, each cut off from the other. His implicit knowledge remained compartmentalized, unable to make contact with the explicit damping instructions he had received at school.

The story of how Sumarsam came to recognize the disparity between his implicit and explicit knowledge of *gendèr* damping technique seems to support an argument of Bourdieu's, to the effect that cultural knowledge acquired implicitly can not normally be made explicit; only culture contact or political or economic crisis can bring to consciousness the taken-for-granted (1977:168). Without motivation from outside the culture, a member of a society will never objectify or take a synoptic view of it (1990a:316 n. 43).

Culture contact is indeed one important catalyst for the cognitive processes of explicitation. In chapter 5 we will meet another example of this phenomenon, in which Sumarsam's exposure to Western theories of *karawitan* enabled him to make some of his implicit musical knowledge explicit.[8] But culture contact is not the only possible stimulus for people to reflect on their tacit knowledge. As Strauss and Quinn point out, this reflexivity is quite common, and is not limited to the "advanced" societies in which it is institutionalized. Indeed, Bourdieu himself quotes Kabyle proverbs and statements that reveal explicit awareness of supposedly unconscious knowledge (1997:46).

However, the act of formulating explicit knowledge is not a personal, isolated intellectual enterprise; it is a social act insofar as it responds to society's conception of the purpose and worth of that act. Music cultures vary greatly in their valuations of explicit knowledge, and the amount of effort people put into explicitation can vary correspondingly. European music history is full of examples of how social, political, and economic forces influence the process of verbalizing knowledge. Indeed, the birth of Western music theory is in part due to such forces: the ninth-century Carolingian attempt to associate itself with the glory of the Roman Empire, and its use of liturgical singing as a symbol of social unity, led to efforts to theorize plainchant (Rankin 1994). The Paris Conservatory's adoption in 1801 of a standard harmony textbook was part of its effort to standardize music pedagogy, which ultimately served its nationalist project, to define and propagate a truly French musical style (Gessele 1989).

"CLASSICAL" ABSTRACTIONS
AND "NONCLASSICAL" PRACTICES

This, then, is the cognitive ecology within which musicians think new thoughts about music. It is filled with a diversity of mental flora and fauna: concepts both classical and nonclassical, knowledge verbalized and unverbalized. The space of disarticulation—the disparateness of isolated cognitive islands, the disjunction between implicit and explicit knowledge, the incongruence of rule-based and family-resemblance concepts—is a space in which new ideas can grow. Motivated to a greater or lesser degree by their society's encouragement or by cross-cultural contact, musicians fill this space with new descriptions and explanations—and sometimes with abstract entities as well.

These entities, occupying the ideal realm of simplicity and order described at the beginning of this chapter, serve to make the real world comprehensible. The manifold complexities of musical practice are to be understood as issuing from the simple abstractions through processes of "derivation and complication." But when these explicitly formulated abstractions take the shape of "classical" concepts there will necessarily be a gap between them and the "nonclassical" real-world categories they are meant to render intelligible—a gap that invites further abstraction. This is easily seen when we consider the role of generalizations in music pedagogy.

Of all the abstractions we formulate to understand music, the simplest and most concrete are generalizations. Explicit generalizations have the form of classical, rule-based concepts; but as such they have built-in limitations for understanding nonclassical categories. They impose strict borders in place of graded structures and fuzzy boundaries; they reduce the criss-crossing similarities of family resemblances to monochrome contrasts. In trying to approximate nonclassical concepts by means of rule-based ones, we often oversimplify, singling out a few regularities within the overall phenomenon. The result is "everyday structuralism."

Psychologists studying how American college students learn nonclassical concepts in artificial laboratory situations have noted that they often use a two-stage strategy. Confronted with stimuli deliberately constructed to elude classical categorization, the students initially try to fit them into classical categories nevertheless. They devise a rule that captures some of the structure in the array of examples. Then they accommodate the exceptions, shoehorning them into the categories they built in the first stage. That is, they initially project too much structure, too much organization, into the examples to be categorized, and only later do they deal somehow or other with the exceptions (Ahn and Medin 1992).[9]

How we feel about the discrepancies between rule and exception depends to a large extent on what we plan to do with the rule. Because of the characteristic looseness, the disarticulation, of cognitive organization, an explicit generalization can often be put to use in various ways. If our interest in the rule is entirely pragmatic we will be more tolerant of exceptions than if we are in search of a theoretical explanation. If our rule of thumb fits reality well enough, and nothing terribly important is at stake, we may not even be aware of the points of mismatch between the two. Or if we do notice the exceptions, we may feel no need to account for them. Or we may offer informal observations about them, noting which seem more, and which less, objectionable; this is especially common in pedagogical contexts.

Consider, for example, the constraints on the use of octaves and fifths in the teaching of European counterpoint. In the most historically influential codification of contrapuntal practice—Fux's *Gradus ad Parnassum* of 1725— the four "fundamental rules" prohibit direct motion into a perfect consonance: that is, two voices may not both ascend or both descend into an octave or perfect fifth. Either they must move in contrary motion or one voice must be stationary.[10] The most conspicuous violations of this principle are the so-called forbidden parallels, parallel octaves and parallel fifths.

In fact, this rule is clearly not intended to be universally valid, even within the scope of Fux's own exercises. The rule only appears to set up a strict dichotomy between "forbidden" direct motion on one hand and "permitted" oblique or contrary motion on the other; in fact we find a graded structure. All cases of direct motion into a perfect consonance are not equally bad; some are more tolerable than others, depending on the context. In three-part writing Fux already allows it in some circumstances (1965:76–77), and also in four-part writing, where "one is sometimes forced to accept a hidden succession of fifths or octaves on account of the requirements of the melody, or of the imitation" (1965:110). For the most part Fux does not attempt to spell out these extenuating circumstances; he does not detail the processes of "derivation and complication" that link the ideal realm of his general rule with the actualities of practice, leaving them in the realm of implicit knowledge. He does, however, offer one simple generalization about gradations of acceptability, remarking that the "prohibited" motion is more tolerable in inner voices than outer ones (1965:123).[11]

The teacher's simple rules need have no more than pragmatic justification as convenient "training wheels" for the student. These overgeneralizations are pedagogically useful, since they aid the student's first efforts without overburdening her memory. They cannot provide a full grasp of the details of the style, but they do not need to; the student will acquire implicit knowledge of those details over many years of exposure. The gap between rule and exception is not intellectually troublesome. Had Fux been challenged by a feisty student to justify his overly general prohibition of parallel perfect intervals, he might simply have replied that not everything in music can be taught by rules: some things "are learnt more by judgement, usage and the observation of works by experienced composers, than by rules" (Fux 1992:240).

But we can also turn our generalizations to more ambitious explanatory ends, and if we do so we will have to take the exceptions more seriously. To close the gap between rule and exception we might complicate the rule, identifying the types of circumstances in which it does or does not apply. Or we might replace the rule with a system of interacting rules, as in some of the computer programs designed by artificial-intelligence researchers to write species counterpoint. Or we might go beyond the immediately observable and postulate abstract entities.

Generalizations of the sort we find in counterpoint treatises are phrased in terms of such easily observable entities as perfect fifths and octaves, or contrary and direct motion. One way we might try to improve the fit between these rough generalizations and the actualities of musical practice is to replace the directly observable with the abstract. This was Schenker's approach to the problem of parallel perfect intervals: he used the power of abstraction to demonstrate that the exceptions to Fux's rule were more apparent than real.

Schenker showed that many so-called forbidden parallels are "surface" phenomena produced by figuration, chromatic passing tones, or rhythmic displacements. When they are reduced to their underlying forms they can be seen to comply with the rule. In other words, Schenker eliminates the exceptions by moving to a level of abstraction—the middleground—at which they do not appear.[12]

This strategy—of using abstract entities to find regularity behind the confusing multiplicity of musical experience—is cognitively more complex than simple generalization. How do we come to postulate unheard musical entities? Given a typically complicated, messy bit of musical reality to make sense of, how do we find within or behind it a pattern of well-regulated but unobservable simples?

We do so by creative thinking. And just as musical knowledge, with its "classical" and "nonclassical" aspects and its "everyday structuralism," exhibits the same cognitive patterning as human knowledge in general, so does creative thinking about music employ the cognitive processes found in creative thinking in general.

COGNITIVE PROCESSES OF CREATIVE THINKING

We do not yet have a general theory of creativity; we cannot say exactly how, when, and why people will think creatively, or what social, cultural, historical, or motivational factors influence the degree and type of creativity they exhibit. Some creative acts are world-changing, bringing undreamt-of things into existence; Boden (1994) calls this historical creativity. Psychologists, however, are also interested in mundane creativity, the creativity of uttering an ordinary sentence that by chance has never been spoken before, or the creativity of the learning process, the creativity of discovering for oneself something that is already known.

Psychologists have proposed several ways to identify the basic cognitive processes that make creative thinking possible (Ward, Smith, and Vaid 1997:5–18). As is often the case, their analytical frameworks differ, and their categories overlap. As before, I will abstract away from the controversies over details, and will describe four general engines of creativity that can also be found in music: combination, extension, differentiation, and analogy or metaphor. These processes are operative in musical creativity—in composition and improvisation—as well as in theorizing about music, and even in the learning process.[13]

Conceptual Combination

One of the most frequently remarked devices of creativity is the combination of two or more existing things to form a new one. This is quite common in music, where new instruments, compositions, ensembles, genres, or styles are often produced in this way. Adolphe Sax invented the saxophone as a cross between a brass and woodwind instrument, essentially combining the body of a bass ophicleide with the mouthpiece of a bass clarinet. Ravi Shankar composed two concertos for *sitār* and orchestra, and combined North Indian instruments with the Japanese *koto* in other works. In jazz, improvising musicians can combine harmonic elements from different genres or compositions: Paul Berliner describes one performance in which bassist Larry Gray filled a blues progression with substitute chords inspired by the distinctive harmonies of John Coltrane's "Giant Steps" (1994:384). Many new developments in popular music take the form of stylistic combinations: rockabilly, jazz/rock fusion, rap metal, or the Afro-Celt Sound System, to name only a few.

The creative power of combination is also available on the conceptual plane. Theorists who devise new accounts of music can combine existing concepts or analytical approaches. In the history of Western music theory, Rameau provides what is probably the most striking example of this, and we shall discuss it in chapter 8. But conceptual combination remains a source of new insights for theorists. For example, in a review of Agawu's *Playing with Signs,* Drabkin praises the author's "synthesis of current thought" in which the best insights of Schenker, Tovey, Rosen, Ratner, and Allanbrook are "fused" (1991:382).

Conceptual Extension/Expansion

People can also create new things by modifying, stretching, or extending old ones. This is common in instrument building, where new instruments are often created by the extension of existing families into new registers. The nineteenth-century expansion of the clarinet family to include piccolo and contrabass clarinets is one example.

On the conceptual level, this process is well known in music theory, and can be seen particularly easily in the recent extension of the concepts and techniques of Schenkerian analysis to repertories for which they had not been intended: medieval and Renaissance music (Salzer 1967, Mitchell 1970), post-tonal or atonal music (Morgan 1976, Baker 1990), popular music (Everett 1987, Gilbert 1995), and non-Western music (Stock 1993).[14]

Conceptual Differentiation

Another means by which people act creatively is by making distinctions within what had previously been undifferentiated wholes. This is evident in the evolution of popular music styles, such as the emergence of acid rock, hard rock, and soft rock out of rock and roll, or the more recent differentiation of electronic dance music into house, jungle, ambient, acid house, drum and bass, and so on.

We will meet examples of conceptual differentiation in music theory in later chapters (in chapter 5, with the separation of the concept of the *balungan* from that of the *saron* part; and in chapter 8, where Thomas Campion discerns the chord root within the notion of the bass note). Here I only wish to point out that differentiation also occurs in the learning process. Bamberger (1991) documents its importance in the story of Jeff, an eight-year-old child learning to play the tune "Twinkle Twinkle Little Star" on a set of bells. Jeff acquires the concept of a scale by learning to differentiate the tune from the tonal resources it employs, as he realizes that its pitches can be ordered independently of the order of their appearance in the song (1991:234).

His insight results from his ability to separate what had seemed inseparable, "a gradual coming apart of the possible features and relations of musical structures that are initially taken as unitary wholes" (1991:264).

Jeff learned a musical concept through a process by which children also learn about the physical world. For example, children develop the concept of density through differentiation, learning to conceptually separate density from weight (Smith, Carey, and Wiser 1985). Scientists, too, arrive at new concepts through differentiation. In the history of physics the pre-Newtonian idea of weight as the property of an object was differentiated into the (pre-relativistic) idea of mass, on one hand, and the concept of weight as a function of the gravitational force between objects, on the other. Similarly with the notions of heat and temperature: starting with an undifferentiated concept of heat, over the course of the seventeenth and eighteenth centuries scientists distinguished between temperature (the average kinetic energy of the molecules of a substance) and the modern concept of heat (the sum of the kinetic and potential energies of the molecules) (Wiser and Carey 1983).

Analogy and Metaphor

Analogical thinking is the cognitive process of most interest to us in this book and thus merits the most detailed treatment here. Analogy and metaphor are also the most intensively researched vehicles of conceptual creativity, and have recently become the focus of several competing theories. They are clearly related phenomena, but there is no consensus on the exact nature of the relationship: some scholars explain analogy in terms of metaphor (Lakoff 1993:235), while others explain metaphor in terms of analogy (Gentner et al. 2001). I take no stand on the issue, and treat them together here.

In everyday life, a metaphor is an unconventional use of language: we speak metaphorically when we use a word to denote not its literal referent, but something else both similar and dissimilar to the literal referent. A piano teacher uses metaphors when he describes a phrase in a composition as a "reverie," or when he tells the student not to use a close-up lens in her playing, but a telephoto lens to see eight bars at a time. However, over the past decades some cognitive scientists have developed a broader understanding of metaphor as a cross-domain mapping in the conceptual system: a general set of correspondences by means of which we understand one domain of experience in terms of another, expressed in conventional patterns of language (Lakoff 1993).

These correspondences are evident in the ways we talk about most abstract concepts. In English, we use a mapping from the domain of space (a source domain) to structure the domain of musical pitch (a target domain): we say that pitches produced by rapid frequencies of vibration are "high," while others are "low" (Zbikowski 2002). This mapping governs more than just the way we talk: it also molds our notation system (where "high" pitches appear "higher" on the page) and the practice of text-painting in vocal music (where composers will set a phrase like "He came down from heaven" to a "descending" melodic line).

Such a pervasive, systematic mapping is called a *conceptual metaphor.* We could represent the English conceptual metaphor for pitch as PITCH RELATIONSHIPS ARE RELATIONSHIPS IN VERTICAL SPACE.[15] It is not the only possible mapping onto the domain of pitch; in Javanese, the sounds produced by rapid frequencies are said to be "small" *(cilik)* while sounds made by low frequencies are "large" *(gedhé).* But both mappings are grounded in the embodied experiences of everyday life through *image schemas:* visual, auditory, kinesthetic, and tactile gestalts derived from our experiences of perceiving, moving through the world, and manipulating objects (Gibbs 1997). The image schema underlying the English conceptual metaphor is based on our experience of space structured by the felt force of gravity into "up" and "down"; the Javanese metaphor depends on our experience of physical objects of different sizes.[16]

Metaphorical understanding is ubiquitous in music; in every society people conceptualize musical phenomena in terms of nonmusical phenomena. We find metaphors on every level, from isolated terms to elaborate theories. These metaphors have been particularly important to ethnomusicologists, since they can be seen as connecting music to its wider context (though over the past few decades they have attracted the attention of music theorists as well). Two of the best-known ethnomusicological examples of metaphorical terminology relate music to the natural environment. The Kaluli of New Guinea describe the descending contours of their *gisalo* song genre using terms for waterfalls: the high opening pitch of a phrase is the waterfall "ledge"; descent to a sustained or repeated pitch is *sa-mogan,* the flow of a waterfall into a level pool (Feld 1981:30–32). The 'Are'are of the Solomon Islands use the word *'au* (bamboo) to refer to individual musical instruments, panpipe ensembles, music in general, and melody (Zemp 1978, 1979).

Scholars have also looked for metaphorical linkages beyond the terminological level. Gay (1998), for example, argues that New York City rock musicians think of the role of technology in rock performance (amplifiers, speakers, reverb, and other effects processors) by using the conceptual metaphor of a conduit: musical communication involves transmitting musical ideas through a technological channel, and the shorter and simpler the conduit, the more direct and "real" the resulting communication. Walser (1991) analyzes the meaning of distorted guitar timbres in heavy metal music by drawing on the notion of image schema: distortion takes on metaphorical meaning, he claims, from the embodied experiences we associate with the image schema of force. From our experiences of the distorted timbres of human screams, we learn to hear distortion as "a sign of extreme power and intense expression" (1991:123), an aural manifestation of force so great it overwhelms its channels.

Others have looked for pervasive metaphors at even deeper levels of connection between music and other cultural realms, and have sought there the key to music's emotional power. Feld, developing a suggestion by the Beckers, argues that a metaphor that permeates several domains of a culture comes to be felt as real, and the cognitive recognition of the "multiple representations of one idea" in "the visual, the verbal, the musical, the choreographic, the ritual, the ceremonial, the everyday, and the mythological" (Keil and Feld 1994b:172–73) becomes transmuted into an emotional response: "The more iconic the metaphor, the more unconscious its coherence, the more affective its resonance" (Feld 1988:133).

Conceptual metaphor theory was not designed as a theory of creativity, but though it focuses primarily on conventional patterns of language it can also encompass new metaphors, usually by showing how they draw on existing conceptual metaphors. Thus the piano teacher's novel metaphor of the telephoto lens depends on the conceptual metaphor UNDERSTANDING IS SEEING, which we normally encounter in conventional expressions like "I see what you mean" (Lakoff and Johnson 1980:48). Consider as well how, over centuries, the arch-metaphor of music as a language has served Western theorists as the basis for a changing series of analytical approaches. Medieval European theorists used grammatical terms to analyze music (Powers 1980), seventeenth- and eighteenth-century theorists devised elaborate systems for understanding music as a kind of rhetoric (Bartel 1997), and some twentieth-century theorists modeled their accounts of music after generative-transformational grammar (Lerdahl and Jackendoff 1983:5).

Conceptual metaphor theory can serve a useful heuristic function in music scholarship, since its emphasis on cross-domain mappings can remind us how a large part of our understanding of music is framed by nonmusical concepts and images. We will encounter some conceptual metaphors in the chapters that follow. But the intense focus on cross-domain mappings in conceptual metaphor theory can distract us from some important sources of creativity in musical thinking. Cross-domain transfers are only one type of mapping, and they are close kin to intra-domain mappings.

This kinship has been recognized in a recent development of conceptual metaphor theory known as conceptual blending (Coulson and Oakley 2000), which takes as central the on-line creation of new meaning (as found in poetry, jokes, editorial cartoons, or imaginative children's books). There are many technical differences between the theories that need not concern us.[17] What is important for our purposes is that in conceptual blending theory there is no principled separation between the metaphorical and non-metaphorical. Metaphorical blends are only one example of conceptual integration. But applying any general concept to a particular is also a kind of integration, in which the particular is identified with a location in a larger conceptual frame (Grady, Oakley, and Coulson 1999).

On this point the conceptual blending theory of metaphor converges with recent research on analogical thinking. Indeed, where it might seem counterintuitive to speak of intra-domain metaphors, when we talk of analogy we can more easily notice the kinship of mappings from close and distant domains; we can more easily see analogy as a continuum.

Analogical thinking is understanding one situation in terms of another that is, in some sense, similar or parallel to it (Holyoak and Thagard 1995). It involves projecting a "source" (a familiar situation) onto a "target" situation so as to help us learn about or think about the latter, or, if the "target" does not yet exist, to create it. The source and target may be closely related or very disparate—though as with metaphors, the most conspicuous analogies are generally the most audacious.

It is indeed true that new insights in many fields come from daring analogies between distant conceptual realms. The notion that culture is structured like a language was revolutionary for anthropology; the notion that the mind works like a computer was revolutionary for psychology. These distant analogies draw attention to themselves. Most of the analogies we read about in histories of science are of this bold type, drawing connections between very distant domains. But conceptual innovation can also come from analogies closer to hand. Even in natural science research, it appears that most analogies stay *within* conceptual domains rather than cross between them.[18] These closer analogies are less spectacular and hence easily overlooked. It can be hard for us to recognize that intra-musical analogies are analogies at all. Yet from a cognitive point of view, analogical reasoning can be used equally well both within a domain and between domains, and there is no dichotomy, no ontological divide between them (Vosniadou 1989:415–16).[19]

The usefulness of within-domain analogical thinking should not be a surprise for composers and improvisers, who routinely use analogies with old music to create new music. There are countless examples of analogy in composition, ranging from the most mechanical to the most subtle. Kirnberger's "Method for Tossing Off Sonatas" (1783) showed how one could construct a new sonata from an old one by writing a new melody to the sonata's bass, then replacing the bass (Newman 1983:442–43). Renaissance composers patterned masses on secular chansons. Debussy composed *Pelléas et Mélisande* with Wagner's example before him, especially *Tristan und Isolde* (Abbate 1981). Analogy functions similarly for improvisers. Jazz musicians model new riffs on old ones (Pressing 1988:162; Berliner 1994:146). Iranian musicians learn how to improvise by absorbing the elaborative techniques embodied in their teacher's *radif*, which they memorize (Nooshin 1998:99–100).

Within-domain mappings can also be found in music theory, though to the best of my knowledge they have not been noticed there. While cross-domain mappings have attracted attention since at least 1980, when Ruth Solie analyzed the organicist metaphors of Schenker and Réti, the presence of intra-domain analogies has gone unremarked. I argue in this book that analogies of this type played an important role in the formulation of Javanese concepts of implicit melody (chapter 6). Furthermore, they are also present alongside cross-domain mappings in the history of Western music theory. I document some examples of these analogies in chapter 8, where I present evidence that the notion of harmonic progression was once framed through an intra-domain analogical mapping.

This completes my survey of the cognitive processes of creative thinking. I have classified them into four categories, but I do not claim this arrangement is exhaustive, or even that the categories are entirely distinct. The boundaries between them can often be blurry, but there is no need for us to patrol these borders. In any particular case of creativity it may be impossible to say which of these processes is primarily responsible. When Wagner designed his tenor tuba, was he *extending* or *combining:* extending the idea of the tuba, or combining the tuba with the horn? When Gene Roddenberry persuaded a television network to support his plans for the *Star Trek* series by describing it as a "space western" (Landy 1997:449), his sales pitch brought together a genre of science fiction with a genre of Americana, but how should we describe this—as conceptual combination or as conceptual blending?

Most important for our purposes, the distinction between intra-domain analogy and conceptual extension is especially fuzzy. The piccolo clarinet can be thought of as the result of extending the clarinet family, or the result of building an instrument on analogy with the sopranino clarinet, but higher. There is often no obvious principled basis for choosing between these two descriptions, and I shall not enforce a strict distinction between them in what follows.

THE MULTIFUNCTIONALITY OF ANALOGY

Analogies, I claim, help musicians populate the ideal realm of simplicity and regularity with abstract entities. But these analogies do different sorts of cognitive work, and the entities we posit with their aid can be interpreted in different ways. Some analogies simply ornament our conversations: they give us colorful ways to say things we could say perfectly well in shades of gray. Other analogies give us convenient ways of coining new terms; yet others serve as guides to action. An analogy—whether intra-domain or cross-domain—may function as the spark of creative insight that leads to a new idea, or as a tool for communicating the idea, post festum, to an audience, or a means of legitimation, a way of attaching the idea to its society's most prestigious intellectual projects. An analogy useful for one of these purposes may be useless for another. As George Eliot noted in *The Mill on the Floss,* "It was doubtless an ingenious idea to call the camel the ship of the desert, but it would hardly lead one far in training that useful beast."

Similarly, once they have used analogical thinking to construct abstract entities, musicians can take various attitudes toward the relations between these entities and the details of their musical practice. They can integrate the new ideas to various degrees and in various ways with existing concepts. And what is particularly interesting for our purposes, the same idea can be put to different uses by different musicians.

Using my earlier image of the team of consultants, we can see the process of analogical thinking as one member of the cognitive team. The analogies she generates can be applied by her teammates in more than one way. In an environment where the needs of teaching are paramount, they can be put to pedagogical use; where the motivation for theoretical reflection is strong they can be put to explanatory use. Hence analogies can serve different purposes because of the disarticulation of cognitive systems: the processes that produce analogies work independently of the processes that use them.

The multifunctionality of analogy is important in the story of implicit-melody concepts in *karawitan.* As we shall see in chapter 6, this idea could bear several different roles: as a hypothesis about the compositional process, an account of the performer's unconscious knowledge of the composition, or simply as a pedagogical convenience. And in chapter 8 we shall meet this multifunctionality again, where it takes a somewhat different form in eighteenth-century France.

CONCLUSION

From a cognitive point of view, musical knowledge acts much like other sorts of knowledge. Like other natural and cultural domains, music is filled with fuzzy, graded and cross-cutting regularities, "nonclassical" rather than "classical" categories. The mind grasps these regularities in cultural schemas, but generalization is limited by disarticulation: local consistency coexists with global inconsistency. In devising explicit accounts of its implicit knowledge, the mind approximates "nonclassical" concepts with "classical" ones, yielding "everyday structuralism."

To return to my earlier comparison, the mind works like a team of consultants, whose members cooperate smoothly but maintain their own personalities and styles. This picture of the mind allows us to understand *both* the unity, integrity, and persistence of experience and culture, *and* their fragmented, fluid instability—what Strauss and Quinn, following Bakhtin, call the centripetal and centrifugal aspects of culture (1997). People are always making sense of experience (and music), finding order and meaningfulness in it by bringing to bear upon it the resources and strategies described in this chapter. But this order can never be total. The cognitive strategies themselves are varied and heterogeneous. Knowledge can be compartmentalized within the individual. Thus the ruptures and fissures of postmodernity are not inconsistent with this vision of human cognition: indeed, they can be deduced from it.

In the chapters that follow we shall see these phenomena exemplified in Javanese music. This tradition is filled with nonclassical categories. I focus on the idea of melodic guidance to show how musicians, attempting to understand the irregularities of guidance in their music, postulated an idealized guide, an unplayed melody, by means of within-domain analogical mapping—though different musicians did so in different ways, for different purposes. At the end of my story I will return to the general cognitive perspective of this chapter, taking some distance from the details of Javanese music to ask if similar processes of musical thinking can be found in other traditions.

2   A Brief Introduction to *Karawitan*

Traditional Javanese music—*karawitan*—includes more than just the gamelan; it also comprises several genres of unaccompanied singing *(tembang)*, the traditional vehicle of Javanese poetry.[1] Even the term "gamelan" refers to more than one kind of ensemble. There are many relatively small ensembles dedicated to particular ceremonial purposes, playing restricted repertories: the *gamelan Sekatèn*, for example, is heard only once a year, performing outside of the Great Mosque during Garebeg Mulud, the commemoration of the birth and death of the Prophet Muhammad.

The ensemble that concerns us, however, is the largest and most versatile, the "complete" *(jangkep)* or "big" *(gedhé)* gamelan of the court tradition. This is the ensemble that encompasses the most tonal and timbral variety, boasts the largest repertory, and serves the widest range of functions: it accompanies several genres of dance *(beksa)* and theater *(wayang)*, sets a dignified tone at weddings, and creates a festive atmosphere at dance parties *(tayuban)*.

A "complete" gamelan ensemble is a set of matched instruments, but also includes male and female singers. Its instrumentation is somewhat flexible: the types and numbers of instruments and singers can shrink or expand depending on the size of the set and the availability of players. (Indeed, much of the repertory can be performed by as few as seven musicians.) But this flexibility is governed by a body of conventions. Each vocal or instrumental part has a more or less strictly defined musical role. Roughly speaking, we can divide these into three categories: the form-defining ("punctuating") instruments; instruments that bear the melodic skeleton or framework; and the "elaborating" parts.[2] No matter how few instruments are available, each of the three categories must be represented: at least one punctuating instrument, one melodic-framework instrument, and a few elaborating parts.

37

The form-defining instruments demarcate the time cycles of the *gendhing* (a composition set in a metric cycle of fixed length).[3] They delineate the boundaries and map the internal contours of each type of time cycle, which range from 8 to 256 beats long. The large gong *(gong ageng)*, producing the lowest, most resonant sound of the ensemble, plays once per cycle, to mark its end (its most important metric point). Hence such a cycle is called a *gong-cycle (gongan)*. *Gongan* are classified into several named categories *(ketawang, ladrang,* etc.) by their overall length and manner of subdivision. The major subunits of a *gongan* are phrases ending with a stroke on the *kenong,* a medium-pitched set of horizontally mounted kettlegongs. These *kenongan* phrases are further subdivided by other instruments (the *kethuk, kempul,* and *kempyang*).

Where the form-defining instruments are diverse in tone-color and construction, the instruments that bear the melodic skeleton are homogeneous; for the most part they carry a single melodic line, though in different registers. These instruments, which we may call the *saron* family, are metallophones with the relatively narrow range of an octave (or slightly more). The three members of the family (the *slenthem, demung,* and *saron barung*) normally perform the same melody in three different octaves, a melody now usually called the *balungan* (literally, skeleton). Though the *balungan* can be played fairly rapidly, it can also be very sparse, with each tone lasting several seconds; the latter practice may explain why the first generation of Western ethnomusicologists compared it to a cantus firmus. There is also an instrument identical in construction but tuned an octave higher than the highest *saron,* which constantly plays simple variations on the *balungan;* known as the *saron panerus* or *peking,* it falls functionally between the melodic-skeleton instruments and the "elaborating" parts.

The rich melodic texture of the gamelan is produced mainly by the diverse group of singers and instruments comprising the "elaborating" parts. These are "elaborate" in that they are more rhythmically active than the *balungan.* They are mostly not concerted parts; that is, these performers do not play or sing in unison with anyone, but need only coordinate with one another in relatively loose ways.[4] They thus possess a great deal of individual liberty and may vary their parts according to their musical personalities or the mood of the moment, or in reaction to the improvisations of the other players.

We may divide them roughly into two groups. On one hand are the so-called loud-sounding parts, dominated by the racks of kettlegongs, the *bonang barung* and *bonang panerus.* It is possible to perform many *gendhing* with no other elaborating parts than these; this kind of "loud" playing is accordingly called *bonangan* in Solo. Most of the time, however, there is a larger group of voices and instruments, including the *rebab* bowed lute, the metallophones *gendèr barung* and *gendèr panerus*, the *gambang* xylophone, a zither *(clempung* or *siter)*, and *suling* flute. The female solo singer *(pesin-dhèn)* will usually be present, sometimes with a male chorus *(gérong)* as well. This larger group, associated as it is with the presence of singers, is sometimes distinguished from the *bonang* kettlegong sets by using the term "soft-sounding." Just as it is possible to play many pieces with only "loud" elaborating instruments, it is also possible to use only "soft" instruments and voices, omitting the *bonang*s.

There is also an instrument that does not really fit into this tripartite schema. The *kendhang* is a set of drums, including a large one (the *kendhang gendhing*), used for the relatively calm *gendhing*, and a smaller one, the *ciblon*, borrowed from dance accompaniment, which plays intricate rhythms to create a lively effect.

GENDHING IN PERFORMANCE: INTERACTION AND LEADERSHIP

Regardless of his or her role in the ensemble, the musician must be familiar with the idioms of the leading parts in order to be able to interpret the clues and signals necessary for ensemble coordination. For while the general course of a composition is predetermined, there are always various alternative possibilities concerning its details. These do not generally need to be specified ahead of time, for they can be communicated as necessary in performance by aural cues from the leading instruments.

The melodic leader of the gamelan is the leading elaborating part: in "soft" playing, the *rebab*, the two-stringed bowed lute, leads; in "loud" *bonangan* playing, where the *rebab* is absent, the *bonang* leads. Complementing the melodic leader is the leader of the tempo, the *kendhang* (drum). The *rebab* or *bonang* indicates to the other musicians what piece they should play next by intoning its introduction;[5] they can also control the timing of the transitions to certain sections within a piece. At finer levels of musical detail, the *rebab* can direct the other "soft" parts to favor one or another interpretive option with regard to ambiguous passages within some compositions.

The *rebab* and *bonang* lead aurally in another sense, in that they forecast the immediate future to some extent; their parts have a certain short-term predictability built in, and can thus quite literally "lead" or "guide" *(nun-tun)* the other parts. Musicians familiar with the idioms of these two parts can often anticipate the shape of a phrase from its opening tones. For example, by listening to the first two notes of a *bonang* phrase, a *saron* player can deduce his part for the next three or four seconds (Perlman 1994:149–50). For musicians who play the skeletal melody, or the secondary elaborating instruments, this predictability can serve as a safety net in case of memory lapses. But it also allows musicians to perform pieces they have not memorized, at least at a minimally adequate level. This sort of playing—in which the performer constructs his or her part phrase by phrase on a just-in-time basis by listening to one of the leading parts—is what musicians call "floating" *(ngambang)* or "being carried by the current" *(ngèli:* Suhardi 19.vii.97).[6]

PITCHES AND SCALES

The "complete" gamelan embraces not only a great variety of instrumental timbres and melodic idioms, but a diversity of scales as well. A *gamelan gedhé* is a double set of instruments, each set tuned to a different *laras* (tuning system). One of these, *sléndro,* is pentatonic, and in its realization on the fixed-pitch instruments it seems to the Western-trained ear to be composed of intervals larger than a major second but smaller than a minor third. (The singers and flexible-pitch *rebab* occasionally introduce smaller intervals approximating semitones.) The other *laras, pélog,* includes seven pitches per octave, but in traditional compositions only five of these appear in any given passage: the other two are exchange tones that substitute temporarily for their neighbors. There is no absolute pitch, or even a standardized intonation, for these two *laras;* each fine gamelan set may have its own distinctive realization of them. The sample tone measurements given in example 3 are therefore only illustrative, not definitive.

The names of the five tones of *sléndro* are also used to denote the tones of *pélog,* though their pitches may be quite different (example 3). This terminological sharing indicates parallels in the use of the two *laras.* Compositions can often be transposed from one tuning system to another (usually from *sléndro* to *pélog*), and a *sléndro* pitch is usually mapped onto the *pélog* pitch that bears its name.

This parallelism is also built into the construction of the fixed-pitch instruments, making such transpositions kinesthetically natural. Some of the elaborating instruments in *pélog* have only five pitches per octave and hence can be played with the same techniques and conventional melodic gestures of their *sléndro* counterparts. Other elaborating parts (the *rebab, suling* flute, and singers) use distinctively different gestures in the two tuning systems.

EXAMPLE 3. Tone measurements of the *pélog* and *sléndro slenthem* of the gamelan used at the Sri Wedhari theater auditorium in Solo, expressed in cents deviations from the Western tempered scale (A = 440 Hz). (This particular tuning pattern is unique to this gamelan; other gamelan differ in various tuning details.)

PÉLOG

Cipher notation	1	2	3	4	5	6	7
Pitch name	*panunggul*	*gulu*	*dhadha*	*pélog*	*lima*	*nem*	*barang*
Western equiv.	D-26	Eb-10	F-45	G+24	G#+43	A+43	B+35

Western equiv.		D+28	F-35		G+17	A+40	C-10
Pitch name		*gulu*	*dhadha*		*lima*	*nem*	*barang*
Cipher notation		2	3		5	6	1

SLÉNDRO

EXAMPLE 4. Skeletal melody *(saron)* and two versions of the male chorus *(gérong)* part for one phrase of Ladrang Pangkur *irama dadi*. Comparison of versions in *sléndro manyura* and *pélog barang*. Source for *pélog* version: Suroso Daladi (n.d., V:27).

saron

3　　　5　　　3　　　2　　　6　　　5　　　3　　　2

pélog

.　　.　　.　　.　　6　　6　　. 7 2̣ 　.　 3̣ 　6　 7 6 5 7 6 5 3 2

sléndro

.　　.　　.　　.　　6　　6　　. i 2̇ 　.　 3̇ 　2̇ i 6 i 2̇i6 3 5 3 . 2

(continued)

Compare one phrase of the male vocal *(gérong)* part for a composition that can be played in both *sléndro* and *pélog* (example 4). The melodic contour of the framework melody is identical in both tuning systems, but the voice part takes distinctively different shapes.[7]

The fact that not all of the *pélog* instruments have all seven tones causes occasional tonal clashes. Some instruments lack the tone 4 [*f*×], and when that pitch occurs in a composition they must substitute a neighboring tone (either 3 [*e*] or 5 [*g*♯]). But *sléndro*, too, has a practice of scalar multiplicity. The *rebab* and *pesindhèn* can play a conventional phrase called *barang miring* ("slanted"; also referred to using a Dutch loanword, *mineer*). This phrase

EXAMPLE 4. *(continued)* Western staff trans-notation.

uses *pélog*-like intervals approximating semitones, smaller than any found on the fixed-pitch *sléndro* instruments.

PATHET

Each of the two tunings systems is home to three *pathet* ("modes"), and a symmetrical arrangement of these six *pathet* governs the overall course of a performance (example 5). Each *sléndro pathet* together with its *pélog* counterpart *(sisihan)* defines a segment of the performance's time frame, during which only compositions in those two *pathet* may be played (at least in theory). The transition from one time period to another is formally marked and irreversible. Hence the progress of a performance is in a sense delineated by the sequence of *pathet*.

The melodic parts are expected to display the *pathet* of a piece in ways appropriate to their respective idioms. The *balungan* distinguishes between *pathet* by emphasizing different pitches at important metric junctions, and also by means of characteristic phrases. The elaborating parts likewise have their own conventional means of signaling the *pathet* of a composition (Perlman 2001).

The apparently clear-cut, formal simplicity of the logic of the *pathet* sys-

EXAMPLE 5. The six *pathet* (modes) within
the two tuning systems. Each of the three rows
corresponds to a time segment of the performance occasion.

Tuning system

	Sléndro	*Pélog*
M		
o	*nem*	*lima*
d	*sanga*	*nem*
e	*manyura*	*barang*

tem belies its actual complexity. As a classification system for *gendhing* it
is full of anomalies; its notional symmetry is not reflected in the transposition of compositions or performance practice between tuning systems. Describing the *pathet* system in these pages would require too long a digres-
sion; *pathet* has stimulated and frustrated generations of Javanese theorists
and has become one of the most heavily researched topics in gamelan scholarship. Making sense of it is a task that must await another occasion.

THE IMPORTANCE OF IDIOMATIC INTEGRITY

The remainder of this chapter will focus closely on the melodic parts. Each
part has one or more strongly defined idioms and is responsible for maintaining the integrity of those idioms. While each part also bears a responsibility to the whole (to match or fit together with the other parts), and while
the elaborating parts must allow room for variation (through which individual players can express their personal tastes and respond to the exigen-
cies of the performance situation), each part must guard the consistency of
its distinctive idiom. Each part should unite with the others *(nunggal)*, but
only as long as it can do so and still maintain its own life *(urip dhéwé:* Sutton 1979:61, 70; Suyenaga 1984).

I will not try to catalog these idioms exhaustively in what follows, but
will briefly illustrate each of the categories introduced above—*balungan,*
soft elaboration, and loud elaboration. I will describe the distinctive aural
qualities of the parts (their characteristic timbres and means of tone production), but because my main concern is to prepare the discussion of in-

terpart relations in chapter 3, I will concentrate on their powers of melodic and rhythmic expression. Since each part can match with the others only as far as the constraints of its idiom allow—since it can express only those melodic features of a composition compatible with that idiom—I pay particular attention to the constraints of range and rhythmic density that strongly define the "character" *(watak)* of each part.[8]

THE IDIOMS OF THE MELODIC SKELETON

The melodic skeleton has three distinct idioms, characterized by three levels of rhythmic density: *nibani, mlaku,* and *rangkep.* Each is roughly twice as dense as its predecessor in the series (example 6).

The middle level, *balungan mlaku* ("walk, travel"), is the most common; *balungan rangkep* ("double"), twice as dense, is the least common. The rhythmically sparsest idiom, *balungan nibani,* is the most rhythmically and melodically regimented. The other idioms have more rhythmic variety, while *balungan nibani* employs notes of a single durational value (represented in staff notation as whole notes). Similarly, where the other idioms can repeat tones, in *balungan nibani* the same pitch can never appear twice in immediate succession (Martopangrawit 11.ii.86). This fact has important consequences for *balungan nibani's* ability to "guide" the other parts: as we shall see, since it can neither repeat nor sustain pitches, it cannot clearly express the kind of melodic motion known as "hanging."

THE IDIOMS OF THE ELABORATING PARTS: AN OVERVIEW

The richness of *karawitan's* melodic texture is found in the elaborating parts. When all nine instruments and both the female solo singer and the male chorus are present, eleven distinct melodic parts entwine around the slow-moving melodic skeleton. The "loud" parts—the *saron panerus, bonang barung,* and *bonang panerus*—are relatively homogeneous in sound: they are all metal percussion instruments and are closely associated with the melodic skeleton. The "soft" parts, led by the *rebab,* are both more varied in tone color and have overall more melodic independence from the *balungan.*

The "loud" parts, though similar in timbre, are distinguished by register or subtle qualities of tonal envelope. The *saron panerus,* playing the most rudimentary elaborations, produces its sounds with an unpadded mallet on metal keys; it is also located in the highest octave of the ensemble. The *bonang barung* and *bonang panerus* are sets of small kettlegongs without res-

EXAMPLE 6. Three varieties of melodic skeleton *(balungan)*, notated as one-octave *saron* melodies. Source: *balungan nibani,* Gendhing Montro *sléndro manyura, inggah; balungan mlaku,* Gendhing Kocak *sléndro nem, mérong; balungan rangkep,* Ladrang Lipursari *sléndro manyura.*

nibani   . 2 . 1 . 2 . 1 . 3 . 2 . 1 . 6

mlaku   . 5 5 5 2 2 3 5 . . 5 6 1 2 3 2

rangkep   32653561 32653561 23..3361 22.3.1.2

Western staff trans-notation.

onators; besides the *saron panerus* they have the strongest attack and sharpest decay of all the metallophones.

The "soft" parts have a variety of means of tone production and timbre. There is one bowed string instrument *(rebab)* and one plucked zither *(clempung* or *siter)*; there is one end-blown bamboo flute *(suling)* and one wooden xylophone *(gambang)*; there are male and female singers. The *gendèr barung* and *gendèr panerus,* though bronze metallophones, are set apart from the *bonangs* and *saron panerus:* they are played with padded mallets, and their metal keys have individually tuned bamboo or metal resonators, giving them a rounded, sustained tone.

The elaborating parts are also distinguished by their melodic and rhythmic idioms, but these are best introduced by means of a concrete example. In example 7 I have aligned selected elaborating parts as they might be played

EXAMPLE 7. Selected elaborating parts (*saron panerus, bonang barung, gender barung, gambang, rebab, pesindhèn*) as they might be played for the *balungan* passage 1232 .126 in the *mérong* (first movement) of a *gendhing* in *sléndro manyura*.

	2	1	2	3	2	.	1	2	6
saron	2								
sar. panerus	2	1 1 2 2	1 1 2 2	3 3 2 2	3 3 2		1 1 2 2	1 1 2 2	6 6 5 5 6
bonang	.	1 2 1 ..	2 1 .	3 2 3 ..	2 3 .	2 1 .55	5 1 ..	5 1 5 . 6	1 . ..
gender	6	i 2̇ i̇ . i̇ 3̇ .	2̇ 3̇ .23̇	2̇ i 6	5 6 5 .	5 6 5 i .	6 . i̇ .	6 i̇ 6	
barung	2	. . .12	3 1 2	6 1 1 .6̣1	2 321 2	. 6.5 6 1	5 6. .53 .	3 .56 .	6 6.
gambang	2	6121612335216366161235661532612			6121212312653653356123352163356.				
rebab	2	. . 21.1 . 3	. 3 ..	. 2 3 212 2	. 1 2 1 .	2 . . 1	. .62 . 1	. . 6.	
pesindhèn	.	. . . .	. . .	. . . 3.	. . . .	3 333 3	. . 2 2 2	3 .12 . .	1 6 . 6.

EXAMPLE 7. *(continued)* Western staff trans-notation.

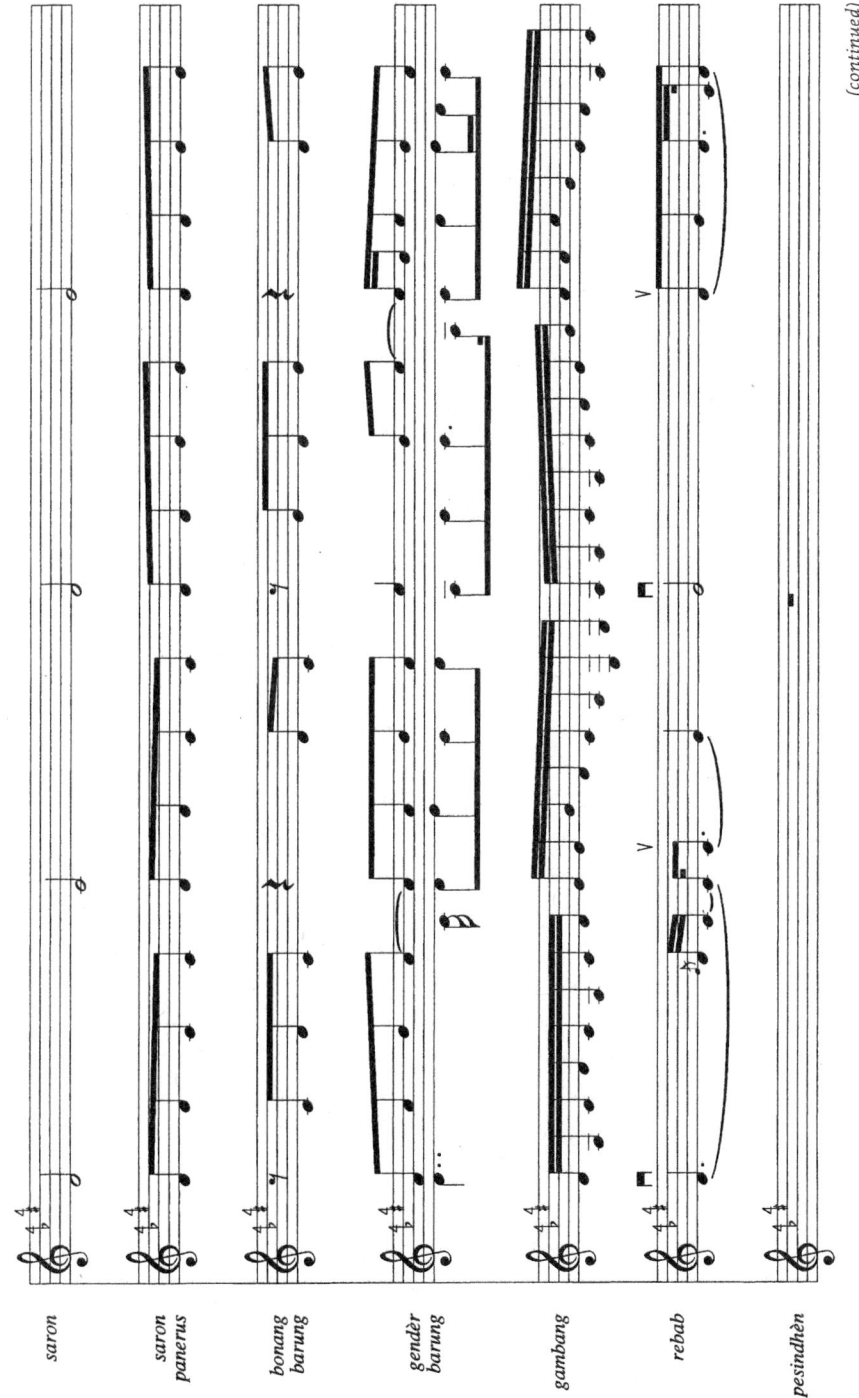

saron

saron panerus

bonang barung

gendèr barung

gambang

rebab

pesindhèn

(continued)

EXAMPLE 7. (continued)

saron

saron
panerus

bonang

gender

gambang

rebab

pesindhen

in a brief passage from a traditional composition.[9] For clarity of exposition, this example and the subsequent discussion omit some of the secondary elaborating parts *(suling, gendèr panerus, clempung, bonang panerus).*[10]

The skeletal melody *(balungan)* of this passage is here represented by the *saron* part, actually played in double parallel octaves by three members of the *saron* family of metallophones. It is slow-moving, notated here in half notes and whole notes.

The elaborating parts are all more rhythmically active than the *balungan.* Some maintain a constant rhythmic density: the *saron panerus* produces a steady stream of eighth-notes, just as the *gambang* rarely breaks its flow of sixteenth-notes. The idiom of the *gendèr barung* has both more rhythmic flexibility and more variety: it can play nearly constant eighth-notes, constant sixteenth-notes, or anything in between. In this example it keeps mostly to eighth-notes but mixes in sixteenth-notes and quarter-notes.

The *rebab* is even more rhythmically supple and is also distinguished by its tendency to play "behind" the beat. (This is hard to represent accurately in notation. The *rebab* part in example 7 has been simplified; in actual performance much more "rubato" would be heard.) But it is the *pesindhèn* who is least regimented by the beats of the meter; she sings almost constantly "out of time" and staggers her phrases to end much later than the other parts. In this example, she ends her phrase about three quarter-notes later than do the other parts.

For our present purposes we do not need to examine in further detail the melodic idiom of each elaborating part.[11] But we do need to understand what it means for each part to preserve its own character. We can most easily do so by observing how the parts can (or cannot) express the various types of melodic movement found in Javanese compositions.

THE RANGES OF THE PARTS

One of the most important determinants of a part's powers of melodic expression is the width of its range. While the parts differ both in their absolute pitch and in their range, only the latter difference has real musical significance for performance practice. Traditional *gendhing* do not exploit the five-octave melodic compass of the ensemble as a whole (example 8) in the way a Western composer might treat the orchestra's total palette by assigning a theme now to the double basses, now to the piccolo. Rather, through the principle of octave equivalence, all of the parts are considered to share a single conceptual tonal space covering two and one half octaves

EXAMPLE 8. The location of selected *sléndro* instruments within the total melodic compass of the ensemble.

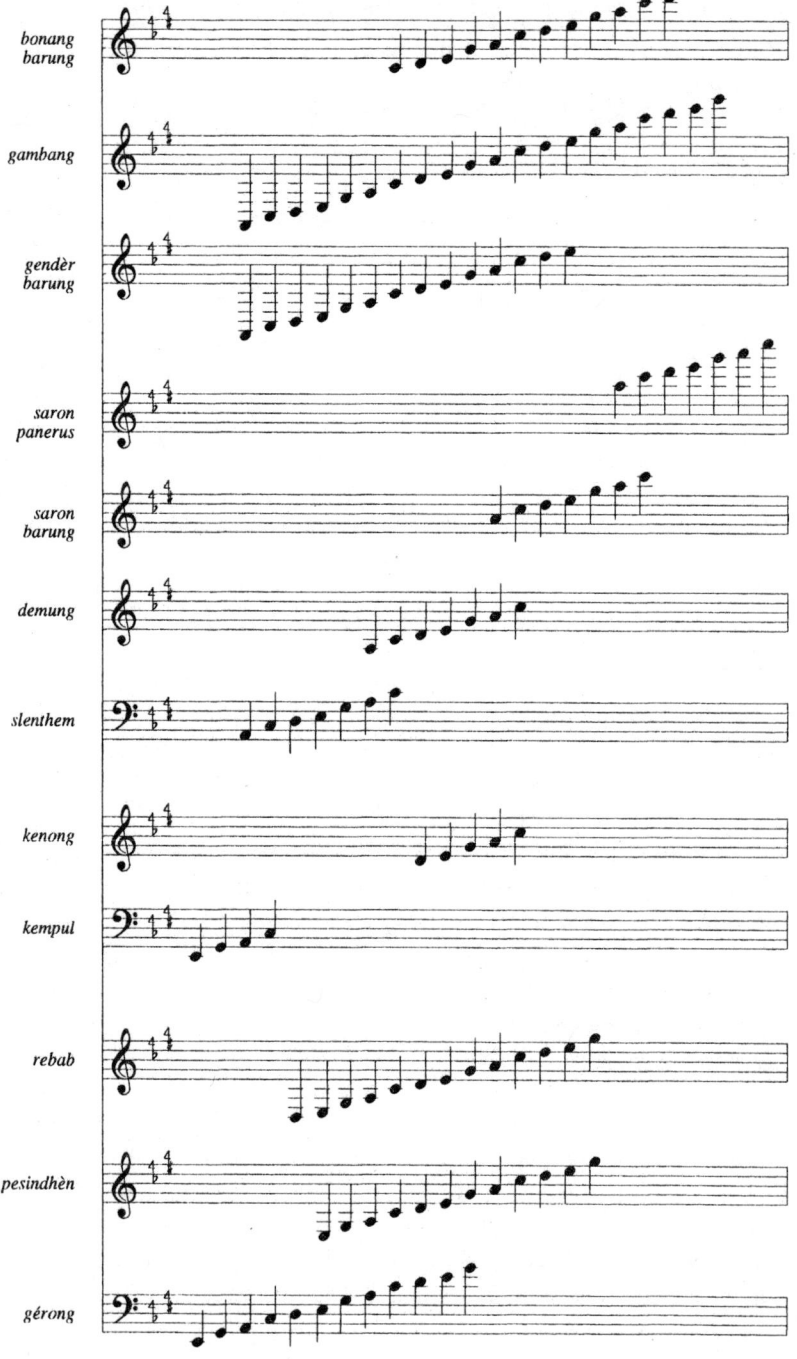

EXAMPLE 9. The conceptual range of gamelan melody. In *pélog*, the low 1 is used only in *pélog lima*.

sléndro

2 3   5̣ 6̣   1 2 3   5 6   1̇ 2̇ 3̇   5̇

pélog

(1̣) 2̣ 3̣ 4̣ 5̣ 6̣ 7̣ 1 2 3 4 5 6 7 1̇ 2̇ 3̇ 4̇

Western staff trans-notation.

sléndro

pélog

(example 9). Different parts realize this conceptual ambitus in different actual octaves. It is this conceptual ambitus that is represented in Javanese cipher notation; in the Western staff examples in this book I locate it arbitrarily from D below middle C to the G above the treble clef. (All mention of specific pitches and registers herein will refer to this conceptual ambitus; thus I will omit further qualifications, referring simply to "low 5 [*g*]" instead of "5 [*g*] in the lower octave of the conceptual range.")

Some of the instruments can encompass this full range, but not all. Example 10 shows the effective ranges of various melodic parts within the conceptual tonal space of *sléndro*.[12] The effective range is not simply the sum of tones available on an instrument, but reflects how they are used. For example, a twenty-key *gambang* can span four octaves. However, since it is played in parallel octaves, and since some of its tones are never used cadentially, its effective range is the same as that of the *rebab*.

The *rebab* and *gambang* clearly have the widest ranges, and the *saron* family the narrowest; the ranges of the other parts fall between these extremes. As a result, there are melodies that can be played on the *rebab* but

EXAMPLE 10. Effective ranges of the widest and narrowest instrumental parts in Solo-style Javanese gamelan music, showing their positions within the conceptual two-and-one-half-octave ambitus of *gendhing* melody.

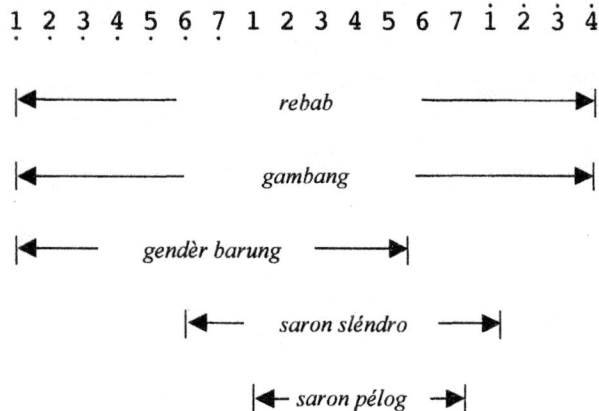

Western staff trans-notation.

that could not be played on (say) the *saron*, if only because of the differences in the width of their effective ranges. In particular, the fact that the *saron* realizes the *balungan* within its narrow range (cf. chapter 3) has played an important role in the development of Javanese theories of melodic guidance (as we shall see in chapter 5).

EXAMPLE 11. Two *gatra* of a melodic skeleton.

Points of main stress
↓   ↓

2356 3532

↑   ↑
Points of subsidiary stress

THE METRIC ORGANIZATION OF CADENCES

In the remainder of this chapter we will explore some of the ways in which the melodic parts move through this conceptual ambitus. Javanese musicians distinguish a few large categories of melodic motion, but in order to understand their distinctions we must first become acquainted with the temporal structuring of melodies around cadences.

A cadential point is called *sèlèh* (literally, to place or put down; also used in the sense of emotionally settled, calm, stable). Melodic cadence-points are closely associated with metrically strong beats, and also with a convention of ensemble coordination: in each phrase of a composition, the different instrumental and vocal parts are expected to cadence on the same tone. They do not always reach the cadence tone at the same moment: as we have already seen, the *pesindhèn* usually delays her phrase to arrive on the cadential tone one to four beats late. But conceptually, the cadential point is the moment when the various parts converge on the same pitch.

Cadences normally occur at metrically important moments: at the most important point in the *gong*-cycle (the stroke of the large gong) and the subsidiary stresses marked by the *kenong*, but also at the ends of a small metric unit not audibly marked by any form-defining instrument. This is a unit of four slow beats, known as *gatra*.[13] Like a Western measure in quadruple meter, the *gatra* has one major point of stress and a point of subsidiary stress halfway through the unit.

In modern Javanese cipher notation a *gatra* is written down separated by spaces from its neighbors (example 11). Since all melodic motion is felt to move toward a goal, *gatra* are written with their most metrically important tones last. Thus the rightmost numeral in each of the groups in example 11 (the 6 and the 2) receive metric stress. Accordingly, in the Western staff examples in this book I notate these tones on the downbeats of measures. Subsidiary stress falls on the second tone of each group (i.e., the 5 in 3532); these tones appear on the third beats of the Western measures.

Melodies typically place their cadences at these points of metric stress, though the relationship is not invariable; the strongest cadences do not always fall at the strongest metric positions. There are many *gatra* downbeats where the melody does not cadence, just as there are *kenong*-strokes that fall on subsidiary cadences.

Now that we have seen the pitch space through which melodies move tonally and the metric space through which they move temporally, we can introduce the three basic types of melodic motion: moving, hanging, and slipping.

THE THREE TYPES OF MOTION IN THE MELODIC PARTS
Moving, Hanging, and Slipping in the Balungan

There is no general term in common use for ordinary melodic motion from cadence-point to cadence-point; the category seems to be unmarked. If a Javanese term were needed for it, the most appropriate one would probably be *mlaku* (to walk, move, travel).[14] "Moving" is normally anticipatory motion, moving *toward* a goal yet to come, not away from something that just happened. Since this goal usually falls on a point of metric stress, we may use motion from a weak beat to a strong beat as paradigmatic of "moving."

In contrast to this type of (unmarked) melodic motion, there are two named types of special motion: "hanging" *(nggantung, gantungan)* and "slipping" *(plèsèdan)*. Hanging is stasis, the absence of motion; slipping is sudden motion.

Hanging contrasts with "moving" precisely because it lacks the motion from weak beat to strong beat characteristic of moving. Hanging is often represented in the *balungan mlaku* idiom by the sustaining or repetition of a single tone from a weak beat to a strong beat. In example 12, the melody hangs for six beats on 3 |e+|. Here, the tone 3 is reached by moving to a strong beat; it is then sustained for four beats and repeated for two beats, at which point moving resumes. (Note that there is no hanging in the final four beats of this phrase, even though two tones are sustained. But the 2 |d| and the 5 |g| are each struck on strong beats—the 2 at a cadential point, the 5 at a point of mid-*gatra* subsidiary stress—and sustained through weak beats. The effect is not one of stasis, but of change in the overall pace of motion: from steady half-notes, we now move in steady whole-notes.)

EXAMPLE 12. Skeletal melody *(balungan)* for a passage from Gendhing Lendhi *sléndro manyura.* The "hanging" part of the passage is bracketed.

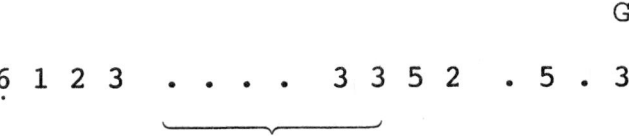

Western staff trans-notation.

Plèsèdan (literally, slipping) is sudden motion. Slipping is implied by the *balungan* when a cadence is immediately followed by hanging on a different tone, as in example 13. Here the melody slips at the end, cadencing on the 2 [*d*] and then slipping to 6 [*a*], where it hangs for four beats.

Slipping is most commonly signaled in *balungan mlaku* by a repeated tone in a weak-beat/strong-beat configuration, as above. (Sometimes the tone is not struck again on the strong beat, but rather the stroke on the weak beat is sustained.) Slipping weakens the previous cadence's sense of completion. When slipping motion occurs immediately after a *kenong*-stroke, the *kenong*, which normally plays the pitch of the cadential tone, plays instead the pitch of the slipped-to note.

I have deliberately chosen to illustrate hanging and slipping using *balungan mlaku* because the three *balungan* idioms cannot all indicate melodic stasis equally well. *Balungan mlaku* is versatile in this regard, and *balungan rangkep*, too, can represent hanging by sustaining and repeating tones. By contrast, *balungan nibani*, since it can never pause and cannot repeat tones, can never clearly indicate hanging.

Let us now observe how the three kinds of melodic motion are manifested in some of the elaborating parts. As we shall see, the parts are not equally capable of expressing all of the aspects of melodic motion. These differences in capability have important implications for the ways the parts can relate to one another.

EXAMPLE 13. Skeletal melody *(balungan)* for a passage from
Gendhing Pujongganom *sléndro manyura*. The "slipping" tones
are bracketed.

N

5 6 5 3   . . . 3   6 5 3 2   6 6 . .

Western staff trans-notation.

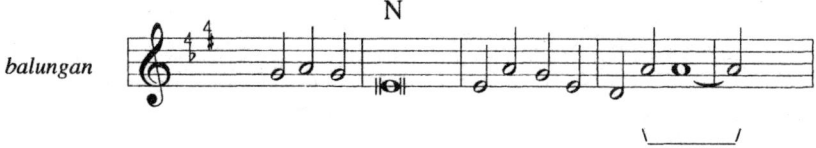

balungan

How the Elaborating Parts Move

Of the three varieties of melodic motion—moving, hanging, and slipping—
it is moving that dominates the melodic landscape. Hanging and slipping
provide variety and contrast, but most melodic gestures in most compositions are of the unmarked, moving type.

How do moving melodies move? All of them tend to move in highly conventionalized ways, but the specific conventions are distinctively different
for each part. We may group them into two large classes, corresponding to
the "soft" and "loud" elaborating parts. The soft parts make extensive use
of phrase types, conventional melodic gestures known as *céngkok*. Some of
the loud parts have such gestures as well, but are often more strictly tied to
the *balungan*. Let us start with a simple example of elaboration in one of the
loud parts, the *saron panerus*.

The *saron panerus* plays the simplest elaborations, often simply repeating two-note segments of the melodic skeleton. Example 14 shows the
saron panerus part for a sample two-*gatra* passage of *balungan mlaku*.[15]
The *saron panerus* takes the eight tones of this phrase two by two. Starting with the tones 3 and 5, it repeats each one (3355) and then plays the
sequence over again (33553355). It then does the same for the last two
tones of the *gatra*, 65. This is its general procedure for a four-note *gatra*,
abcd. As long as no two consecutive tones within this *gatra* have the same

EXAMPLE 14. *Saron panerus* part for a sample two-*gatra balungan* passage *(irama dadi).*

balungan

3 5 6 5 3 2 1 2

saron panerus

.33553355665566553322332211221122

Western staff trans-notation.

pitch, and as long as there are no large leaps, the *saron panerus* will play *aabbaabbccddccdd.*

When musicians talk about the soft elaborating parts, they often use the term *céngkok.* This is a way of referring to the conventionalized aspect of melody. It is a word with varied meanings, but in this context it describes the stable melodic content of a stock phrase, one or two *gatra* long, which can be varied and embellished in indefinitely many ways but which remains recognizable.[16]

Musicians sometimes speak of *céngkok* as things, and of the quantity of *céngkok* as a measure of musicianship. An accomplished player can be said to "have many *céngkok*"; a young musician can self-deprecatingly say that his "vocabulary" *(perbendaharaan)* of *céngkok* isn't very large. The sense of *céngkok* as distinct "riffs" with their own identities is further reinforced by the practice of referring to some of them by name *(dua lolo, puthut gelut, ayu kuning,* etc.). One of the most easily identifiable is the double-length *céngkok* called *ayu kuning.* This *céngkok* has a distinctive vocal part, and its name is taken from the words that can be sung to it (they describe a woman's appearance: "beautiful, fair-skinned, and shapely"). Example 15 shows two

EXAMPLE 15. The melodic pattern called *ayu kuning* in the *gérong* (male chorus) idiom. 15a: A basic version in *sléndro pathet manyura*, cadencing on 1 [c–]. Source: Martopangrawit (1975:I, 4–5; 1984:14). 15b: The same, transposed to *pathet sanga*.

15a.

6 . 1̇ . 3̇ . 2̇ . 6 . 3 3 2 2 1

a – yu   ku – ning   bén – trok maya   maya

15b.

5 . 6 . 2̇ . 1̇ . 5 . 2 2 1 1 6̣

Western staff trans-notation.

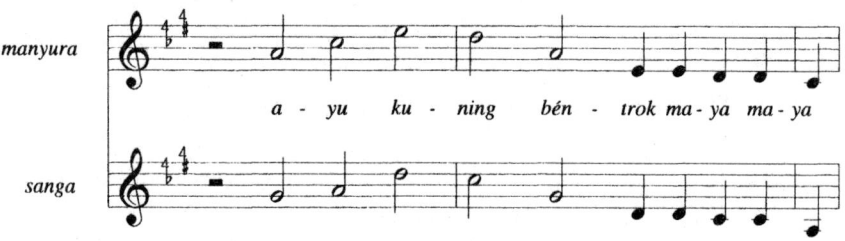

versions of this gesture at two different transposition levels (in *pathet manyura*, where it is used to cadence on the tone 1 [c–], and—one tone lower—in *pathet sanga*, where it cadences on 6 [a]). The soft elaborating parts such as the *rebab*, *gendèr barung*, and *gambang* have their own versions of *ayu kuning* suited to their respective idioms.

But a *céngkok* need not have a single invariable melodic outline. For example, the very common pattern *puthut gelut* has no conventional vocal line associated with it and takes two or three different shapes in both the *rebab* and *gendèr* parts. And some elaborating phrases are even less distinctive; there are also unnamed phrases used as transitions. These phrases are not thought of as integral wholes, but are referred to generically as "bridges" *(jembatan)* or *rambatan* (literally, a trellis for climbing plants).

EXAMPLE 16. *Saron panerus part for a sample "hanging" balungan gatra (irama dadi).*

balungan	2	2	.	.

saron panerus   .3322332211221122

Western staff trans-notation.

How the Elaborating Parts Hang

The elaborating parts differ in the extent to which they can represent hanging. For example, among the loud elaborating parts, the *saron panerus* is as limited as *balungan nibani*. The idiom of the *saron panerus* does not allow it to repeat tones immediately, and thus it has no special way of distinguishing hanging from moving. When the *balungan* is hanging, the *saron panerus* generates movement of its own by using the upper or lower neighbor of the sustained tone (example 16). But this introduces a certain degree of ambiguity. Notice that the *saron panerus* part for this hanging phrase is identical to that used for the moving phrase, 3212, in example 14. That is, the *saron panerus* cannot reflect the melodic stasis of the *balungan* phrase 22.. while remaining true to its own idiom.

Most of the other elaborating parts can represent hanging, though they use a variety of means to do so. Some parts sustain the hanging tone, some reiterate it in a cross-rhythmic pattern, some make small circling motions around the tone. Hence we find with melodic stasis the same diversity that we found with melodic register; in each case, the parts differ widely in their expressive abilities. (Slipping is akin to hanging in that the parts that cannot clearly represent hanging tend to be unable to slip as well. Thus neither *balungan nibani* nor the *saron panerus* can represent slipping.)

GARAP

Before concluding this survey of the melodic parts, I must briefly return to one of the most important dimensions of contrast between the elaborating parts and the *balungan*. This contrast is more than a contrast of melodic idiom: it is also a contrast in kinds of performance practice, kinds of knowledge, and in the roles different musicians play within the ensemble. One word that summarizes many of these dimensions of contrast is *garap*. This term, though meaning literally "work," is untranslatable. In its broadest sense it refers to performance practice in general, but it is also used to distinguish the elaborating parts from the *balungan*. Mitropradongga, for example, advised me to "know the *balungan* first [*ngerti gendhing dhisik*], then study the *garap*." *Garap* connotes the individual latitude and autonomy of the performer of an elaborating part; Martopangrawit considered it an art of interpretation, requiring insight and judgment. The performer has some liberty in the choice of *céngkok* to use for any given passage in a *gendhing*, and flexibility in how to realize a *céngkok* on any given occasion. This latitude, which has been called improvisational by ethnomusicologists, distinguishes the elaborating parts from the *balungan*;[17] for while the *balungan* of a *gendhing* can exist in different versions, the musicians entrusted with it are not expected to spontaneously vary it in performance.

CONCLUSION

The melodic parts are expected to match or "unite" within the limits established by their respective idioms. In this chapter we have seen how these idioms provide more or less scope for the parts to traverse pitch space and to display different kinds of melodic motion. Some of the parts—in particular, the *saron*—have quite narrow ranges. Some idioms, such as *balungan nibani* and the *saron panerus*, cannot represent hanging movements. Within these limits the parts must fit together. How they do so is the subject of the next chapter.

3   *Karawitan* as a Multipart Music

The Relations between the Melodic Parts

As we saw in chapter 2, the parts guard their own musical identities. But they also need to guard their relations with one another. Musicians must coordinate their conceptions of the composition to produce the best musical results; they should be united (*kompak:* Martopangrawit 7.xii.85). While maintaining their musical individuality, they should strive for *kerukunan,* social accord and goodwill (Suhardi 13.ix.85).

But good musical citizenship does not require a constant, unvarying acknowledgment of the demands of the group. To change the metaphor, we could say that the parts do not always walk in as tight a formation as the terrain permits. While always maintaining the same general direction of movement, they sometimes wander from one another, singly or in small groups. Thus the relations among the parts are constantly changing. Drawing on distinctions my teachers made, I describe these shifting relations in terms of degrees of congruence and divergence among the parts.

I then describe how musicians use the relations among melodic parts to facilitate ensemble coordination. Two of the elaborating parts, the *rebab* and *bonang,* have leadership roles that depend on the ability of the other performers to relate their own parts to these two guiding lines. But there is another sort of guidance as well, which I introduce in the remainder of the chapter by focusing on the relationships between the *balungan* and the elaborating parts.

The conventions of interpart relations guarantee the flexibility of the elaborating parts within the set melodic framework of the composition. Only the *balungan* is considered fixed; the elaborating parts derive their melodies from it by interpreting it according to these traditional conventions. Because there is considerable leeway and wide tolerances built into these conventions, they preserve the personal latitude of the performer without detriment to the stability of the composition.

The idea of the *balungan* as a guide for the elaborating parts demands extensive discussion, which I provide in chapter 4. To prepare that discussion, I conclude this chapter by introducing two aspects of *balungan-garap* relations that play important roles in the story of Javanese theorizations of melodic guidance. I first show how awareness of the wide-range parts transforms learners' conception of the *balungan*, helping them unfold it in the imagination from the one-octave *saron* line to an expansive but unplayed multi-octave line. Finally, I consider the rhythmic relationships between *balungan* and elaboration, known in Javanese as *irama*.

CONGRUENCE AND DIVERGENCE

Since at least the 1920s, ethnomusicologists have described Javanese gamelan music as heterophonic. This is a murky term, introduced a century ago by Western scholars to stand for a generic musical Other. It was defined by the gap it filled, being whatever was neither monophony nor polyphony. As the "simultaneous variation . . . of what is identified as the same melody" (Cooke 1980), heterophony remains a concept defined largely by what it is not.[1]

There is no standard set of technical terms to describe the range of possible relationships among melodic parts, but my teachers tended not to describe them as variants of one another. Rather, they used a variety of metaphors: social metaphors or spatial metaphors of proximity, distance, and motion in similar or different directions. For example, Mloyowidodo (21.ii.85) referred approvingly to players that "walk (or travel) together" *(jalan bersama)* when they play. Martopangrawit (1983:41) used *mengikuti* (Indonesian) and *ngendhel* (Javanese) to describe the relation between two parts; both words mean "to follow" or "accompany" someone, as on a journey. He also referred to two parts as being far *(tebih)* from each other.

Martopangrawit also had a technical term to describe this sort of melodic distance, though it was a personal one: he used *salah gumun* to refer to elaborating parts that don't follow the course of the *balungan*. (Interestingly, he had no antonym for *salah gumun*.) Suhardi was the only musician I knew who had a set of technical terms to describe a range of interpart relations: *nunggal* and *misah*. *Nunggal* means "to be the same; to become one"; *misah* means "to separate" (11.x.85).

To make my exposition easier to follow, I will introduce standard terms of my own to subsume these varied personal metaphors and idioms. I use *congruence* to refer to the sense that different parts are walking together, keeping each other company, or matching; the opposite case I call *divergence*.

Congruence and divergence are both essential, but do not have the same status. Congruence is clearly central and primary. My teachers thought of it as natural, as easier than divergence. This is clear from both Suhardi's statements and his pedagogic practice. Congruence is easier to learn than divergence (30.i.87); melodic passages with *misah* are difficult *(berat)*. In teaching beginners, Suhardi used pieces with relatively little divergence (21.iv.84; 30.i.87). Similarly, Martopangrawit characterized congruent passages free from *salah gumun* as "natural" or "proper" *(wajar)*.

Congruence is a complex notion, and it makes sense only within the set of conventions governing the melodic idioms described in chapter 2. Without a knowledge of these conventions we cannot expect to be able to know when Javanese musicians would judge two parts to be congruent or not.[2] Parts that are congruent may be melodically similar, but need not be. I will not try to further analyze the notion here, but will instead describe the varieties of divergence.[3]

Types of Divergence

Divergence is a complex phenomenon, as the melodic parts can diverge from one another in a dizzying multiplicity of ways. To present this overwhelming variety clearly to the reader, I need to organize it. I do so in terms of three distinctions. The first concerns the temporal location of divergence: I distinguish parts that diverge on their way to a common cadential tone from parts that diverge *at* a cadential point. The latter is less common and more likely to excite remark. My second distinction concerns the regularity of divergence: I separate out divergence that is predictable and occurs in the same form in many compositions from divergence that is unique to a particular composition. Finally, I distinguish between types of divergence in terms of the specific parts involved. Some divergence accentuates the cleavage between the "soft" elaborating parts and the other parts, in that the soft parts all diverge as a group from the *saron* and *bonang* parts. Other cases of divergence are more piecemeal, splitting the unity of the soft parts.

Let us start with the temporal location of divergence. To understand the difference between divergence at cadences and divergence between cadences, recall that the parts are expected to show their mutual awareness and affirm their unity by sounding the same pitch at cadentially important moments. Because cadences are normally so strongly correlated with regular metric stress, this amounts in practice to the expectation that parts will converge at the ends of *gatra*.

Divergence Approaching a Cadence   Let us start by examining the relations among parts that share a common cadential goal. This is the most common situation. In the next section we will look at parts that diverge at a cadential point.

In the following discussion, I assume that all of the parts have certain basic resources in common, in particular a shared set of pitch-classes. This is true most of the time, but there are a few important exceptions. As we saw in chapter 2, not all of the *pélog* instruments can play the tone 4 [*f*ˣ]. But more significant, in *sléndro* the *rebab* and *pesindhèn* have *céngkok* called *barang miring*. They are not used in every *gendhing*, but when they do appear, they open a gap between the *rebab* and vocal lines on one side and the fixed-pitch parts on the other. As Suhardi put it (7.ix.84), when the *rebab* plays *barang miring*, the *gendèr* "can't be of any assistance" *(tidak bisa membantu apa-apa)*.

Some cases of divergence are due to differences in the ranges and idioms of the parts. For example, the *gendèr* does not always "walk together" with the *rebab*, even when its limited range would permit it to do so. This is because it needs to "stay alive," to be faithful to its own idiom (Perlman 1994:113–15).

There are, however, cases of divergence that cannot be attributed to factors of range. Even parts with more or less equivalent ranges can approach a cadence tone from opposite directions. The bracketed portion of example 17 illustrates this phenomenon. Here the *gérong* and *rebab* cadence on 2 [*d*], but arrive at it from different directions, the *gérong* from above, the *rebab* from below.

Divergence at Cadential Points   Divergence at a cadential point comes in several varieties. Sometimes it involves a disparity of conceptual pitch but not of pitch-class: that is, sometimes the diverging parts cadence on conceptual pitches separated by an octave. However, the examples I present in this chapter all involve divergence in pitch-class. These cases may be divided into two types, predictable and unpredictable. What I call predictable divergence is divergence common to many *gendhing*. For example, the *puthut gelut céngkok* in *sléndro manyura* is often used for the *balungan* passage 33..6532. In the middle of this passage, where the *balungan* and *bonang* parts hang on 3 [*e+*], the "soft" elaborating parts play 6 [*a*]. Hence the soft parts diverge from the others, but this divergence is highly conventional (example 18).

Unpredictable divergence is composition-specific. It cannot be deduced from any general conventions; it simply must be learned, piece by piece. Martopangrawit had a term for this. *Salah gumun pamijèn* ("special"; also called *gawan*, "characteristic," "inherent") is divergence between *balungan* and *garap* for no other reason than that "the composer wanted it that way" (6.x.81).[4]

This kind of divergence seems to be a peculiarly Solonese phenomenon;

EXAMPLE 17. One *kenongan* phrase from Ladrang Siyem *sléndro nem*. Source: Martopangrawit (1988:73), Djumadi (1986:147).

Western staff trans-notation.

original Yogyakarta-style *gendhing* never diverge in this way (Suhardi 3.v.85). Even within the Solonese tradition it seems to be limited to *sléndro*. Interestingly enough, Martopangrawit could think of no examples of *salah gumun pamijèn* in *pélog* (21.iii.84; 8.v.84).

The clearest example of composition-specific divergence is undoubtedly the relatively uncommon Gendhing Lagu Dhempel *sléndro sanga*. The passage from the first movement *(mérong)* of this piece shown in example 19 consists of two identical *balungan* phrases: each descends conjunctly from 6 to 2, where it hovers for several beats, then ascends to 5.

The soft elaborating parts do not interpret these two phrases identically, however. This is most easily seen from the vocal part *(sindhènan bedhayan)* sung when Lagu Dhempel is used to accompany dance (example 20).

The voice part distinguishes between these phrases in the following way: on the first occurrence, the voices approach the *kenong* tone 5 [g] from above,

EXAMPLE 18. *Balungan, bonangan, rebaban, gendèran,* and *gambangan* for the phrase 33..6532 in Ladrang Wilujeng *sléndro manyura*. Source: Suhardi (*gambang*); other parts, Sumarsam (1976:21; 1984:265). The tones in parentheses represent the beginning of the *rebab*'s subsequent pattern, which it starts early.

balungan	3	3	.	6	5	3	.	2

```
bonang    3 . . 3 . . 3 . . 3 6 5 6 . . 5 6 . 3 2 3 . . 2 3 .
          3. . . 3. . . 3. . . 3.

rebab     . . . . . 3 . 5 6 . 6 . . 6 . 6 . . . i . . . 3 . 1 . 2 . . 2 3 2 . (3 . 5)

gendèr    5 i 5 3 6 .56 i 5 6 5 i 5 6 i 6 i 2 i .6i 2 i 3 i 2 i 3 i 2 i 6
          ----- ----- ----- ----- ----- ----- ----- -----
          3 3 . .21 6 3 . 1 . 5 6 35.56 . . .12 3 1 2 6 . 3 . 1 2 321 2
          3. . .

gambang   3335612333321233561233..i2333212623i6333212i26356321661616611221261i2
```

EXAMPLE 18. (continued) Western staff trans-notation.

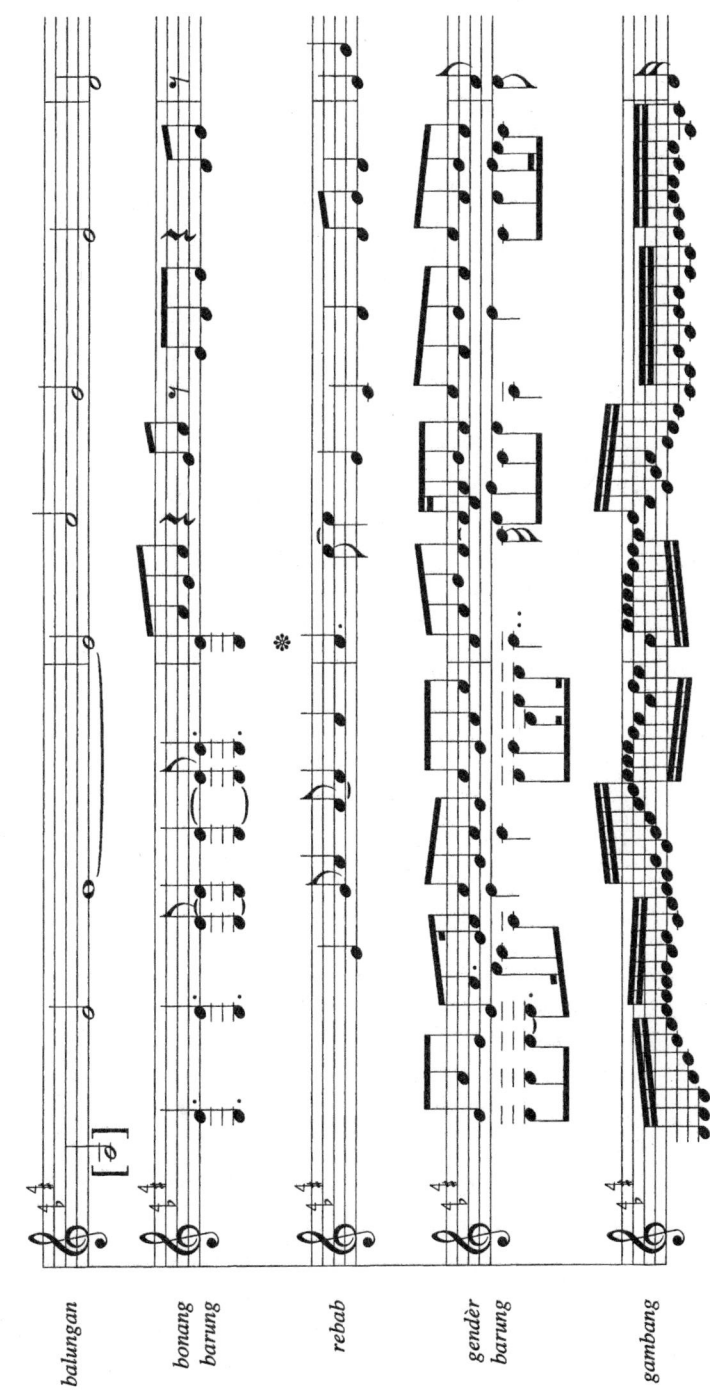

balungan

bonang
barung

rebab

gendèr
barung

gambang

EXAMPLE 19. *Balungan* notation for one *gongan* of the first movement *(mérong)* of Gendhing Lagu Dhempel *sléndro sanga.*

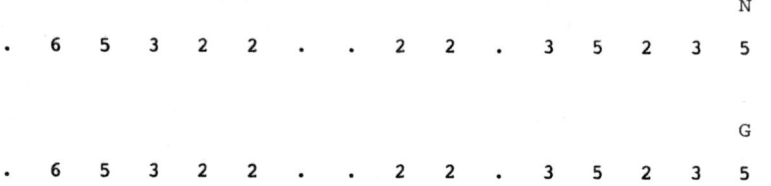

Western staff trans-notation.

thus in contrary motion to the *balungan.* On the repetition of the phrase, the voices approach the 5 from below, more or less as the *balungan* does. Hence the first occurrence is marked by a vocal leap from 2 to 6. From 6, the voices rise to 1 as the *balungan* ascends to 3; then the two parts converge. We find precisely the same pattern of divergence in the other *garap* parts, even when this piece is played outside of the dance context (Perlman 1994:157–58).

The example of Lagu Dhempel is particularly useful, since congruent and divergent versions of the same phrase are juxtaposed. This is rare, however. In most cases of unpredictable divergence, the phrase in question is not repeated, or if it is, the *garap* does not change. The very well-known *gendhing* Cucurbawuk *sléndro manyura* is perhaps more typical in this regard (example 21).

Here, after hovering with the *balungan* on 3 |*e+*| for a moment, the soft

EXAMPLE 20. *Balungan* and *sindhènan bedhayan* for one *gongan* of the *mérong* of Gendhing Lagu Dhempel *sléndro sanga*. Source: Martopangrawit (1976:77).

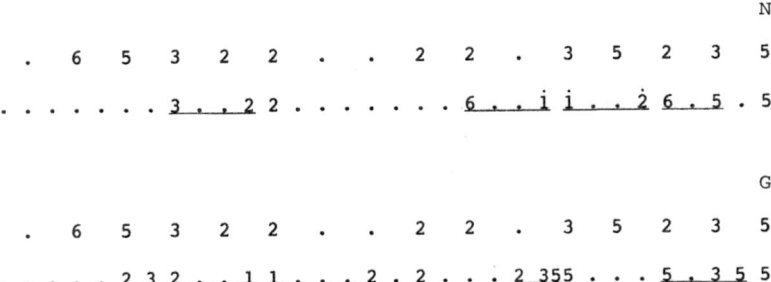

Western staff trans-notation.

EXAMPLE 21. *Balungan* (top), *rebaban* (middle), and *genderan* (bottom) for one *kenongan* of Gendhing Cucur-bawuk *sléndro manyura*. Source: Suhardi (17.x.86).

```
bal.   ·   ·   2   3   ·   3   3   ·   5

reb.  · · · 5 · 6 · · 2 · ·1263 · · · · 6· i · · · i· · · · i

       i·6i 5   2 3 5 6   ·5·35 3   6 ·56 3   i· ·6i   6i6·2   6i6·2   6i2·i

gnd   ------- ------- ------- ------- ------- -------
      ·35 5· · 1656 656· 5 23i23 ·23 3 3 · 1· · · ·6i2·2· 16i 16i 2·321·1·

                                                                        N
bal.   6   i   ·   6   5   3   5   6

reb.  · · · 6· · · · i 2· · · ·2· · · · · 2· i· 6 i 2· · ·3· · ·2· i· 6 · ·

       6 ·56 i 5 6 i 6 ·i·6i 2· ·i·6i 6 ·i·6i 6 i 6 i 2· ·3· 2·3 ·2· i 6

gnd   ------- ------- ------- ------- ------- -------
      · 2 6 3  ·216216 1 1 ·6· 12 12612 16 6· · 1·161·12 123·1212 3·216·6·
```

EXAMPLE 21. *(continued)* Western staff trans-notation.

(continued)

EXAMPLE 21. *(continued)*

parts leap up to high 1 [*c*–], where they hang for four *balungan* beats, ignoring the *balungan*'s sustained 3 and the subsequent 5 [*g*]. They then proceed to high 2 [*d*] (while the *balungan* lands on 6 [*a*]). The parts converge again only at the *kenong*-stroke. (We will meet this example again in chapter 6, example 40.)

Soft/Loud Bifurcation versus Piecemeal Divergence   The examples of predictable and unpredictable divergence given above have a common feature: in all of them, the melodic parts bifurcate into two groups, following the dividing line between the soft parts and the other parts. That is, the *balungan* and the *bonang* parts remain congruent with each other, and the soft parts are congruent among themselves. This is not the only kind of divergence, however. The soft parts can split among themselves: some of them can remain congruent with the *balungan* while others diverge, or several of them can diverge from the *balungan*, but in different ways.

These possibilities are represented schematically in examples 22 and 23. The ovals encircle parts that are congruent with each other. The vertical dotted line separates the *balungan* and *bonang* from the soft elaborating parts. Example 22 depicts the situation of Lagu Dhempel: the soft parts diverge from the *balungan* as a unit. Example 23 shows a more piecemeal type of divergence.

To illustrate the latter sort of divergence, consider example 24. Here we find the *rebab* part using the *puthut gelut céngkok*, stressing 6 [*a*] at the

EXAMPLE 22. Schematic representation of divergence between *balungan* and the "soft" elaborating parts (as found in Gendhing Cucur-bawuk or Gendhing Lagu Dhempel). The soft parts are congruent with one another, and the *balungan* and *bonang* are congruent with each other, but the two groups diverge.

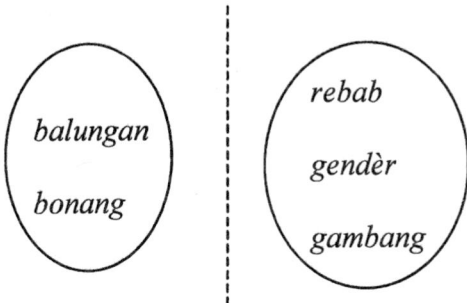

EXAMPLE 23. Schematic representation of divergence cross-cutting the distinction between the *balungan* and the "soft" elaborating parts (as found in *Ayak-ayakan manyura*). The *balungan, bonang, gendèr,* and *gambang* parts are congruent; the *rebab* is congruent neither with the *balungan* nor with the other soft parts.

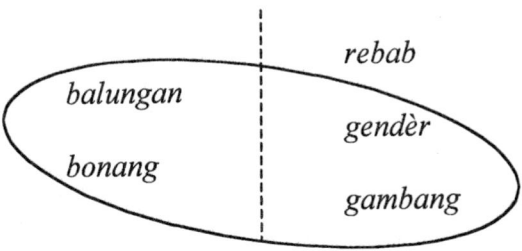

midpoint as it did in example 18. In that example, the *gendèr* and *gambang* followed the *rebab* to 6 [*a*]. But in *Ayak-ayakan manyura*, according to Suhardi, this is not possible. In example 24 I show the most common *gendèr* interpretation, cadencing on 1 [*c*–] instead of 6 [*a*]—that is, remaining congruent with the *balungan*. This is not the *gendèr*'s only option. It may play to 3 [*e*+] instead of 1 [*c*–], for example; but it may not play to 6 [*a*].[5]

EXAMPLE 24. One phrase from *Ayak-ayakan sléndro manyura.*
Source: Simplified *rebab* notation from Djumadi (1986:40); *gendèr*
part from the playing of Joko Waluyo (8.v.93). The arrow indicates
where the *rebab* deviates from the *gendèr* and *balungan.*

balungan	1	2	3	2	1

rebab	1 2 3	3	5 6 . 6 .	6	6

```
                i 2̇ 3̇ 2̇ i 2̇ 3̇ 2̇ i 6 5 6 2̇ 6 i 2̇ i
gendèr          -  - - - - - - -  - - - - - -  - - - - - -  - - - - - -

                1 . . . .61 2 1 2 3 .21 2 . 3 3 321
                                                  ↑
```

balungan	3	5	3	2

rebab	. 6 .	3	2	1 6̣ 1	2	2

```
                6.65 6 i 5 6 i 6 . 2̇ .3̇. 3̇ 2̇ i 6
gendèr          - - - - - - -  - - - - - - -  - - - - - - -  - - - - - - -

                . 23 3. .216̣216 . 1 6̣ .12 2 212
```

THE *REBAB* AS GUIDE

The relationships among the parts have great practical importance for musicians, since they form the basis of the system of guidance that governs the
interaction among the performers. There are two types of melodic guidance:
one unfolds in real time, as it were, during the course of a performance; the
other is the conceptual guidance afforded by the melodic framework *(balungan)* to the elaborating parts. The former type of guidance requires that
the players understand the systematic relationships among the parts, so that
they can respond to musical signals given during performance and even play
an unfamiliar piece by letting themselves be carried by the current *(ngèli)*,
figuring out their parts as they go by listening to the other parts. Two of the
parts exercise this "real-time" guidance function. One of them—the
bonang—is less important for our purposes (for an example of its guiding

EXAMPLE 24. *(continued)* Western staff trans-notation.

role, see Perlman 1994:149–50). But the ultimate melodic authority is the *rebab*, and so we should understand something about how it acts as a guide.

The *rebab* is usually called the *pamurba lagu*, "that which has authority over melody." The *rebab* player signals the tuning system and *pathet* of the piece to be played next by intoning a short phrase called a *senggrèngan*, and determines the piece to be played by playing its *buka* (introduction). Sumarsam adds (1976:11–12) that "throughout the *gending* the *rebab* gives direction to the melodic motion. Frequently, the *rebab* anticipates the notes that will appear in the following line."

At a *klenèngan* the *rebab* does indeed have the right to determine the *gendhing*, and need not announce it in any way except by playing its *buka*. Once the *gendhing* has begun, the *rebab*'s decision-making powers do not evaporate. For example, the *rebab* decides when to play the high-register *(ngelik)* section of a *gendhing*. Again, when more than one version of a *gendhing* is current in a community of musicians, the *rebab* usually has the authority to choose which one will be played on any particular occasion.

This "real-time" leadership function is evidently related to the hierarchy of knowledge, skill, and status implicit in *karawitan*. The *rebab* player is expected to have a trustworthy memory, which the ensemble can rely on if the other players' memories fail them. According to Mloyowidodo, the *gendèr* and *bonang* follow the *rebab*'s melody *(wilet)*—unless they are expert *(pandai)* and know the *gendhing* on their own. It was not automatically assumed that one really knew a piece just because one could play it in ensemble. Mloyowidodo pointed out that many *gendèr* players in particular could play *gendhing* they didn't know by listening carefully to the *rebab*: this is called *bliru tahu* ("to be able to do something one doesn't really know"; to "play by ear"). Many *gendèr* players would just *nginthil* (trail along after; follow) the *rebab*'s playing.

Therefore the *rebab* constantly gives clues to the course of the *gendhing*. The *rebab*'s job is to anticipate, to move in advance, as if to say: "Go here next!" According to Mloyowidodo, the *rebab* player must never stop playing during a *gendhing*, even if the strings have slipped out of tune, for the *rebab* is the guide *(pedoman)*.

THE *BALUNGAN* AS GUIDE

Besides the *rebab* and *bonang*, the part most commonly described as a guide *(pedoman)* is the *balungan*. But the *balungan* does not offer the same sort of real-time guidance. It is more of a conceptual basis for the elaborating parts, a point of reference. It is the melodic anchor of the composition, from which the other parts can be derived. A musician can construct an elaborating part based on the *balungan* thanks to his or her knowledge of the relations among the parts, and this knowledge is in large measure what musicians refer to when they talk about the importance of "knowing *garap*."

The *balungan* has a special responsibility as guide that the *rebab* part does not have. For Martopangrawit, the *balungan* needed to be such that all of the elaborating parts could interpret it in idiomatic ways. A *balungan* passage that could be elaborated gracefully on the *gendèr* but was awkward for the *bonang* was perhaps a sign of carelessness on the composer's part. Martopangrawit was especially critical of composers of the popular *kreasi baru* genre, who seemed to compose a unison choral part first, then construct a *balungan* that slavishly followed it, heedless of whatever contortions the elaborating parts had to endure to track the twists and turns of the resulting *balungan*. Such a *balungan* was obviously not planned with the idioms of all of the elaborating parts in mind; it was no longer a "pattern" for all of the parts, but rather "just an accompaniment to the singing" (1975:49).

We will examine the role of the *balungan* at length in chapter 4. Here I only wish to point out that the relations between the *balungan* and elaborating parts are not one-to-one but many-to-many: that is, a given *céngkok* can almost always appear with different *balungan* phrases, and a given *balungan* phrase can almost always occur with different *céngkok*. But these relations are not perfectly regular.

As an example of this complexity, consider the *gérong* phrase in example 25, below which I have placed several different *balungan* phrases that it accompanies in different pieces.

At the midpoint of this phrase (at the end of the first *gatra*), the *balungan* tones are all different and thus relate differently to the *gérong* part. Here the men are circling 6 [*a*], and at the cadential point they are singing 5 [*g♯*] as a long lower neighbor to the following 6 [*a*]. *Balungan* B, from Ladrang Wilujeng, is the closest to this, as it too simply "hangs" on 6 [*a*]. The most distant is *balungan* D, from Ladrang Kutut Manggung, which strongly cadences on 2 [*d*] and then "slips" to 6 [*a*]. The *gérong* part ignores this 2 [*d*] and starts directly on 6 [*a*], anticipating the motion of 6356.

Thus this vocal part generalizes over four rather different *balungan*. But the *gérong* line can also make distinctions when an identical *balungan* phrase occurs in different *gendhing*. Thus for example, Ladrang Sri Widodo has the phrase ..6. 7576, just as does Ladrang Wilujeng, but it is normally sung as in example 26. You could give it the same *gérong* part as in Wilujeng, but people will say, "That's not Sri Widodo!" (Darsono 19.vi.85).

What is true of the *balungan* and *gérongan* phrases in example 26 is true, to greater or lesser degrees, of all *balungan* and all elaborating parts: there are no simple rules that will get from one to the other. Differently put, the category of possible elaborations of any *balungan* phrase is not a "classical," rule-based category, but a "nonclassical" one. The same is true of the category of possible *balungan* phrases that can accompany a given phrase in an elaborating part (as we saw in example 25). Hence the relations between *balungan* and *garap*, viewed as a whole, are a mass of "nonclassical" categories, and, as we might expect, the musician's knowledge of these relations is mostly implicit knowledge, built up slowly from experience, not from learning explicit rules.

There is enough orderliness in these relations to suggest that they can

EXAMPLE 25. A phrase from a *gérong* part in *pélog barang*, along with the skeletal melodies it is sung with in four different compositions. A: Ladrang Moncèr; B: Ladrang Wilujeng; C: Ladrang Sri Biwadha; D: Ladrang Kutut Manggung. All are taken from notation by K. R. T. Wasitodiningrat except C, which is from Suroso Daladi (n.d., V:7). (The ciphers in parentheses indicate the preceding cadential tones.)

part							
gérong	· · · · · · · · · 6 · 6 · ·	6̇7̇5	· · · 6	· · · 7̇	· 2̇ · ·	· · 2̇ 3̇ 2̇ 7̇	6
bal. A (6)	·	6	3	5	6	7	6
bal. B (6)	·	6	·	7	5	7	6
bal. C (3)	·	3	5	6	7	5	6
bal. D (7)	5	3	2	6	3	5	6

EXAMPLE 25. *(continued)* Western staff trans-notation.

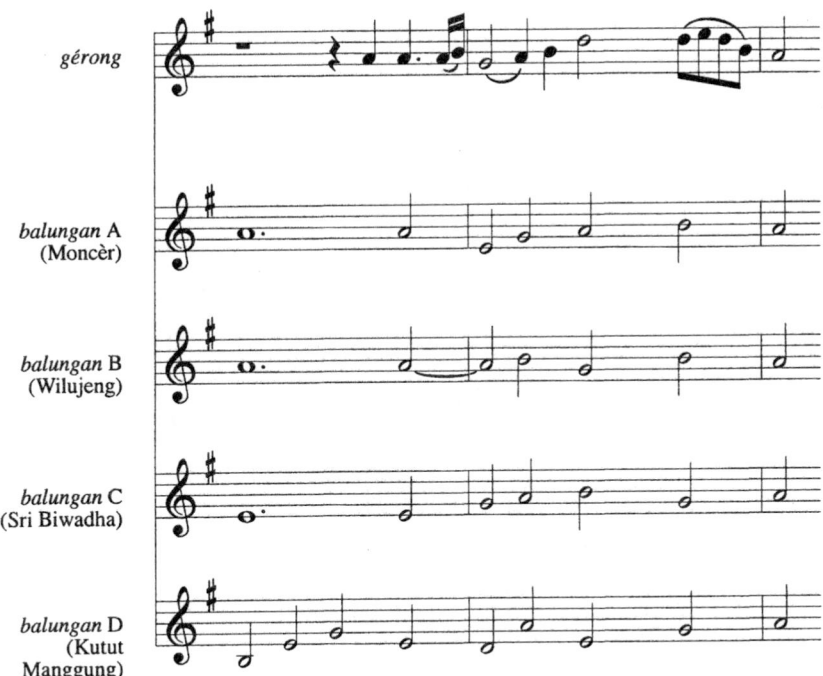

be given systemic presentation, and a few musicians have occasionally tried to do so. Martopangrawit, for example, wrote a multivolume inventory of *céngkok* for the *gendèr* (1973), attempting to specify general rules for their use. Unfortunately, these rules are not as general as they seem. Martopangrawit admitted to me that they are only provisional and cannot be applied without taking the local context into account (26.vi.84). Thus his attempt to reduce "nonclassical" interpart relations to "classical" rules produced only "everyday structuralism," an apparently precise body of formal, explicit norms that in fact could not be used without intuitive, unformalizable adjustments on a case-by-case basis.

This example has important implications for the *balungan*'s ability to serve as a guide to the other melodic parts, implications we will consider in chapters 4 and 6. But before we leave the subject of the *balungan/garap* relationship, there are two aspects of it that we need to examine in some detail. The first concerns the impact of the musician's awareness of the multioctave parts on his or her conception of the *balungan*; the second concerns the rhythmic relationships between *balungan* and *garap*, as expressed in the

EXAMPLE 26. A phrase from the *gérong* part of Ladrang Sri Widodo *pélog barang*, along with the skeletal melody it accompanies. From Suroso Daladi (n.d., V:15).

gérong   . . . . 6 . 6 . . 6̣7̣5 . . . 6̣ . 7̇ . 5 . . . . 6̣ 7̇ 2̇ 3̇ 6

balungan (6)   .   6   .   7   5   7   6

EXAMPLE 26. *(continued)* Western staff trans-notation.

Javanese notion of *irama*. The latter in particular has important implications for the idea of melodic guidance.

From Saron *Line to Multi-Octave* Balungan

Although the *balungan* is said to guide the *garap* parts, there is one respect in which the relationship between them is dialectical. For in learning the elaborating parts, the musician's conception of the *balungan* changes. The *balungan* is played by the *saron* family of instruments, which have the narrowest range of any part; as a *saron* line it is thus naturally sounded within the compass of about an octave. Young musicians typically start by identifying the *balungan* with the *saron* part. Even Suhardi memorized the *saron* line at first (27.ix.85). At this stage, they have no sense of a determinate multi-octave melody, and if they get a chance to play an elaborating instrument like the *bonang*, they use its low and high octaves arbitrarily, choosing a register by guesswork (*ngawur:* Suhardi 8.xi.85). But as they become aware of the relationships between the *saron* and the wide-range parts, their conception of the *balungan* is transformed. They begin to think of it as a multi-octave melody with a range as wide as that of the *rebab* or *gambang,* but folded in on itself to fit the *saron's* narrow range.

Sumarsam (1984:254) gives an example of a multi-octave *balungan* from Lancaran Tropong Bang *pélog nem* (example 27). Here the pitch-classes of the *balungan* correspond to the pitch-classes of the *saron* line, but certain leaps in the latter are converted to steps by means of octave transposition. Where the *saron* line is concrete, this *balungan* is abstract. The *saron* line is played by the *saron*, but no instrument plays the *balungan* in the same straightforward way.[6]

Nevertheless it is sometimes possible to hear this abstraction. Sumarsam has testified to experiencing this auditory illusion; indeed, so have I. When I brought this up with Suhardi, he said (17.v.85):

EXAMPLE 27. *Saron* melody and multi-octave *balungan* from Lancaran Tropong Bang *pélog nem.*

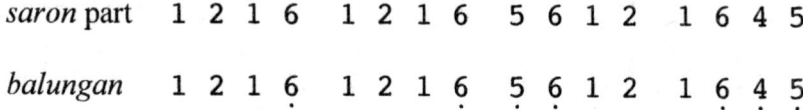

saron part	1	2	1	6	1	2	1	6	5	6	1	2	1	6	4	5

balungan   1   2   1   6̣   1   2   1   6̣   5̣   6̣   1   2   1   6̣   4̣   5̣

Western staff trans-notation.

The point [*maksud*] of *karawitan* is for us to hear .165̣ 33.. rather than .165 33.. when the gamelan plays. This can happen if the *saron* sound is rounded [*empuk*]—like the *saron* in [the ensemble at the Mangku-nagaran court,] Kyai Kanyut Mèsem—and if they're played softly, so the sound of the *bonang* and *rebab* is clear; and maybe also if the *saron* player *feels* it as .165̣ 33̣..

Although there is no traditional terminological distinction made between these two senses of "*balungan,*" for the purposes of this book it will be helpful to adopt one. When necessary, I will distinguish between the *saron* line (or the "single-octave *balungan*") and the "multi-octave *balungan.*"

When musicians hum the *balungan,* they often hum the multi-octave *balungan.* In Solo, modern archival notation usually indicates the multi-octave *balungan,* not just the *saron* part. The multi-octave *balungan* is more memorable than the single-octave *balungan,* since the melodic patterning that is evident in the former is obscured in the latter. There are many regularities in *gendhing* that are apparent in the multi-octave *balungan* but are obscured in the single-octave *balungan.*

Nevertheless, the relationship between the *saron* line and multi-octave *balungan* is more complex than this. The multi-octave *balungan* is not always preferred over the *saron* line in notation, nor is it completely consistent between performers. Fully documenting this complexity would lead us too far afield, however, so we must postpone discussion of it to another occasion.

EXAMPLE 28. Four *irama* levels illustrated in terms of the density ratios of the *balungan* (*bal.*) and the *saron panerus* (*s.p.*). The *balungan* phrase (represented by the *saron* line) is the first *kenong*-phrase of Ladrang Pangkur *sléndro sanga*.

irama tanggung

bal.	5	2	1	2	6	2	1	6	5

s.p. 55 22112266 22116655

irama dadi

bal.	5	2	1	2	6	2	1	6	5

s.p. 55 221122112266̣2266 221122116656655

irama wilet

bal.	5	2	1	2	6	2	1	6	5

s.p. 55 33223232311221 33223322116̇1166̣ 33223322311221 5566i166̇33556655

irama rangkep

bal.	5	2	1	2	6̣	2	1	6	5

s.p. 55 33223322112211225533553322112211 3355335533223322112211221166̣1166̣ 33223322112211225533553322112211 556655661166i166335533556656655

(continued)

EXAMPLE 28. *(continued)* Western staff trans-notation.

Relations of Rhythmic Density between Garap and Balungan

There is one very important factor still unmentioned affecting the relations between the elaborating parts and the *balungan*. Most sections of most compositions can be played with the *balungan* and elaborating parts in at least two different kinds of rhythmic relationship. Roughly speaking, the tempo of the *balungan* can be doubled or halved while the pulse of the elaborating parts remains the same. These rhythmic relationships have names and are arranged in a system called *irama*.

The term *irama* has two senses. It can refer to the overall tempo of a performance and in that sense is characterized as fast or slow. But it can also refer to ratios of rhythmic density: specifically, to the relationship between the beat of the *balungan* and the pulses of the elaborating parts. Javanese theorists often demonstrate this concept by comparing the *balungan* and the *saron panerus* parts. Example 28 shows the same eight-beat *balungan* phrase played at four different *irama* levels. In *irama tanggung*, the *saron panerus* plays two notes for each *balungan* tone. In each successive level the rhythmic values of the *balungan* tones are doubled while the *saron panerus* pulse remains more or less constant; hence the latter is able to fit in twice as many strokes. Thus at the second *irama* level represented, *irama dadi*, the *saron panerus* plays four strokes for each *balungan* beat; at the next level, *irama wilet*, eight strokes. At the final level, *irama rangkep*, it plays sixteen strokes for each *balungan* beat.

Change of *irama* has different effects on the rhythmic density of the *garap* and *balungan* parts. Most of the elaborating idioms (like that of the

EXAMPLE 28. (continued)

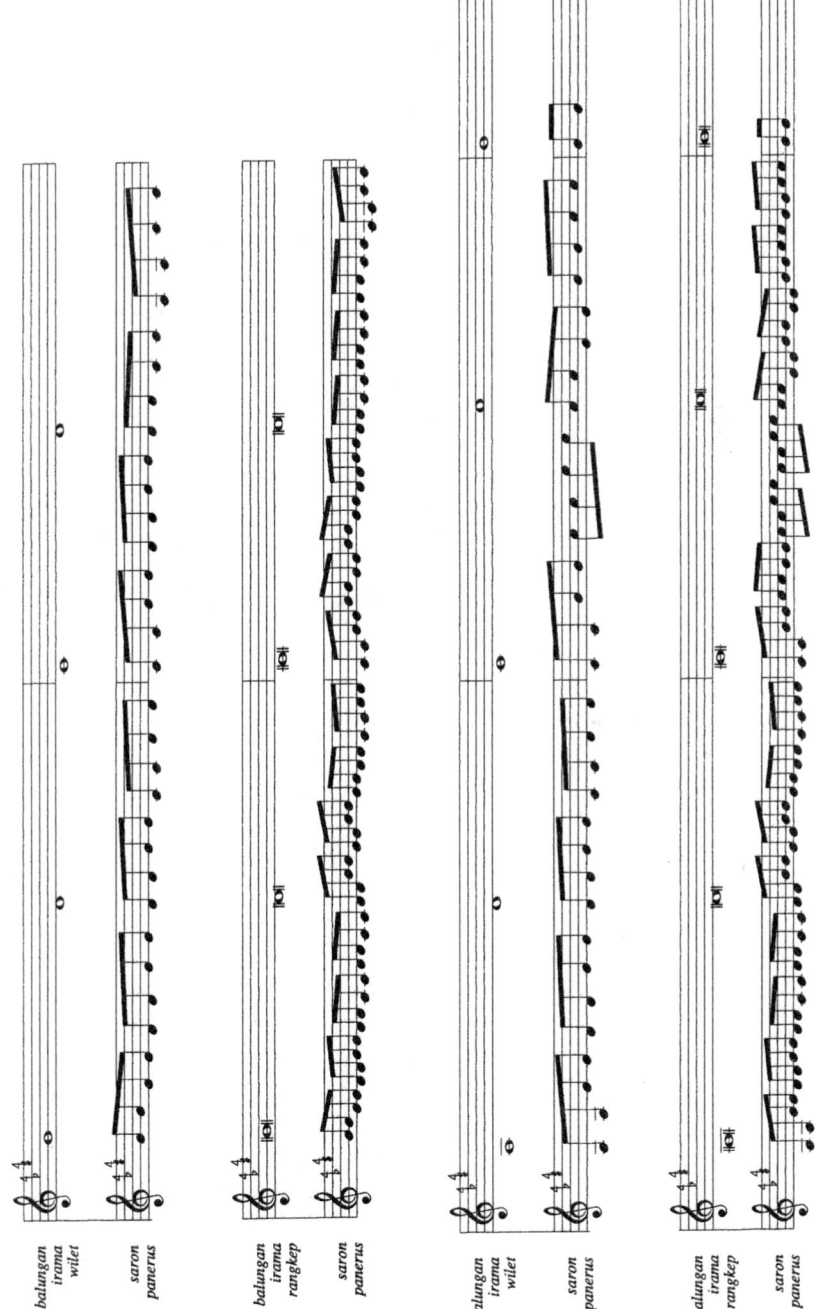

balungan
irama
wilet

saron
panerus

balungan
irama
rangkep

saron
panerus

balungan
irama
wilet

saron
panerus

balungan
irama
rangkep

saron
panerus

saron panerus in example 28) keep a set density regardless of the *irama*, while the *balungan* cannot: in most cases it can only respond to an *irama* shift by becoming sparser. This is especially noticeable in *balungan nibani*. In *irama dadi* the strokes of *balungan nibani* fall about once every three or four seconds (MM ca. 14–17). In *irama wilet* there are about 7.5 seconds between strokes (MM ca. 7.5–8.5). In *irama rangkep* each stroke lasts over thirteen seconds (MM ca. 4.25).

In terms of melodic shape, then, the *balungan* is the most stable element of the melodic texture. But the *balungan* purchases this stability at the expense of its role as a melodic guide. When a composition using the relatively sparse *balungan nibani* idiom is played in *irama wilet* or *irama rangkep*, each *balungan* tone becomes a potential cadence. There is no melodic motion left in the *balungan*, no melodic continuity; every tone becomes a comma, semicolon, or period. The *balungan*'s ability to guide the elaborating parts from cadence to cadence consequently shrinks to a minimum. This is visible in example 28, where the *saron panerus* part in *irama tanggung* and *dadi* can be fairly easily derived from the *balungan* by repeating the *balungan* tones singly or in pairs (compare chapter 2, example 14). In *irama wilet*, however, it introduces tones not present in the *balungan*, and in *irama rangkep* it makes each *balungan* tone the endpoint of a new melodic phrase. We will return to this effect of *irama* in chapters 4 and 6, when we explore the question of melodic guidance in depth.

CONCLUSION

The subject of interpart relations touches virtually every aspect of gamelan music, and an attempt to treat it in one chapter will therefore range widely indeed. We have surveyed types of congruence and divergence, noted the leadership role of the *rebab*, considered the *balungan* as a guide for the elaborating parts, distinguished the multi-octave *balungan* from the *saron* line, and reviewed the variety of *irama*. Congruence is basic to the music, but it is constantly flickering as it is interrupted by moments of divergence. Divergence takes myriad forms, sometimes predictable, sometimes unique to a composition, sometimes reinforcing the unity of the group of "soft" parts, sometimes cutting across it. The relationships among the parts, though far from arbitrary, cannot be captured in general rules: they are "nonclassical" categories. In chapter 6 we shall return to this topic, to see how the almost-regularity of melodic guidance suggested to some Javanese musicians that there might be a deeper aspect of melody in their music.

4 The *Balungan* as Melodic Guide

THE *BALUNGAN* AS RULE:
THE IDEA OF GUIDANCE

On my second visit to Martopangrawit (12.ix.81), he talked at length about the difference between Javanese music and Western music. Western music, he said, has a "score" *(partitur)*, by which he meant that each vocal or instrumental part in the ensemble is fixed. But *karawitan* typically uses a different system, what Martopangrawit called a "rule" or "law" *(hukum)*, centered around the *balungan* (Javanese: "skeleton, framework"). "The *balungan* alone is fixed; the other players and singers derive their parts from it." The composer of a *gendhing* tries out all of the instrumental and vocal parts in his mind but writes out only the *balungan*. If he does his work well, the performers of the elaborating parts will use the performance practice he envisioned. Martopangrawit acknowledged that it is possible to notate the elaborating parts, though fixing them would rob the players of their creativity *(kreativitas)*. These creative parts do *garap*, which he defined as "interpretation" *(tafsir)*.

Thus Martopangrawit had an explicitly formulated view of the way gamelan music works, a view accepted as common sense by many musicians. Each composition has a fixed melodic framework that musicians interpret and upon which they improvise. This framework is a "guide" *(pedoman:* Martopangrawit 12.ix.81, Suhardi 2.i.87), a conceptual melodic basis for the ensemble, a reference point, a fulcrum about which the other parts turn. Martopangrawit seemed quite proud of this system, wondering if it was perhaps unique in the world. He seemed to regard the *balungan's* guiding role as virtually a defining feature of Javanese gamelan music.

And yet, on other occasions he was equally emphatic in his denials that the *balungan* played any such role. He once demonstrated for me how an identical *balungan* phrase must sometimes be interpreted differently in different *gendhing*.[1] How, then, could we derive the elaborating parts from it? "The *balungan* is not a guide," he concluded flatly (11.ii.86). At most, he allowed that the *balungan* might seem to be a guide to the musically immature: "Are all of the parts oriented to the *balungan*? I don't agree! Though maybe it's true for beginners."

Indeed, in many ways the *balungan* is a very irregular guide. It does not guide in the same way that the *rebab* does; it does not have the same importance for the musical imagination. It does not provide the impetus for the compositional process, nor is it the most important factor in the performer's mental image of a piece. Even considered as a purely conceptual guide, as the basis for musical interpretation, the *balungan* often fails to offer a clear basis or point of reference for the elaborating parts.

In this chapter I survey these "failures" (some of which will be familiar to the reader from chapter 3), not to "debunk" the concept of the *balungan*'s guidance, but to demonstrate its irregularity, to show how it is possible that Martopangrawit could declare with equal conviction that the *balungan* does, and does not, guide the elaborating parts. The idea of the *balungan*'s guidance role is a handy cognitive tool, a schematized approximation; it is an example of "everyday structuralism," the use of a straightforward, "classical" concept to refer to the "nonclassical" complexity of the relations among the parts. The notion of the *balungan* as melodic guide presupposes a simplified world, one in which all *balungan* is *balungan mlaku*, the *balungan/garap* relationship is perfectly regular (that is, there are no cases of unpredictable divergence), and it is always clear when the *balungan* is serving as a guide rather than "living its own life."

Perhaps as a result of the "failures" in the *balungan*'s guidance function, some scholars have expressed suspicion of the very concept of the *balungan*. Since it seems to distort the reality of Javanese melodic practice, they have assumed that it must be a foreign body, a conceptual extrusion from a different thought-world, the result of misinterpretation—perhaps the remains of a colonial-period attempt to understand Javanese music using inappropriate Western terms.

I suggest that there is little historical evidence for this conjecture and good reasons to reject it. It assumes the indigenous and original must be pure and self-consistent; irregularity and inconsistency must be belated, the result of admixture and foreign influence. But irregularity and inconsistency are ubiquitous in Javanese music, as no doubt they are in all music. It is true that the concept of the *balungan* as guide does not perfectly describe the nature of Javanese performance practice, but then neither does the sixfold *pathet* system or the concept of *irama* levels as density ratios. We cannot for this reason regard the notion of the *balungan* as an alien interloper in the conceptual world of gamelan.

Indeed, despite its occasional "failures," the idea of *balungan*-as-guide works well enough most of the time. However, when Javanese musicians reflect on their practice, the contrast between the clear cases of guidance and the "failures" can seem to beg for explanation. Why is the *balungan*'s guidance sometimes unambiguous, sometimes ambiguous, and sometimes entirely absent? Is the *balungan* a guide or isn't it? Musicians have tried to make sense of the irregularity of the *balungan*'s guiding function in various ways. In chapter 6 we shall see how some of them found regularity of guidance by postulating unplayed melodies.

THE COMMON SENSE OF THE *BALUNGAN*'S GUIDANCE

Since the rest of this chapter and the next will seem to attack the idea of the *balungan*-as-guide, I must emphasize at the start that many musicians— with good reason—take the *balungan*'s guidance for granted. The *balungan* is the common currency of musical discourse. When musicians talk about *gendhing*, they hum bits of *balungan* at each other to clarify their meaning. Martopangrawit couched his written discussions of *pathet* and phrase structure in terms of the *balungan* (1975; 1984). His oral explanations of diverse questions of performance practice also were presented in terms of the *balungan*. Furthermore, *gendhing* are taught by means of the *balungan*, and it is precisely notation of the *balungan* that has documented *karawitan* over the past century. These practices presuppose the guiding role of the *balungan*, a role that many musicians explicitly affirm. "The musicians do *garap* starting from the *balungan*. They translate, elaborate, interpret the *balungan*, improvising on their particular instruments in various ways . . ." (Supanggah 1985:125). The *balungan* is the "frame of reference and point of departure for the playing [*penggarapan*] of the gamelan instruments" (Supanggah 1990:134; 1988:9). "The various elaborating instruments . . . realize the *balungan gendhing* by filling it out and embellishing it in ways appropriate to the particular instruments" (Hastanto 1985:39). Or, in Martopangrawit's succinct formulation, "The *balungan* is what is *garap*-ed" (1.iv.86).

The *balungan* can guide the other parts because of the systematic relationships between them. Learning *garap* is in large part learning this system of traditional correspondences. These relationships allow musicians to use what they learn in one composition to interpret others. If they find a *balungan* passage in a newly encountered piece that is identical to a passage in a piece they already know, they can transfer the *garap:* "If the *balungan* is the same, then the elaborating parts should be the same" (Martopangrawit 22.i.85). Using this principle, musicians can draw analogies between compositions. Such analogies are powerful tools in learning pieces and in devising creative new interpretations of them (Perlman 1994:406–14; Brinner 1995b:27–28, 64–65).

Ultimately, a musician who "knows *garap*" can construct an elaborating part based on the *balungan*, without consciously needing to draw analogies to a specific piece. As Supanggah (29.x.84) put it,

> We are equipped [*dibekali*] with *garap*. If the *balungan* is like this, then the *rebab* has to play that, the *gendèr* has to play such-and-such, the *pesindhèn* has to sing like so, etc. It is fixed [*fixed*] by the tradition.

What is thus fixed is rarely a single possibility, but a range of melodic options. Each *balungan* phrase dictates a smaller or larger set of possible interpretations. Thus the *garap* system provides for both individual autonomy and social coordination (among players in an ensemble, and within the community of musicians generally). Different performers prefer different interpretive options, allowing them to express their personal taste and to vary their playing from one day to the next. But as long as they agree on the *balungan* for a composition, they are able to play together. The *balungan* guarantees the identity of the musical composition as an intersubjectively shared cultural entity, while leaving space for individual musicians to interpret it in individual ways. The musician who knows *garap*—the "*garaper*" (*tukang garap:* Suhardi 16.viii.85)—can decide for him- or herself how to elaborate on the *balungan* of a composition without having to imitate a teacher's example. In this way are independence of individual judgment and the needs of social cooperation reconciled.

Thus the *balungan* would indeed seem to be "a very important factor, even the most important factor" in Javanese performance practice (Supanggah 1990:134). It seems to function for the improvising performer as the necessary "something given to work from" that Nettl calls a model (1974:11). In that way it serves as a charter for the musician's creativity. Furthermore, for Martopangrawit the *balungan* was intimately tied up with the very *identity* of Javanese music, distinguishing it from Western music—and, he thought, perhaps from all other musical traditions.

This, then, is the simplified world of the *balungan*. But the real world is more complicated, and the elaborating parts cannot always or with equal ease be derived from the *balungan*. In the rest of this chapter we shall survey some of the reasons why the *balungan* is not a perfectly reliable guide for the other melodic parts.

THE *BALUNGAN* IDIOMS AND DEGREES OF GUIDANCE

Let us start with what is perhaps the most pervasive of these complicating factors. As we have seen, there is no one *balungan* idiom. There are three densities of *balungan*, each of which relates in a different way to the elaborating parts, depending as well on the *irama* level. The amount of potential guidance to be found in *balungan* depends on its rhythmic idiom and the prevailing *irama*, more or less in inverse relationship to the latitude it affords the interpreter. The sparse *balungan nibani* allows the most freedom *(kebebasan)*; by comparison, *balungan mlaku* is more restricted *(terikat)* (Suhardi 17.i.86). According to Supanggah (25.ix.81), the dense *balungan rangkep* is the most limited *(terbatas)*, while *balungan nibani* is the most free—and hence the most difficult.

Balungan mlaku is conceptually central (prototypical). It is easier to interpret than *balungan nibani* (Suhardi 13.ix.85). Suhardi felt that the *balungan* is the basic melody *(lagu pokok)* only when it is *balungan mlaku;* in the case of *balungan nibani* the player must "discover" a corresponding *balungan mlaku* (31.i.86). Similarly, Martopangrawit said that *balungan nibani* is derived from *(mengambil dari)* *balungan mlaku* (21.v.85).

Perhaps the centrality of *balungan mlaku* is due to its ability to represent all three varieties of melodic motion. As we have seen in chapter 2, *balungan mlaku* can express the differences among moving, hanging, and slipping. *Balungan nibani* cannot, and consequently it cannot guide the elaborating parts as clearly. To see this, let us compare *balungan mlaku* and *balungan nibani* versions of the same composition (example 29, Ladrang Srikaton). The cadence tones (on the downbeats of each measure) are identical throughout. The tones halfway between the downbeats, at the secondary points of stress, are often identical as well. But the *balungan mlaku* version is more informative, twice indicating melodic slipping by means of repeated tones (once indicating slipping motion to 3 [e+], once to 5 [g]). The *balungan nibani* version gives no clue to these.

In example 29 the *irama* level remains constant. Both versions are played in *irama dadi,* and so the density ratio between them is simply the usual density ratio between *balungan mlaku* and *balungan nibani,* two to one. But *balungan nibani* gives even less guidance when it is played in *irama wilet.* To see this, consider example 30. Here we find two possible *balungan*

EXAMPLE 29. Two versions of Ladrang Srikaton *sléndro manyura*. *Top:* the standard *balungan mlumah* version. *Bottom:* a nonstandard *balungan mlaku* version learned in the village areas near Yogyakarta by Suhardi (21.iv.84). The arrows locate slipping motions clearly indicated in the *balungan mlaku* version (by repeated tones).

	N	N	N③	G N⑤	N↘①	N	N	G N
.2.1	.2.6	.2.1	.2.6	.3.6	.3.2	.5.6	.5.3	.i.6	.5.3	.2.1	.2.6	.2.1	.2.6

| 2321 | 3216 | 2321 | 3216 | 2321 | 3216 | 3356 | 3532 | 55i6 | 1523 | i2i6 | i523 | 2321 | 3216 | 2321 | 3216 |

EXAMPLE 29. *(continued)* Western staff trans-notation.

balungan nibani

balungan mlaku

(continued)

EXAMPLE 29. *(continued)*

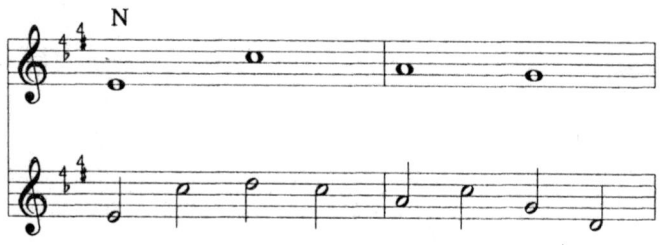

EXAMPLE 30. Two *balungan* phrases used for the *céngkok ayu kuning* in *sléndro sanga*. Top: Ladrang Pangkur *sléndro sanga*. Bottom: a *balungan nibani* phrase from Gendhing Gambirsawit *sléndro sanga, inggah.*

Pangkur	5	6	2̇	1̇	5	2	1	6̣

Gambirsawit	.	2	.	6̣

Western staff trans-notation.

instantiations of the *ayu kuning* phrase type (chapter 2, example 15). One of these (from Ladrang Pangkur) is four times as dense as the other. Its greater density allows it to outline the pattern closely. By contrast, the sparse *balungan nibani irama wilet* (from the *inggah* of Gendhing Gambirsawit) provides only two tones to guide the interpreter. Pangkur's *balungan* exhibits the shape of *ayu kuning* much more clearly than Gambirsawit's *balungan* does. As Martopangrawit commented, *ayu kuning* "isn't visible" *(tidak tampak)* in the latter *balungan* (17.v.84).

In fact, the guidance offered by *balungan nibani irama wilet* is so ambiguous that in many village areas (at least in the Yogyakarta and East Java regions) this sparse *balungan* is replaced with *balungan mlaku* four times as dense. This makes it easier to memorize, although to musicians used to the canonical Solonese practice the extra activity in the *balungan* may detract from the elaborating parts, creating too busy an effect (Harjito 27.viii.00). Consider example 31, where we can compare two versions of one *kenong*-phrase from the *inggah* of Gendhing Bondhèt *pélog nem:* the canonical Solonese version and a village version.

The denser *balungan* here is four times more specific, more informative, than the *balungan nibani* version. In the latter, we seem to find only two different two-tone phrases, each appearing twice: 6 5 [*a g♯*], and 3 2 [*e d*]. In

EXAMPLE 31. The first *kenong*-phrase of the *inggah* of Gendhing
Bondhèt *pélog nem.* Top: the standard *balungan nibani* version.
Bottom: a nonstandard, rhythmically denser version for *irama wilet,*
learned by Suhardi in the village areas surrounding Yogyakarta.

N

. 6 . 5 . 3 . 2 . 3 . 2 . 6 . 5

12162165 33536532 32536532 65262165

the denser version we see that there are in fact four melodically distinct
phrases. In its two occurrences, 6 5 [*a g♯*] has different melodic contents, and
similarly with 3 2 [*e d*]. For example, at the first appearance of 3 2 [*e d*] there
is a moment of melodic slipping, indicated in the dense *balungan* by the repeated 3 [*e*]. There is no slipping at the second occurrence of 3 2 [*e d*], and
hence no repeated notes.

DIVERGENCE

The *balungan's* guidance is clearest when the elaborating parts are congruent
with it. As we saw in chapter 3, congruence is thought to be natural or proper
(*wajar:* Martopangrawit 21.viii.84). It is easier to learn than divergence
(Suhardi 30.i.87), which is why Suhardi started beginners off with *gendhing*
that have relatively little divergence (21.iv.84; 30.i.87).

What happens when the *garap* parts diverge from the *balungan,* sounding different pitch-classes at cadence points? Some divergence is regular. Consider the *balungan* phrase 33.. 6532 in *pathet manyura,* which is quite regularly interpreted with the *puthut gelut céngkok* (chapter 3, example 18). Even
though the "soft" elaborating parts diverge from the sustained 3 [*e+*] at the
downbeat, stressing 6 [*a*] instead, this divergence is relatively predictable.

But there are many occasions of divergence where the *balungan* does
not guide the *garap* at all, where the *garap* simply cannot be deduced from
the *balungan.* We have seen this in chapter 3; it is the unpredictable,
composition-specific divergence that Martopangrawit called *salah gumun
pamijèn.* On these occasions, Martopangrawit's rule ("If the *balungan* is the
same, then the elaborating parts should be the same") fails to hold. To play
such compositions, knowledge of the *balungan* is insufficient; the musician
must also "know the particulars of the case" *(tahu persoalannya)* for that

EXAMPLE 31. *(continued)* Western staff trans-notation.

balungan
nibani
(standard)

non-
standard

N

gendhing in order to be able to play *garap* parts for it (Suhardi 2.i.87). As we have seen, unpredictable divergence seems to be unique to the Solonese tradition, and it is found only in certain parts of the repertory. In numerical terms it occurs in a relatively small percentage of *gendhing*, though many of these are very well known.

AMBIGUITIES OF GUIDANCE

The *balungan's* guidance function is necessarily compromised by the fact that the *balungan* is one element of the melodic texture like any other, with its own idiom to which it must remain faithful. We have already seen some examples of this phenomenon. *Balungan nibani* has a strictly regulated idiom, one that does not permit the immediate repetition of a tone; hence it cannot represent hanging (example 29). As a result, in any given *balungan* passage there may be aspects with no relevance for the elaborating parts, but which are necessary if the *balungan* is to "stay alive." As my teachers explained, not all *balungan* tones have equal meaning for the elaborating parts. Some of them—the ones that "speak" or have "significance" (Perlman 1994:425–30)—need to be acknowledged by the *garap* parts; others do not.

The clearest example of the latter sort of tone is the *pancer*, a tone inserted between each stroke of a *balungan nibani* passage. If a piece uses *pancer* for an entire *gongan*, typically the *balungan* is played normally (without *pancer*) once, and the *pancer* is added for all subsequent repetitions. This is the case with Gendhing Okrak-okrak *sléndro manyura*, whose second movement *(inggah)* uses *pancer* 3 |e+| (example 32). Notice that the *balungan* tones 3 |e+| change to 5 |g| or 1 |c−| when the *pancer* is applied. The *balungan* cannot accommodate a phrase like 3332; this is because *gendhing* with *pancer* may not immediately repeat any tone. Hence if a tone with the same pitch as the *pancer* appears in the *balungan*, it must be changed to keep the *balungan* "alive": 3332 must change to 3532 or 3132 to preserve the consistency of the *balungan* idiom.

If a *pancer* tone has only idiomatic value to the *balungan*, then the other parts should not feel obliged to "walk together" with it. This is in fact the general advice my teachers gave. According to Martopangrawit (19.ii.85), a *pancer* should not be taken into consideration *(dihitung)* by the other parts. In the case of Okrak-okrak, Mloyowidodo (17.x.85) told me to ignore the *pancer* when playing *bonang*: I should play exactly the same as I would for the *pancer*-less *balungan*.

EXAMPLE 32. The use of tone 3 as a *pancer* tone in the first two *kenong*-phrases of the *inggah* of Gendhing Okrak-okrak *sléndro manyura,* as played on the cassette "Gending Bonang" (Lokananta ACD-050). Arrows indicate *balungan* tones that are changed to accommodate the *pancer* tone.

normal *balungan*

.6.5 .i.6 .3.2 .6.5 .6.5 .i.6 .3.2 .3.2

with *pancer*

3635 3136 3532 3635 3635 3136 3532 3132
          ↑   ↑   ↑

Western staff trans-notation.

normal
balungan

with
pancer

Theoretically, then, a *pancer* can be discounted when interpreting *balungan.* But to discount it a performer must first identify it. Sometimes a *pancer* is easy to spot, for the application of a *pancer* often produces a phrase that could not possibly be mistaken for ordinary *balungan.* For example, applying the *pancer* tone 5 [g] to the *balungan nibani* phrase .1.6 produces 5156, which is completely unidiomatic as *balungan mlaku* (Suwardi 9.i.85).

In this instance we are obviously dealing with a *pancer*. But there are ambiguous cases: it is not always obvious whether a tone is a *pancer* and thus whether it should be taken into consideration. See, for example, the passage from Gendhing Kembanggayam *pélog nem* in example 33. We can read this *balungan* as incorporating a *pancer* tone 5 |g#|. The phrase 5653 would then be an altered version of .5.3, modified to avoid the repetition of the tone 5 (just as in Okrak-okrak the *balungan* was altered to avoid repetitions of the tone 3). On this interpretation, the 6 |a| is present only so that the *balungan* can "stay alive," and the elaborating parts should ignore it. But 5653 is itself a very common *balungan* phrase. Hence it is possible to treat this 6 |a| not as a negligible by-product of the application of a *pancer* tone, but as a fully fledged, "significant," *balungan* tone, one that the elaborating parts should "walk together" with.

Both interpretations are possible, as we can see in the two versions of the *gérong* part in example 33. By acknowledging the 6 |a|, Martopangrawit's version implicitly confers greater reality on it. Wirawiyaga's version, by ignoring the 6 and singing to the 5, implicitly dismisses the 6 as an artifact of the use of the interpolated *pancer* tone, as something the *balungan* must do to remain idiomatic.

BALUNGAN AND MELODY IN THE MUSICAL IMAGINATION

Thus far we have seen the limitations of the *balungan* considered as a conceptual guide, a melodic reference point from which the elaborating parts could be derived. We saw that the relations between the *balungan* and *garap* parts are sometimes clear and regular, sometimes ambiguous, and sometimes entirely unpredictable. Considered as a conceptual reference point, the *balungan* is an uneven and irregular guide.

Might the *balungan* function as a guide in another sense, as a phenomenological or mnemonic reference point? Do musicians orient themselves in the gamelan's texture by listening for the *balungan*? Do they remember *gendhing* by memorizing *balungan*? Does the *balungan* dominate the sound-image of a *gendhing* in their musical imaginations? Does a composer compose *gendhing* by trying out the *balungan* in his mind's ear?

As we have seen in chapter 3, Javanese musicians are familiar with the idea of "real-time" melodic guidance, since they need to be alert to the moment-to-moment guidance provided by the leading parts, the *rebab* and *bonang*. But the *balungan*'s guidance is not of this sort. It is not enacted in real time: the other parts cannot (without great difficulty) follow the

EXAMPLE 33. Notation of *balungan* (B) and two versions of the *gérongan* for a passage from Gd. Kembanggayam *pélog nem*. Top: hypothetical *balungan* as it would appear without the interpolated *pancer* tone, 5. *Second line* (B): actual *balungan*, with the *pancer* tone. *Third line* (W): *gérongan* as given by Wirawiyaga (1937). *Fourth line* (M): *gérongan* as given by Martopangrawit (1988:23). The arrow indicates the position of the alternate interpretations. (*Gérongan* similar to Wirawiyaga's can be heard on *Gending Kembang Gayam*, Borobudur cassette, Riris Raras Iromo led by "Ki Cipto Suwarso.")

```
                                                        N ↘①

           .       .      2̇      .      i      .      5      .      3

B:         5      2̇      5      i      5      6      5      3

W:  . 2̇ 2̇  . 2̇3i2̇ . 3̇ 3̇  i3̇2̇ i  i2̇.3̇i2̇i65  . 6  i̇ .2̇5  653i

M:  . 2̇ 2̇ 2̇3i2̇ . 3̇ 3̇  i3̇2̇ i  i2̇.3̇i2̇i6 i 2̇3̇6 5  . 5 653 56i
                                        ↑
```

(continued)

EXAMPLE 33. *(continued)* Western staff trans-notation.

balungan. (At best, a player of one *balungan* instrument, such as the *saron*, might follow the player of another, such as the *slenthem*, by noting which key the latter is about to strike.) A *gendèr* player, for example, in playing an unfamiliar or nearly forgotten *gendhing* in ensemble, would listen to the *bonang*, not the *slenthem*, for clues to the future course of the *gendhing*.

The *balungan*, then, is not a melodic focal point in the practical sense in which the *rebab* or *bonang* are real-time melodic guides. Nor is it the composer's starting point or the mnemonic handle musicians use to memorize *gendhing*. For these purposes the *balungan* is inferior to what musicians called "melody" *(lagu)*.

Lagu means "melody," especially sung melody (Perlman 1994:207). Given the strong association between the vocal parts of the gamelan and the *rebab*, it should not be surprising that musicians also frequently use the term *lagu* in reference to the *rebab* part. The *balungan* is not melody: it is a skeleton or framework *(rangka)*, a melodic pattern *(pola lagu)* but not a melody (Martopangrawit 27.xi.84; 24.xii.85).

Those musicians who described their compositional processes to me said that melody is prior to *balungan*. Thus Martopangrawit (27.xi.84): "In composing a *gendhing*, the melody [*lagu*] comes first, then the *balungan* appears [*timbul*]." Similarly, Darsono (8.xi.84) said he composed starting with the melody *(lagu)*, which he characterized as somewhat like the *gérong* part; then he fit *balungan* to it.

Musicians also emphasized the difference between *balungan* and melody when suggesting ways to commit *gendhing* to memory. Suhardi and Martopangrawit both stressed the importance of "reciting" *(membaca)* the *balungan;* that is, of singing it, "knowing where it's high[-octave] and where it's low" (Martopangrawit 27.xi.84). It is possible to memorize a *gendhing* by such recitation, but Martopangrawit felt that there is another, easier way (27.xi.84):

> It's hard to memorize *balungan*, especially in the *inggah* [section] of *sléndro* [*gendhing;* i.e., the relatively sparse *balungan nibani*], like .6.5 .3.2, for example. But if you use melody [*lagu*], it's easy to memorize. *Balungan* is a framework [*rangka*], it's not melody.

Of course, musicians have several ways to memorize *gendhing*. It is clear that many musicians do memorize *balungan;* indeed, in the earlier stages of the learning process they have few alternatives. Furthermore, there is evidence for a nonmelodic, structural mnemotechnic strategy, one that parses *gendhing* into a hierarchical structure of goal-tones (Perlman 1994:216–17). But many of my teachers insisted on the mnemonic importance of melody, especially where the *balungan* is sparsest. In *balungan nibani irama wilet* and especially in *irama rangkep*, a *saron* player who had nothing else to hang on to might be forced to fill up the long pauses in his part with silent rehearsal of the *balungan* tones to come:

> When Suhardi was still young and wasn't yet able to *garap* [*nggarap*]— didn't yet know the melody [*lagu*]—he memorized the *balungan* for

Gendhing Onang-onang *pélog nem* from notation. He subsequently played *slenthem* when his gamelan group performed it. When it entered *irama rangkep* he had a hard time of it. The first *gatra* after the *kenong* is .2.1, and so after the *kenong*-stroke he thought to himself, "Next comes .2.1." As the seconds passed he kept repeating to himself, "Two one . . . two one . . . still two one . . ." until the moment finally arrived for him to play the 2. (13.ix.85)

Suhardi concludes that it's bad to play *balungan* before you know the *lagu*, before you know the *isi* (the "filling" or "contents").

Several of my other teachers also considered the sparser kinds of *balungan* as harder to remember, and they also recommended reliance on the melodic material that fills the long empty intervals in the *balungan*. Mitropradongga (15.xi.84) also emphasized the importance of "filling" the *balungan*, and not only when *irama*-shifts rendered it extremely sparse. This sort of filling is essential to the memory technique he called *ijoan* and defined as "memorizing *gendhing* without a gamelan."[2] If you try to memorize the *balungan*, you'll easily forget it *(gampang lali)*, but if you fill it with *rebaban, kendhangan, gendèran*, or whatever else you're familiar with, it will stick *(leket)*. He later (22.xi.84) emphasized further the importance of memorizing *balungan* with its filling *(isènipun)* so as not to forget it: you should sing *(ura-ura)* or hum *(rengeng-rengeng)*, filling it with all sorts of stuff *(wrena-wrena)*, whatever you need: *gendèran, sindhènan*, etc. If you memorize this way, you can instruct *(muruki)* the *gérong, pesindhèn*, and so on by singing their parts while you play *bonang* (or another instrument).

Among all the types of filling, the *rebab* part has a special place. For Martopangrawit (13.viii.85) the *rebab* played the full melody of the *gendhing (lagu gendhing penuh)*, and the *rebab* part was the part favored by skillful musicians—"the masters" *(empu-empu)*—when memorizing compositions (27.xi.84). In part this was because of the *rebab*'s wide range; parts with narrower ranges (like the *gendèr*) could not as clearly display the register of the melody of the composition (24.ix.81).[3] Martopangrawit seemed to rely on the *rebab* part even when he had the notation of a piece in front of him, as on one occasion (27.viii.85) when he refreshed his memory of the second movement *(inggah)* of Gendhing Mawur *sléndro sanga* by humming the *rebab* line while perusing the *balungan* notation.[4]

Martopangrawit allowed a special place for the *rebab* part in the mnemonic technique he called humming *(rengeng-rengeng)*. Before notation was invented, he claimed (17.iv.84), people learned *gendhing* by humming. Even Martopangrawit learned this way, though notation already existed, since it is much easier to memorize *gendhing* by humming than by notation:

Humming unites *rebaban, balungan,* and *kendhangan.* The melody would be hummed using the drum syllables as words.[5] Even humming a *gendhing bonang* would incorporate *rebaban,* moving smoothly, never intermittently [*putus-putus*].

Martopangrawit used this fact to explain "why many musicians have versions of *gendhing* that differ slightly from each other" (17.iv.84; 3.iv.84):

In the past, musicians didn't have notation, so they relied on humming the *rebab* part. You would teach someone to hum the *rebab* part and then he would interpret it himself to make the *balungan.* This is why there are *gendhing* that exist in different versions, all of which have the same feeling [*rasa*].

Although the *rebab* part was central to Martopangrawit's concept of humming, in fact his own practice of humming included more than just the *rebab* line. This became clear to me when I recorded Martopangrawit (30.x.84) humming a few well-known *gendhing.* Martopangrawit found the idea of recording his hums somewhat amusing, but the exercise quickly revealed that they were not well-defined entities, nor were they confined to the *rebab, balungan,* and drum parts. They also incorporated *gendèr, bonang,* and vocal parts. As he himself admitted (9.x.84),

Which part he hums at any given moment isn't something he plans [*disengajakan*]; it's sort of unconscious. He doesn't decide, "Now I'll hum the *bonang* (or *kendhang*)." So each repetition of the *gendhing* might be hummed differently.

He explained that humming depends on what it is used for *(kebutuhan):* if you're learning to play *gambang,* you'll put more *gambangan* in your humming. But if you're humming to memorize the piece, then *everything* should be in it.

It is obviously not possible to unite in a single hum all of the vocal and instrumental parts in their entirety, or even the subset of parts Martopangrawit considered essential in the process of composition *(rebab, gendèr, bonang, balungan, kendhang, kenong).* The hummer can jump back and forth between parts, however; and this is what Martopangrawit in fact did.

Examples 34 and 35 show how Martopangrawit hummed passages from Gendhing Gambirsawit *sléndro sanga.* Underneath the *balungan* notation I have indicated the part or parts Martopangrawit hummed at each moment.

Clearly, a good deal more than the *rebab, balungan,* and *kendhang* parts entered into Martopangrawit's hums. The *rebab* part, though prominently featured and never absent for long, shares the hummings with the *gendèr, bonang, pesindhèn,* and *gérong* parts. Martopangrawit's humming is rather

EXAMPLE 34. Analysis of Martopangrawit's humming of Gambir-sawit *(mérong)*. Where *"kendhang"* is indicated, Martopangrawit pronounced the syllables that conventionally represent drum strokes. When no other part is indicated beside that of the *kendhang*, Martopangrawit sang the drum syllables to the *balungan* part.

                                                        N

. 3 5 2   . 3 5 6   2 2 . .   2 3 2 1

                                      rebab   *rebab*

kendhang   *kendhang*   *kendhang*   *kendhang*

                                                           N

. . 3 2   . 1 2 6   2 2 . .   2 3 2 1

rebab   *rebab*   *rebab*   *rebab*

kendhang   *kendhang*   *kendhang*

                                                           N

. . 3 2   . 1 6 5   . . 5 6   1 6 5 3

rebab   *sindhèn*   *gérong*   *gérong*

kendhang   *kendhang*   *kendhang*   *kendhang*

                                                           G

2 2 . 3   5 3 2 1   3 5 3 2   . 1 6 5

gendèr   *gendèr*

                  kendhang   *kendhang*   *kendhang*

what Supanggah called a "miniature *klenèngan*," a multipart texture turned into a single, singable line. It thus represents a sophisticated form of what Arom calls diagonalization (1991:453, 504).

Martopangrawit's hums were virtuoso performances, obviously out of reach of a beginning student. Learners probably start out memorizing compositions by singing the *balungan;* as they master the other parts, they can

EXAMPLE 35. Analysis of Martopangrawit's humming
of Gambirsawit (first half of the *inggah irama wilet*).
(See the caption for example 34.)

```
.            6            .            5̣
kendhang                  kendhang


.            1            .            6̣
rebab                     rebab
                          kendhang


.            1            .            6̣
        sindhèn                 sindhèn
            kendhang
                                                    N

.            2            .            1
     gendèr                      gendèr


.            2            .            1
gendèr sindhèn                  sindhèn
                 kendhang


.            2            .            6̣
     rebab                       rebab
kendhang                  kendhang


.            1            .            6̣
     sindhèn
kendhang     kendhang

                                                    N

.            2            .            1
     gendèr                      gendèr
kendhang
```

incorporate more elements into these personal rehearsals. Ultimately they can perform Supanggah's "miniature *klenèngan.*"

"Humming" seems to draw its mnemonic power from the psychologically salient elaborating parts—especially the *rebab* and vocal parts—that dominate it. Richer and more vivid than the bare *balungan* line, it can impress itself on the memory more easily. But it gains mnemonic utility by leaving behind the realm of relative fixity, the realm of the *balungan,* and entering the realm of interpretation *(tafsir),* the realm of *garap.* It is a kind of performance, and hence as personal, variable, and improvisational as all gamelan performance.

IS THE *BALUNGAN*'S IMPORTANCE
A RECENT DEVELOPMENT?

The use of the *balungan* to represent *gendhing* in notation, and the explicit affirmation of the *balungan*'s importance by Martopangrawit and other musicians, would seem clear testimony to its centrality. But as we have seen, the *balungan* does not consistently guide the elaborating parts, nor does it dominate the musical imagination of the expert performer. Is it, then, as central as it seems? And if it is not, where does the idea of the *balungan* as guide come from?

Over the past twenty years scholars have made increasingly strong claims for the role of Westernization in the development of the *balungan* concept. Starting with the position that it is historically belated, the product of an artificial notational dilemma, they have questioned its foundational role in the tradition. The idea of the *balungan*'s guidance, they suggest, may be an oversimplification produced directly or indirectly by an inaccurate analogy with Western music.

In this view, the importance of the *balungan* is a recent development, a product of the late colonial period. It was a response to two turn-of-the-century innovations, both the result of foreign influence: the introduction of gamelan notation and the growth of descriptive and instructional writings about the music. The *balungan* melody, they claim, was arbitrarily singled out for notational and theoretical attention.

How plausible is this argument? It rests largely on a single lexicographical fact: that in the extant manuscript and published writings about gamelan music we do not find the term *"balungan"* used until the 1910s, about four decades after the invention of notation. But it is dangerous to infer history from negative lexicographical evidence, especially in Javanese music, where there is a great deal of variability in the uses of words. I suggest that there were sound musical reasons for notating the *balungan* rather than any other part. Before I detail these reasons, however, I must clear the historical ground.

It is true that the term *"balungan"* acquired a musical sense only in the twentieth century. Judith Becker was perhaps the first to point out its essential novelty. She described it as a modern coinage, called into existence by the introduction of gamelan notation in the late nineteenth century. Notation itself was introduced from preservationist motives, she claimed; it was absorbed by the Javanese from the Dutch—neither of whom "understood oral traditions in which through a process of continual re-creation every piece is at once contemporary and the cumulative result of ageless tradition" (1980:13). The idea of the *balungan* was a response to the dilemma faced by the first generation to commit *gendhing* to writing (1980:13–14):

> The initial question faced by those developing notation systems must have been, Of all the different polyphonic lines of the gamelan, which shall be chosen for notation? Gamelan music is composed of a series of layers of melody, increasing in density in proportion to the higher registers of the instruments. Most traditional Western music is not constructed in this way, but rather has a main melody with supporting, but subordinate harmonic structure. Western notation was developed to accommodate European musical structure. Where is the main "melody" in a Javanese gamelan piece? In a series of polyphonic layers this is not at all clear. . . . There is nothing in the traditional practice of gamelan to indicate emphasis of one part over another. On the contrary, musicians will often say that ideally all parts should be equal. Given an impossible choice, a compromise solution was accepted. A middle register part of medium density was designated as the "melody," the part to be notated. Since this part was singled out by notation and placed in a special focus, a new word had to be found to designate that part.

Lindsay (1985) arrived at a similar conclusion from her investigation of the history of *karawitan* in Yogyakarta. After observing that the term *"balungan"* is not reported by the earliest Western writers on Yogyanese gamelan (in the late 1880s), and that "the introduction to the Yogyakarta *gendhing* collection, the *Pakem Wirama*, does not mention the term *balungan*," she concludes that "the *saron* line was not chosen to be notated because it was inherently or exclusively the *balungan* of a *gendhing*, but rather the word '*balungan*' came to be applied to the *saron* part to refer to its role as the notated *gendhing* outline" (1985:195).

Sumarsam, too, agrees with Becker, though he amplifies her remarks with a more detailed and thorough historical study and makes even stronger claims of Western influence. He points out that the earliest Javanese writings to mention the term postdate published Western analyses that treat the *saron* line as a "theme" or "cantus firmus." He asks, "Were these Javanese authors' writings inspired by the works of the Dutch intellectuals?" (1995:149). The historical record does not allow us to answer this question. But Sumarsam concludes that notation was not the only factor at work in the genesis of the *balungan* concept (1995:151–52). In the decades surrounding the turn of the century, the interaction of Dutch intellectuals with learned Javanese aristocrats and leading artists stimulated the production of teaching manuals for gamelan and attempts to theorize the music. "Consequently, a fixed idea of the medium density, the most easily represented line of the multi-layer gamelan texture—the *saron* part—was notated and designated as the theme, cantus firmus, nuclear theme, or *balungan* of the *gendhing*." Sumarsam admits that, despite the important role of Western thinkers in the early history of the *balungan* concept, this concept was not a pure Western fabrication. Javanese musicians already had a concept of a melodic abstraction of *gendhing*; however, this concept was "misinterpreted" (1995:149). But the *balungan* concept, though it arose from a "combination of indigenous and non-indigenous perspectives on gamelan," over the course of the twentieth century "has gradually been accepted as an 'indigenous' aspect of *gendhing*" (1995:153).

Is the idea of *balungan* in fact a colonial-era innovation, a response to an artificial notational dilemma, a result of misunderstanding, a product of foreign influence? Is it an "invented tradition" whose Western origins in the recent past have been forgotten? I believe that the historical record supports a different interpretation. I suggest that, while *"balungan"* may be a recent *term*, there is no reason to suppose that the *concept* is also new. I believe that other words were used in the nineteenth century to refer to what is now called the *balungan*. The importance musicians attach to the *balungan* concept today is not, I argue, a side effect of the introduction of notation. For the idea of the *balungan*, under whatever name, helps musicians make sense of certain regularities in their music. (Not perfect sense, to be sure; but if perfection is our standard, we will have to question the credentials of most or all of the concepts musicians use to understand their music.)

The Prehistory of "Balungan"

Sumarsam establishes the appearance of the word *"balungan"* (as applied to music) in the early years of the twentieth century and points out how it is confined to instructional literature; earlier belletristic writings on music do not use the term. For example, it does not appear in the *Serat Gu-*

lang Yarya (1870), one of the earliest surviving manuscript treatises on music.

But suppose *"balungan"* simply replaced or supplemented some earlier words? If so, the innovation might not have been conceptual, but terminological. The vocabulary of *karawitan* even today displays a great deal of semantic overlap: different people use different words to refer to the same things, a single word can refer to several things, and certain senses of one word may be identical to certain senses of some other word. We also know that terminology can change over time.[6] It is thus conceivable that other terms were once used in the same sense that *"balungan"* is today.

A careful reading of historical sources supports this view, and carefully listening to the conversations of musicians shows that several other terms can be used to refer to the *balungan*. Prominent among these terms is the word for composition itself: *"gendhing."* Musicians sometimes say *"gendhing"* in contexts that clearly indicate they are talking about the *balungan*.[7] Such polysemy—the use of a musical term in both a relatively concrete sense (in this case, a single musical part) and a relatively abstract one (a musical composition)—is common in many traditions. It suggests that the *balungan* is in some sense the *gendhing* par excellence, but we should not assume that musicians who use the term this way naively identify the composition with the *balungan*. After all, Western musicians who call the notated form of a composition "the music" are not necessarily incapable of distinguishing the composition from the score. But just as this usage reflects the importance of notation in the life of the Western musician, the polysemy of *"gendhing"* suggests that the *balungan*, more than any other part, is conceptually central to the idea of the composition.

Furthermore, musicians seem to have other ways of referring to the *balungan*. Some of my teachers used *thuthukan* ("strokes"), a word that also appears in the *Gulang Yarya* (Canto 5, stanzas 13–14), in a context that clearly refers to the *balungan*. Kunst (1973:I, 157) mentions *baku*, "the principle, real thing," as another term for the *balungan*.

It may be that the word *"céngkok"* also once referred to the *balungan*.[8] There are several passages in the *Gulang Yarya* that bear this interpretation. Canto 2 of this work contains poetic descriptions of the gamelan instruments where we find recognizable melodic technical terms associated with certain instruments. Significantly, in this canto *"céngkok"* is used only of a *balungan* instrument, the *demung*.[9] *"Céngkok"* is further used (in Canto 5, stanza 8) in parallel with *lagu* (melody, tune) to refer to basic, unornamented melodic forms. *Lagu*'s place is in *tembang* (sung poetry), while *céngkok*'s place is in *gendhing*, but they mean the same (*sami kéwala pika-*

jengipun): "[something] pure and unmixed from the start, which indeed is made the sonic standard" *(tulèn sawantah saking wit yektènira kinarya watoning swara).* Both *lagu* and *céngkok,* the pure standards, are contrasted with *wilet,* variable embellishment. Thus it is possible to find variants of *tembang* melodies that differ in *wilet* but share the same melody *(lagu).* After discussing this possibility, the *Gulang Yarya* (Canto 5, stanza 13) goes on to talk about changes in the actual melodies of *tembang:* in such cases, the *tembang* should be given a new name. The text then addresses the same topic with regard to *gendhing:*

makaten ugi yèn gendhing	Similarly, with regard to a *gendhing*
nyimpang céngkokirèki	[whose] *céngkok* deviates,
inggih wenang nama santun	its name too may be changed

Thus different versions of *tembang* are said to have different melodies; different versions of *gendhing* are said to have different *céngkok.*[10] Given the earlier association of *"céngkok"* with a *balungan* instrument (the *demung*), it is highly likely that the author of this text meant by *"céngkok"* (in this context) what we would now call *balungan.*

Thus the emergence of the word *"balungan"* did not usher in a radically new concept, but simply added a new entry to the lexicon of *karawitan.* But there was nothing arbitrary about singling out the *balungan* for such attention. Becker implies that notational convenience, not musical considerations, motivated the generation of musicians who designed Javanese notation. But it is far more likely that those musicians chose to notate the *balungan* because of its centrality than that they chose it more or less at random and then were beguiled by its new visibility into giving it a special status it had never had. Choosing to notate the *balungan,* and terminologically equating it with the *gendhing,* makes good musical sense. For the *balungan* is uniquely well suited to serve as a point of reference.[11]

The Centrality of the Balungan

First, the *balungan* is a concerted part. Unlike most of the other parts, the *balungan* is not a solo part; it is usually performed in more or less identical form by three different people (the players of the *slenthem, demung,* and *saron barung*) and followed closely by the *saron panerus* (and, sometimes, the *bonangs*). Though the players of the *balungan* sometimes differ among themselves on small details, and musicians tolerate such differences, individual latitude and spontaneous variation are not prized as they are in other parts (Suhardi 16.viii.85).

Furthermore, the *balungan* (particularly in its concrete one-octave form) is a typical entry point for the learner. The advice of the old masters was to learn the *gendhing* (i.e., the *balungan*) before studying the elaborating parts (Mloyowidodo 2.iv.87). Indeed, before they understand the relationships among the parts, musicians often use the one-octave *balungan*, the *saron* melody, as a point of orientation (Suhardi 27.ix.85).

But most important, the *balungan* can be used as a melodic anchor amid varying interpretations and transformations. Change of *laras, irama,* and performance context often alter the *garap* of a composition but leave its *balungan* unchanged. Thus it is often a uniquely stable point of reference, and as such it is reasonable for musicians to have oriented themselves toward it even in a purely oral tradition.

At the most detailed level, different musicians can use different *garap* for the same *balungan* passages in the same *gendhing*. But considered more broadly, processes of tonal and temporal transformation frequently affect the *garap* parts without altering the *balungan*. When a *sléndro* composition is played in *pélog,* the *garap* parts can change (especially those of the singers and *rebab*) while the *balungan* does not.[12] When the *inggah* section of a composition is played in *irama wilet,* the *garap* changes (Martopangrawit 9.i.85; Suhardi 8.ii.85) and the feeling changes (Martopangrawit 11.vi.85), but the *balungan* usually stays the same. Even more radical transformations occur when a *gendhing* is played in *bonangan* style (cf. chapter 2), for the "soft" *garap* parts are simply omitted while the *balungan* remains the same. Finally, when a *gendhing* is played on the Sekatèn ensemble, even the *bonang's garap* changes. The only elaborating instrument in the ensemble is a one-octave *bonang;* hence the composition's register information is lost, and all that remains is the concrete *balungan,* the *saron* melody.[13]

It is true that the *balungan* is not invariable; it sometimes alters when it changes *laras* or *irama.* But there is no other melodic part that is more stable. Thus there are sound reasons for the centrality of the *balungan.* It is a concerted part, not spontaneously varied in performance. It remains relatively constant across changes in performance context, tuning system, and *irama.* It is accessible to both beginning and advanced players. *Contra* Becker, the inventors of Javanese notation were not confronted with an "impossible choice." The *balungan* is the ideal part to notate; no other part could provide similar advantages.

The idea of the *balungan's* guidance function is a useful construct that nevertheless does not quite fit the reality of musical practice. It evokes a simplified world, one in which *balungan nibani irama wilet,* unpredictable divergence, and ambiguities (like those involving *pancer* tones) do not exist. But as we have seen, such simplifications are endemic to human cognition.

All human culture is filled with self-typifications and self-objectifications, stereotypes and "everyday structuralism." The concept of *balungan* as guide provides only a rough approximation to Javanese melodic practice, but there is no reason to think that it is therefore a distorted concept inspired by foreign models.

THE COGNITIVE CONSEQUENCES OF IMPERFECT GUIDANCE

I hope the reader can now understand why Martopangrawit could on separate occasions both affirm and deny the *balungan*'s guidance function. His apparent ambivalence, evident in these contradictory statements, raises a few questions: How do musicians relate to the fact that the *balungan* is an imperfect guide? How do they deal with it? How do they think about it?

Many (perhaps most) musicians may take no general attitude toward it at all. The idea of the *balungan*'s guidance is a theory of interpart relations, and its success or failure at accounting for them is of interest only to musicians who pay careful attention to those relations. Of course, all competent musicians must have a minimal knowledge of the relations among the melodic parts, so as to be able to follow the cues of the *rebab* and *bonang*. But it is perfectly possible to play gamelan music without scrutinizing interpart relations any more closely than that. For example, Suhardi (8.xi.85) noticed that among the musicians who played *saron* under his direction in the radio station's studio ensemble were some who seemed insensitive to the congruence or divergence of the melodic parts: they played the *balungan* from memory, not noticing what the elaborating parts were doing. Suhardi could tell if they learned to feel a little more, if they became more aware of their melodic surroundings, for they would start to be troubled by divergence. When the elaborating parts diverged from the *balungan*, these musicians would look unsure of themselves, as their memories and their newly opened ears were telling them different things.

It is impossible to estimate what percentage of Javanese musicians pay what level of attention to interpart relations. Suhardi complained that most musicians just play by imitating, without thinking about the relations among the parts (7.ix.84)—though presumably he was measuring them against his own extremely high standard. Insofar as a musician's knowledge of the melodic parts remains disarticulated—insofar as he or she maintains them in cognitive isolation from one another—we would expect him or her to be relatively unconcerned about the "failures" of the *balungan*'s guidance.

Even musicians who do listen panoramically, who hear the parts shifting between congruence and divergence, who are challenged by the "failures" of the *balungan*-as-guide, are hardly likely to feel that those "failures" are something that needs explaining. Nor are they likely to be troubled by the *general* inconsistency of the *balungan*'s guidance. Few musicians, in the course of their day-to-day activities, are likely to wonder abstractly why the *balungan* sometimes guides clearly, sometimes obscurely, and sometimes not at all. For to do so they would need to integrate the idea of the *balungan*'s guidance with their case-by-case knowledge of its occasional "failures" in a connected conceptual whole and to judge that whole by a standard of logical coherence.

For even the best musicians, their knowledge of the overall pattern of interpart relations—in all its heterogeneity—is probably implicit knowledge. Like a native speaker's knowledge of verbs, it encompasses both regularity and irregularity but is activated on a word-by-word (or composition-by-composition) basis. Like other examples of "everyday structuralism," the idea of the *balungan*'s guidance effaces these irregularities. It describes the patterning of *karawitan* only to a rough approximation, one that serves musicians well enough in their daily business.

As must be obvious from my many quotations in this chapter, my teachers were well aware of the *balungan*'s varying degrees of guidance, but few of them seemed to feel the need to theorize it. Even Martopangrawit, for all his interest in theory and despite his awareness of the inconsistency of the *balungan*'s guidance function, did not seem to have a general account of that function, but was capable of strong affirmations and equally strong denials of it (as we saw at the start of this chapter). Other musicians, however, did theorize the inconsistency of the *balungan*'s guidance.

CONCLUSION

Javanese musicians treat the *balungan* as the point of reference for the elaborating parts, as their "guide." While these parts can often be easily derived from the *balungan*, there are many situations in which the *balungan*'s guidance is obscure or even nonexistent. Furthermore, the *balungan* is not as useful as a *rebab* or vocal line to a performer trying to remember a composition, or to a composer trying to create one. Perhaps for these reasons, some scholars have been tempted to suppose that the concept of the *balungan* is a recent one, based on a misinterpretation fostered by colonial-era modernization and Westernization. I believe that these suspicions have no historical basis, and that the *balungan* concept has a firm grounding in the reality of Javanese musical practice. The idea of the *balungan*'s guidance (like the *pathet* and *irama* systems) evokes a "simplified world," but it is no less indigenous for that. However, the disarticulation between the ideal and reality of the *balungan*-as-guide left a conceptual space that some musicians could fill with virtual melodic guides. The coexistence of clear and obscure guidance, once it came to seem incongruous, stimulated them to creative thinking. I will tell that story in chapter 6; but first I must describe the social and historical circumstances under which the idea of melodic guidance came to seem problematic.

5 Theorizing Melodic Guidance

*The Social and Historical Context
of Javanese Music Theory*

As we saw in chapter 1, the act of formulating explicit knowledge is a social act, responsive to social pressures, and Javanese theories of the *balungan* have doubtless been shaped by such pressures. Javanese reflection on the nature of melodic guidance emerged within a rapidly modernizing society, where colonial and postcolonial political, social, and technological changes affected the circulation of knowledge. In traditional Javanese society there had been no formal institutions charged with disseminating musical knowledge; like most other forms of knowledge, it flowed within familial and personal circles. Learners were expected to be self-reliant, to figure things out for themselves based on deliberately cursory and cryptic hints. Over the past century, however, social changes accumulated that encouraged the explicit formulation of musical knowledge and provided new criteria of musical explanation. In this chapter we will see how the spread of formal music education, the valuation of explicit theorizing as a perceived attribute of modernity, and encounters with Western ethnomusicology created a new climate for the verbalization of musical knowledge.

THE TRADITIONAL LEARNING PROCESS

Traditionally, musical knowledge was not considered a public good, and the larger institutions of Javanese society—in particular, the courts—did not formally transmit it. Knowledge was a status marker, and among court musicians (the most strongly hierarchical area of musical society) specialized knowledge was treated as a possession to be guarded. It flowed not through public institutions, but through personal relationships: either informal ties of kinship and friendship or a somewhat more formalized apprenticeship.

The traditional "ethnopedagogy" of Javanese musicians placed great value on the initiative of the learner, who was expected to take an active role in "searching" for *(nggolèki)* knowledge. Musical regularities were not often explicitly articulated; students had to abstract general features or principles from the compositions and improvisations they heard and infer widely applicable techniques for interpreting or embellishing the models they encountered (Brinner 1995b:64, 147). This focus on autodidacticism rewards the learner who can "take a hint" *(tanggap ing sasmita)*, who does not need explicit instruction but can profit from cryptic, indirect, or abstract clues. (As we shall see in chapter 7, the valuation of such abilities is consistent with the status awarded in Javanese society to the ability to respond to indirect suggestions and subtle, unspoken undercurrents in social interaction, and the ability to interpret symbols in general.) To their own observations the learners could add whatever they might glean from the remarks of older performers, but these were not necessarily easy to understand. Javanese musicians traditionally were sparing with explanations, and when they did give them, they were often gnomic, bafflingly banal, or apparently unhelpful; at any rate, they called for a great deal of interpretation on the part of the student. For example, Martopangrawit (1975:II, 5) wrote that the explanations about *karawitan* given by the old masters *(empu)* "seemed straightforward but were not easy to understand" *(katon yen prasaja nanging ora gampang ditampa)*; the listener would have to "figure out for himself" *(ngonceki dewe)* what the speaker meant. Wahyopangrawit (3.xii.84) confirmed that the court musicians would give "instruction without explanation" *(pituah tanpa penjelasan)*, and the student was told to "search out for yourself" *(golèkana dhéwé)* the meaning.

Of course, verbalization was hardly unknown to the Javanese before the twentieth century; there was a centuries-old tradition of historical, moralistic, divinatory, mythographic, lexicographical, and other sorts of writings, and we have literary and theatrical depictions of verbal debates or duels *(bantahan)*. Musicians had their own tradition of commentary on matters musical. These oral traditions have left few historical traces (Perlman 1994:78 n. 24), but to judge from the lore recorded from musicians born in the early decades of the twentieth century, many of them involved allegorical, homiletic, or symbolic interpretations of instruments, *gendhing* titles, performance practices, and so on (Perlman 1994:585–91; Warsodiningrat 1987; Wong and Lysloff 1991:319–22). For example, there were allegorical interpretations of the *pathet* (Kunst 1973:I, 76–77). The three *sléndro pathet* could be compared to the three basic emotions (happiness, anger, and sadness) or the three basic tastes (salty, bitter, and sweet) or the three stages of life (childhood, maturity, and old age).

These allegories represent a type of metaphorical or analogical thinking. They are based on equinumerosity, linking one set of three elements with another set of three elements—what Beatty calls numerical puns (1999:250 n. 8). Like all analogies, they bind together disarticulated knowledge, building links between otherwise unrelated conceptual schemas, and in this way create meaning. We can regard them as explanations of a sort, though they do not satisfy modern Western scholarly criteria of explanatory value.

WIDENING THE CHANNELS OF CIRCULATION

Modernization has not completely changed this situation, but it has made musical knowledge more accessible in certain respects and has marginalized traditional allegorical explanations in favor of styles of verbalization that meet what were felt to be the scholarly and scientific demands of the modern age. The twentieth century saw a gradual lowering of the barriers restricting access to musical knowledge. This came about through a series of mutually reinforcing developments, including the invention of music writing, the publication of notation and guidebooks, the founding of courses of musical instruction, the staging of musical performances open to the public, the introduction of radio broadcasting, and the founding of state conservatories, statutorily open to all, which now transmit the court tradition.

Starting apparently in the late nineteenth century, Javanese writers on traditional culture display a sense of obligation to an epistemic public sphere. Knowledge should not be hoarded, but made available to all: "Knowledge which is hidden away is like buried iron; it will only rust and disappear without a trace." Again and again, authors who commit traditional knowledge to writing describe their efforts as intended "for the general good" *(amaédahi ing ngakathah).*[1]

In the musical realm we can more or less arbitrarily trace the influence of this attitude to 1901, when the first articles about music and compilations of notation began to appear in print.[2] By the 1920s courses of musical instruction were offered. The most famous of these was the *kursus* (course) offered by the Prime Minister's Radya Pustaka foundation from 1923 to 1942 (*Nawa Windu* 1960:13). There were also courses in vocal music and gamelan courses for children.

With Independence, new institutions arose to supplant the authority of the courts, institutions whose mission was to put music and musical knowledge into circulation. The Solonese studio of the national radio service, Radio Republik Indonesia (RRI), has a permanent gamelan ensemble. Until the 1990s it sponsored an annual gamelan competition for amateur musicians, with both male and female divisions; these had a certain standardizing effect on performance practice (Suhardi 28.iv.84). Starting in 1950, the Indonesian government established performing arts conservatories. These institutions have unquestionably brought villagers into the court tradition. Indeed, in the early 1980s most of the *karawitan* students at the Music Academy came from rural areas.[3]

There were also numerous opportunities to learn music outside of the conservatories. Local amateur gamelan groups proliferated. Starting in the early 1950s, high school and university students formed their own ensembles (Waridi 1997:40). Neighborhoods, factories, and government offices had their own amateur groups.

Finally, the growth of the recording industry has made examples of certain performance styles and repertories widely available, especially after records were replaced by cassettes as the medium of choice in the 1970s (Sutton 1985; Yampolsky 1987).

The increasing availability of musical instruction widened the circulation of musical practices and repertories, but it also created new incentives for verbalization about music and new styles of verbalization. With the spread of formal training and the use of written texts, an emphasis on immediate intelligibility came to compete with the deliberately cryptic teaching style of the old masters; as Martopangrawit put it, "Now things are written down, so they have to be clear |*terang*|" (12.vi.84). But writing was probably not the sole cause of this new need for clarity. Throughout the twentieth century, the changing social environment of colonial and postcolonial Indonesia, and the availability of Western epistemic models, introduced a "modern," "progressive" style of verbalization quite unlike the allegories and Delphic utterances of the past.

EXPLICITATION AS MODERNIZATION

Over the past century verbalization about music responded to increasing opportunities and rewards for discourse of various kinds. It increased in quantity and altered qualitatively in response to new material conditions, such as the increased availability of paper and the increased publishing activity it encouraged (Sumarsam 1995:132), and in response to new state policies, such as the expansion of the school system, which enlarged the market for textbooks. But it also responded to a widespread feeling that explicit verbalization was *modern,* a tool of enlightenment and self-improvement, and hence necessary for progress.

This attitude is plainly evident in the plan of one Javanese administrator to prepare his fellows for the twentieth century. In 1907 Tjokro Adi Koesoemo, the native ruler *(bupati)* of the district of Temanggung, proposed to foster the progress of the Javanese people by establishing reading clubs for the *priyayi* elite (the ruling class of minor aristocrats and civil servants). In these clubs, the *priyayi* would meet to "mingle their knowledge" *(bergosokan pengatahoewannja).* These clubs, with their libraries, newspapers, pictures, maps, and blackboards (and if possible a terrarium, microscope, or other scientific implements), were to be places for speeches, lectures, debates, questions, answers, and discussion (1907:455–56): in other words, forcing-beds of verbalization.

Tjokro Adi Koesoemo wanted to make his fellows use their brains *(pikiran).* Hence it was essential to make them read newspapers or books, or to listen to lectures. But it was also necessary to get them to talk. For this reason, no Dutch members were allowed—for in the presence of the Dutch most of the Javanese would become yes-men (1907:458). But even in the absence of the articulate Dutch it might happen that no Javanese volunteered to talk. If so, by drawing lots they could be gently *forced* to talk (1907:458–59):

> Someone who speaks, however briefly, and not well, must be encouraged, and must absolutely not be laughed at or criticized; rather, as much as possible he should be helped willingly so that he can progress.
>
> The reason most *priyayi* can't speak well is certainly because [they are] shy, afraid, and don't know what to say; as a result no one talks. If [on a given occasion] no one used to talking is present, they should draw lots. For example, if 50 members are present, make 50 lots, 46 of them blank, four with the numbers 1, 2, 3, and 4. Whoever draws one of the numbers must speak in the order his number indicates. He can talk about whatever he likes: knowledge [*ilmu*], thoughts, news from a newspaper or journal, [something from] a book, or a *wayang,* [something he has] seen or heard, something from a history [*babad*], and so on. It is forbidden only to lie or speak falsely. [They] must practice speaking believably.

The new inducement to discourse did not promote all types of verbalization equally. It introduced a new set of criteria for "useful" talk, a new idea of what was "believable," inspired apparently by Western science and scholarship. For the next century the kinds of talk prescribed by this new set of standards—sober, worldly, practical, empirical—would coexist with the mystical, allegorical, hermetic discourses that had long circulated through Javanese society.

In 1923, Soelardi, a painter and the author of one of the earliest published books on Javanese music, complained that the Javanese traditional arts were not making progress. He attributed this to a lack of explicitly formulated knowledge *(kennis)*, the absence of a theory of art *(ngélmi kagunan)* that could function as the basis for artistic practice and instruction (Soelardi 1923:135). In 1935, Ki Hadjar Dewantara (1889–1959), nationalist agitator turned pedagogue, told a conference on Javanese music that musical knowledge based on scholarship *(kasardjanan)*, and teaching methods based on scientific *(wetenschappelijk)* pedagogy, were necessary to reverse the decline of the art (1957:43). This respectful attitude toward theory remained in evidence after Indonesian independence, when the new Republic set up a *karawitan* conservatory in Solo. In one of its publications, this institution gave theory *(teori)* an important place in the learning process, "especially for the young generation today, who demand in all fields of instruction—those of an artistic as well as scientific nature—the use of reason |*ratio*| and intellect [*akal-pikir*]" (*Kursus* 1959:28–29).

WESTERN KNOWLEDGE AND JAVANESE MUSIC

The first generations of Javanese to formulate explicit theories of their music used European epistemic models to understand their own culture, though in other respects they were often strongly nationalist. This is only an apparent paradox; it is in fact typical of what Partha Chatterjee (1986:79) called "the characteristic form of nationalist thought at its moment of departure . . . born out of the encounter of a patriotic consciousness with the framework of knowledge imposed upon it by colonialism." Like the Javanese who wrote grammars of their language based on the principles of Dutch grammar, the first music theorists applied the colonizer's knowledge to understand their own culture. For example, Dewantara invented a notation for Javanese music explicitly modeled on the European "moveable *do*" solmization system (1941:3–4; Sumarsam 1995:135–39). His student, R. M. Sindoesawarno (1905–1964), drew on Western ethnomusicological theories to understand *karawitan:* he read von Hornbostel and Jaap Kunst, and in later life worked with Mantle Hood (Sumarsam 1995:142).

THEORIZING MELODIC GUIDANCE

The *balungan* did not entirely escape this Westernizing treatment; for example, one Dutch-educated amateur compared it to a figured bass (Soorjo

Poetro 1920:46). But at the earliest stages of Javanese musical theorizing the *balungan* did not occupy the spotlight of theoretical attention. Topics such as *pathet* had a greater fascination for the first generations of theorists, while the concept of melodic guidance was relatively neglected. The late-nineteenth-century inventors of notation who chose to notate the *balungan* had implicitly signaled their belief in its importance, but there were no explicit investigations of its general function for a long time. Even Martopangrawit never tried to formulate a general, comprehensive account of the nature of melodic guidance. That task was taken up by two of his students, Sumarsam and Supanggah. We will examine their ideas in chapter 6. But first we must note the social context of this new direction in Javanese music theory, and in particular the catalytic role of Western scholarship.

Sumarsam started thinking about the nature of the *balungan* as a result of his exposure to Western ethnomusicological ideas about the gamelan. But he did so in an intellectual environment quite unlike that of Dewantara. Born one year before the declaration of Indonesian independence, Sumarsam never fully experienced the Dutch colonial grip. He reached intellectual maturity in a world where Western ideas did not automatically command uncritical respect. Although his thinking was stimulated by his encounter with ethnomusicological theories, he formulated his ideas in reaction *against* them.

ETHNOMUSICOLOGICAL THEORIES OF THE *BALUNGAN*

From the start, Western discourse on the melodic organization of *karawitan* has dealt with two problems: the nature of its melodic texture and the basis of that texture. From early on it has been customary to describe *karawitan*'s melodic texture as *heterophonic,* composed of simultaneous variations of a single melody. It therefore makes sense to ask what that melody is.

The first answer to this question to emerge in Western discourse identified the melody played by the *saron* family as the melodic focus. This "theme" was compared to a Western figured bass (Soorjo Poetro 1920:46) and to a cantus firmus (by Linda Hofland-Bandara, according to Brandts Buys 1921:64). Jaap Kunst adopted this theory: he called the *saron* melody the "cantus firmus" or "nuclear theme" (1973:I, 167, 247) and identified it with what the Javanese called the *balunganing gendhing.* He described how it was punctuated by certain instruments and "paraphrased," syncopated, and resolved into smaller note values by other instruments (1973:I, 175, 230). Yet other instruments and voices provided variations that sometimes approached true polyphony (1973:I, 129).[4] But Kunst was not greatly concerned with the precise nature of this "nuclear theme," and he said little about it. He was far more interested in scales and modes, in his eyes "the most fascinating province of the whole Indonesian world of music" (1937:2).

Kunst's student Mantle Hood looked somewhat more closely at the melodic basis of *karawitan*—though significantly, he presented his ideas in the context of a study of *pathet*. In general, he followed Kunst (except that he came to deny the applicability of the term "cantus firmus" [1971:238]). For him, the *saron* melody "is actually the nuclear theme or melodic core of the composition" (1954:3); he called it the "principal melody" and, like Kunst, identified it with the *balunganing gendhing* (1954:9). He wrote of his "conviction that the nuclear theme and the instruments entrusted with this principal melody were the most important elements of the gamelan. . . . The nuclear theme or principal melody of the gending distinguishes that piece from all others" (1954:17). This melody "predominates all others as it is sounded by the normally large numbers of saron(s)" (1954:4). Noting that most Javanese systems of musical notation record this melody but not any of the so-called elaborating parts, he remarked that this kind of score "is sufficient because the panerusan parts are guided by the nuclear theme" (1954:18).[5]

THE "NUCLEAR THEME" COMES TO JAVA

The Kunst-Hood identification of the *saron* part as the melodic basis of gamelan compositions was the Western theory that stimulated Sumarsam's thinking. Sumarsam was one of Martopangrawit's closest students and was recognized as having a gift for theory *(teori)*. At the Music Academy he was Martopangrawit's teaching assistant for the "Knowledge of *Karawitan*" course. This is perhaps why, when a visiting American arrived in town with questions about music, he gravitated toward Sumarsam.

In May 1971, the American composer and researcher Vincent McDermott came to Solo to study *karawitan*. He took lessons and had discussions with several musicians. Although he also worked with court musicians and teachers at the Konservatori, it was with Sumarsam that he had the most stimulating discussions. (When he asked a technical question of a court musician, the answer might be about "birds in the forest"; Sumarsam, by contrast, gave McDermott answers he found more useful [17.xii.92].)

These conversations proved mutually beneficial. McDermott, of course, learned a great deal about *karawitan;* but Sumarsam, too, profited from his effort to answer McDermott's questions, questions he had never before been asked. It was in the course of these talks (and subsequent correspondence) that Sumarsam made his "discovery" (as he called it [14.xii.92]) that the *balungan* is not the same as the *saron* melody.

The Konservatori library had a copy of Hood's book on *pathet* (1954), and Sumarsam had long wanted to read it. His English at the time was not equal to the urbane modulations of Hood's prose style, and he had tired of consulting the dictionary several times for each sentence (19.xii.92). McDermott, however, read the book and explained some of its main points to Sumarsam in the course of his questions.

The *saron* part is Hood's major tool in his analysis of *pathet*. He places great stress on the melodic shape of cadential passages as they are played by the *saron*, especially on the pattern of steps and skips that result.[6] This seemed mistaken to Sumarsam. As McDermott and Sumarsam later wrote (1975:237),

> Javanese musicians today, if asked to sing such a balungan melody [2165], will more likely sing it with a conjunct downward motion. The rebab, too, as it outlines the balungan will move conjunctly wherever possible, and indeed balungan notation as used at ASKI today is based on the rebab and not on the saron as dots are consistently used to indicate upper and lower octaves in, wherever possible, conjunct order. In sum, it appears that the leaps characteristic of the saron's performance of standard melodic patterns are not tied in closely with pathet nor even with the basic melodic shape of the balungan.[7]

But if the *saron* is incapable of representing the true melodic shape of the *balungan*, why wasn't it modified—in particular, why wasn't its range expanded? Hood believed that the *saron* presented the "nuclear theme" as the Javanese preferred to hear it, skips and all. Had the Javanese felt the *saron* distorted the *balungan*'s true shape, they need not have maintained the *saron*'s limited compass over the years: they could have added extra keys.[8]

McDermott felt the force of this argument, and he conveyed it to Sumarsam. Sumarsam's hesitant answer shows that he was not expounding any received ideas or the fruit of years of meditation, but was thinking out loud, as it were (1975:237):

> From our side we are not sure we have a thoroughly convincing answer, but it may be a general rule that Javanese musicians hear the downward pattern anyway, even in the saron, feeling it pass conjunctly from a higher to a lower saron, in other words that the line may be heard as passing stepwise from one instrument to another, ultimately to be swallowed by the gong ageng.[9]

In his talks with McDermott, Sumarsam was experimenting with a conceptual distinction he had never heard expressed, and which he himself had never articulated. He had never discussed it with anyone at ASKI, and Martopangrawit had never talked about it (14.xii.92). At that time, Sumarsam was a teacher of *teori* in the conservatories, but he taught the subject as he had learned it from Sindusawarno and Martopangrawit. This *teori* not only did not address the question, it blocked Sumarsam from even posing the question (19.xii.92). It took a stimulus from outside the culture to liberate Sumarsam's thinking. In correcting the flaws in Hood's theory, Sumarsam was forced to formulate a distinction between the *saron* part and *balungan* that had not been previously articulated. Before meeting McDermott, he had been unable to "explain" the distinction (19.xii.92); it was through their conversations that he was able to make his implicit knowledge explicit.

As we saw in chapter 3, there is no standard terminological distinction made between the *saron* line and the abstract *balungan*. Sumarsam's realization thus required a cognitive operation of conceptual differentiation. Just as in the history of physics the prereflective idea of weight was separated into the modern concepts of mass and weight, or the prereflective idea of heat fissioned into the modern concepts of temperature and heat, so the prereflective idea of the *balungan* was separated into the distinct concepts of the *saron* part and the unplayed, multi-octave *balungan*.

In August 1971, McDermott returned to America and Sumarsam left to teach gamelan for a year in Australia. The following year he became a Visiting Artist at Wesleyan University. In the summer of 1974 he had an opportunity to return to Surakarta, where Martopangrawit confirmed his ideas about the *saron* part/*balungan* distinction. Humardhani, the director of ASKI, arranged for a group of junior faculty *(asisten dosen)* to meet with Sumarsam to discuss his ideas; most of them seemed to find it unproblematic (14.xii.92).[10] Sumarsam proceeded to broadcast his "discovery" through written channels, publishing an English article with McDermott (McDermott and Sumarsam 1975). But by that time he had already become dissatisfied with his "discovery" and had set out in search of a "deeper" concept of melody. The result of that search—his theory of "inner melody"—will concern us in chapter 6.

6 Three Concepts of Unplayed Melody

Melodic guidance is, as we have seen, a basic aspect of Javanese *karawitan*, but not an entirely systematic or consistent one. It pervades the music, but in differing degrees, and admits of many exceptions. In chapter 4 I documented the limits of melodic guidance, but not to show that Javanese music is somehow incoherent. For I am not interested in these irregularities for their own sake: my real concern is how musicians deal with them.

Insofar as musicians absorb the swirling mass of general rules and apparently arbitrary exceptions through learning-without-teaching—insofar as they acquire implicit knowledge of it—they may never feel the need to account for the irregularities. But once they reflect on the overall relations among the parts, a gap becomes visible between the ideal of the *balungan's* melodic guidance and the mottled reality of interpart relations. The attempt to bring together their piecemeal, disarticulated knowledge of particular cases within a synoptic view can inspire creative thinking, stimulating musicians to understand their music in new ways. In this chapter I show how the irregularities of melodic guidance described in chapter 4 have led three musicians to postulate new musical entities, melodies neither played nor heard.

Suhardi, Sumarsam, and Supanggah formulated their ideas in late-twentieth-century Java, where decades of modernizing influences had transformed the cognitive landscape (as described in chapter 5). These men worked in two distinct regions of that landscape. Suhardi was a civil servant, a member—and eventually, the director—of the ensemble at Yogyakarta's branch of the national radio service. He also performed in, and eventually directed, the gamelan at the Paku Alaman court. But he started out in the world of informal, neighborhood gamelan instruction. He had no institutional musical tuition, but he had a strong desire to teach, and he taught for much of his life, though always privately in his home, not at a formal institution.[1] By contrast, Sumarsam and Supanggah, though also civil servants, graduated from and taught at institutions of higher learning. They both studied theory with Martopangrawit and were both interested in the writings of Western ethnomusicologists. Both eventually obtained graduate degrees abroad (Sumarsam at Wesleyan University and Cornell University, Supanggah at the Université de Paris VII), and both produced scholarly publications. All three men were thus committed to the spread of musical knowledge, but in different ways. Suhardi worked informally, on a small scale, training future performers, and wrote nothing but musical notation. Sumarsam and Supanggah worked in an academic environment, produced much expository prose, and participated in a transnational theoretical discourse. As we shall see, these differences may have affected the uses to which these three men put their concepts of unplayed melody.

SUHARDI'S *"LAGU"*

The 1950s were a time of burgeoning grass-roots gamelan activity throughout Central Java. Amateur gamelan groups emerged in countless villages and city neighborhoods. Suhardi, eighteen years old and already well known on the outskirts of Yogyakarta as a *gendèr* player, dreamed of leading one of these groups. In 1958 he founded Ngudyo Wiromo, which would rehearse in his house under his direction until his death.

Sometime in the mid- or late 1960s, the *rebab* player in this group was having trouble remembering the *garap* for the second movement *(inggah)* of Gendhing Onang-onang *pélog nem*. He apparently found the sparse *balungan nibani,* played in *irama wilet,* too vague to use as a guide. Each tone of the *balungan* functions as a cadence, giving no clue as to the shape of the *céngkok* to use to connect these cadence tones. Suhardi suggested that he flesh out his notation by writing additional ciphers between those of the *balungan*. With these added notes, each tone of the *balungan* became a four-beat phrase of *balungan mlaku* (as it would be played in *irama dadi*). (See example 36.)

Suhardi found this device so useful that he made it a regular feature of his teaching. He wrote out this more informative *balungan*-like part—which he called the *lagu* (melody)—in a wide range of cases: not just to supplement *balungan nibani irama wilet,* but to replace *balungan nibani* in *irama dadi* as well, and even to replace *balungan mlaku* in compositions where it was not congruent with the *garap* parts. Suhardi emphasized this *lagu* in his teaching, calling knowledge of it a master key of *garap* (23.xi.84): "The

EXAMPLE 36. An excerpt from Suhardi's notation of the *lagu* of Gendhing Onang-onang *pélog nem (bottom)* compared with the *balungan* for the identical passage *(top)*. Source: Suhardi (26.x.84).

Western staff trans-notation.

secret [*rahasia*] of *garap* is that, no matter what part we play—*rebab, gendèr, gambang . . .*—we have to know the *lagu*."

In a sense, Suhardi's "melody" is a substitute *balungan*. In most instances it has the idiomatic shape of the *balungan*; the *saron* section could easily play the *lagu* phrases in example 36. This is not invariably the case, however. In particular, Suhardi almost never indicated sustained tones in his "melody," but would repeat tones instead. Thus he would write four beats of "hanging" on 6 as 6666—something rarely found in actual *balungan* parts.

How did Suhardi know what to write? He himself explained that one could learn the *lagu* for a certain *céngkok* (say, *ayu kuning*) by comparing the *balungan* phrases used in different compositions for that *céngkok*. Suhardi (26.x.84) described the relatively dense *balungan mlaku* idiom as a clue to the *lagu*:

> If you can play a *gendhing* with *balungan mlaku*, you can discover
> the *lagu* of that *gendhing*. So, for example, in Ladrang Pangkur, when
> the melodic pattern *ayu kuning* appears, the *balungan* is 6132 6321,

EXAMPLE 37. Martopangrawit's (1984:14) notation of the *céngkok ayu kuning* in *sléndro manyura* (top line), with the *balungan mlaku* phrase that represents it in Ladrang Pangkur *sléndro manyura (middle)* and the *balungan nibani* phrase in Gendhing Titipati *sléndro nem* for which *ayu kuning* is played *(bottom)*. The *balungan mlaku* version also represents Suhardi's *lagu* for the passage from Titipati.

ayu kuning	6	i̇	3̇	2̇	6	3 3 2 2 1

balungan mlaku irama dadi	6	i̇	3̇	2̇	6	3	2	1

balungan nibani irama wilet	.	2	.	1

Western staff trans-notation.

and the *rebab, gendèr*, etc. all play this too. So when they play the same way [in some other *gendhing*] where the *balungan* is .2.1, you can discover for yourself the *balungan* that we construct [*yang kita buat*].

We can represent the situation Suhardi describes here in example 37, a comparison of two *balungan* phrases used for the *ayu kuning* pattern. The denser one *(balungan mlaku)* shows the melodic outline of the pattern much more clearly than does the sparser *balungan nibani*. Suhardi's statement implies that a musician confronted with *balungan nibani* could draw on his experience of playing the congruent *balungan mlaku* version to construct an equally congruent implicit melody. Indeed, this is how Suhardi claims he learned the *lagu*. The musicians of Gedhong Kuning, where he learned to play, used versions of many common pieces that differed from the current standard court-style versions. Often these nonstandard versions used a *balungan* that was denser or more congruent than the standard versions (cf. chapter 4, example 31). Suhardi learned these versions, in which the *balungan* was very close to the *gendèr*, *gambang*, vocal, and other parts. When he later encountered the standard versions, he interpreted them in terms of the highly congruent *balungan* he had already memorized (28.xi.86).

This explanation does not quite explain everything, for Suhardi would sometimes write out *lagu* phrases that made for unidiomatic *balungan*, phrases he could not have learned in this manner. For example, his *lagu* for Ladrang Siyem *sléndro nem* (21.xii.84) contained the phrase 2̇563, which (as he noted himself) is not idiomatic for the *balungan*. In such cases he did not merely select the most congruent possible idiomatic *balungan* phrases from among those actually used, but generated phrases more congruent than any actually played. What made such phrases unidiomatic was their faithfulness to the *garap* parts: they hewed closer to the *garap* parts than any actual *balungan* phrase would. They were, so to speak, hyper-congruent. Suhardi produced them by extending the principle of congruence, extrapolating it, applying it more strictly, more minutely, than usual.

In practice the *lagu* represented an outline of the shared melodic content of the "soft" elaborating parts. Suhardi did not try to summarize all of them in this way, but mainly the *rebab, gendèr, pesindhèn*, and *gérong*, the four parts that most strongly determined the *lagu* (16.xi.84). Of these, the most important is the *rebab* (Sutton 1979:65–66). Sometimes Suhardi referred to the *gambang* as well, but never to the *gendèr panerus*, which, he felt, made no melodic gestures *(nyéngkok)* and made no melody (12.x.84). Nevertheless, as we shall see, constructing a *balungan*-like guide congruent with even just the *rebab, gendèr, pesindhèn*, and *gérong* parts could be difficult enough.

Suhardi's idea of *lagu*, and his way of notating it, remained confined to Yogyakarta; I never found anyone in Solo familiar with it. But it became known among students and scholars of Javanese music abroad. His student Andy Sutton described it in his master's thesis (1975) and brought it to the attention of Western ethnomusicologists in a journal article (1979). Meanwhile, however, another Javanese musician, unaware of Suhardi's thinking, had formulated his own idea of unplayed melody.

SUMARSAM'S "INNER MELODY"

As we have seen, Sumarsam arrived in the United States in 1972 having come to an explicit realization of the distinction between the sounded *saron* line and the unplayed multi-octave *balungan*. He was not satisfied with this formulation, however. Even the multi-octave *balungan* did not seem really to fulfill the guidance function it was credited with. He therefore set out on a search for the "source" of the multi-octave *balungan*. After teaching for two years at Wesleyan, he enrolled there as a master's candidate and concentrated his efforts on this search, which was to lead him to what he called the "inner melody."

Sumarsam articulated the idea of the unplayed *balungan* as a contribution to an ongoing ethnomusicological conversation, and the concept of inner melody was a further response to Western scholarship. Sumarsam found encouragement for his critical stance in Wesleyan's academic environment. His first formal exposition of the inner melody idea was in a class paper, written in February 1975 for David McAllester's "Seminar in Ethnomusicology" (30.v.93). "This is a highly interesting answer to the notion of nuclear theme," McAllester wrote in his comment on Sumarsam's paper. "It's exciting to see Hood and Kunst et al. turned right around backwards." Sumarsam expanded and developed his argument in his master's thesis, which also locates itself as an answer to Western thinking; it begins by criticizing both Kunst and Hood (1984:249–50).

Thus Sumarsam formulated the concept of inner melody under circumstances quite unlike Suhardi's. He worked in an international academic context, driven more by motives of intellectual inquiry than by the practical challenges of gamelan instruction. He sought a theoretical corrective to Western scholarship rather than a teaching aid for aspiring Javanese musicians.

But why did he undertake his search for the source of the *balungan*? His stated reasons (7.iv.82) all correspond to the "failures" of the *balungan*'s guidance function we examined in chapter 4. First, in *irama wilet*, the *balungan* is played so slowly relative to the *garap* parts that it loses its melodic character and becomes a "point-like" series of goal-tones. Second, in certain *gendhing*, the *garap* parts diverge from the *balungan* (e.g., Gendhing Cucurbawuk *sléndro manyura*).[2]

These examples of irregularity in guidance could be interpreted in various ways. They could be tolerated as exceptions to the rules, no more inexplicable than any of the other mysterious irregularities found throughout the realm of gamelan music. Or they could be used to call into question the concept of melodic guidance: they could be taken as evidence that there is no single melodic line in the musician's imagination from which the others could be derived, that the musician must hear the entirety of the sonic texture in his mind's ear.[3] Sumarsam had a different solution. He did not abandon the search for a single melodic line. The *balungan* was problematic, but there was yet a "deeper" sense of melody to be discovered. That melody would provide a key to many questions of *garap*.

Let us follow Sumarsam's own written exposition of these ideas (1976). His aim in his master's thesis is to discover "how the musicians intuitively conceive of the melody of *gendhing*" (p. 71), on the assumption that "the musicians' conception of melody is the true and only essence of melody" in *karawitan* (p. 10). He starts by expounding the difference between *saron* melody and *balungan* (as explained in chapter 4). He criticizes Jaap Kunst and Mantle Hood, who identified the *saron* melody with the *balungan* because they neglected to analyze "the relationships between the musicians' conception of the melodic motion of the *gendhing* and the melodic patterns of each of the instruments" (p. 3). Now, "based solely on what each individual instrument plays, it is difficult to determine what musicians feel is the melody of a *gendhing*" (p. 10). Therefore Sumarsam examines the relationships among the various vocal and instrumental parts, taking into account their different limitations of range and their different performance techniques (p. 3). He concludes that the *saron* melody is not the core of a piece or the basis for the other parts. The *saron* does play the *balungan*, but within its narrow range, making octave transpositions when necessary. The *balungan*, therefore, is "felt by the musicians" (p. 8) but is not actually played in its complete or integral form by the *saron* or any other instrument.

To this point Sumarsam has simply recapitulated the distinction between *saron* line and *balungan* that he first formulated in 1971. However, this is not the end of the story, for "musicians have an intuitive understanding of the *gendhing* melody deeper than *balungan*" (p. 9). To uncover this "deeper melody" Sumarsam examines briefly the *rebab, pesindhèn, gérong, gendèr, bonang,* and *gambang* parts in terms of their "melodic motion, melodic range, playing technique," and "position in the ensemble" (p. 10).

Starting with the *rebab*, described by Javanese musicians as the *pamurba lagu* or "authority over melody," Sumarsam shows how it "directs the melodic motion of the *gendhing* by anticipating the tone or tones which will be approached" (p. 12). Also, its "voice-like," "continuous or smoothly flowing" sound (p. 13) and its wide range (1978:2) make it suitable for the role of *pamurba lagu*.

And yet, in *gendhing* that accompany dance, the *rebab* part is not clearly audible; in certain pieces (such as *gendhing bonang*) and certain ensembles (*cokekan* and *siteran*), the *rebab* is never played; and the *rebab* might be temporarily absent (or, as in some villages, permanently absent) from the ensemble without crippling the other parts. These facts suggest that "actually the *rebab* does not necessarily lead the melodic motion of the ensemble. Who, then, does direct the melodic motion of the *gendhing?*" (p. 14).

It cannot be the *pesindhèn*, since she does not sing continuously, nor the *gérong*, since they do not sing in every *gendhing* or section of a *gendhing* (pp. 14–15). The *gendèr* and *bonang* are unsuitable for the task, since, besides having percussive, nonvocal tone colors, their melodic ranges are not as wide as the *rebab*'s (p. 16). Finally, the *gambang* is disqualified because, although its range is as wide as the *rebab*'s, its percussive quality, high rhythmic density, and characteristic ornamentation prevent it from clearly "guiding the melodic direction of *gendhing*" (p. 16).

These considerations lead Sumarsam to posit an inner melody *(lagu batin)* that is "unconsciously sung by musicians." This inner melody or humming in the heart (*rengeng-rengeng di hati* |1978:3|) is "the essence of melody in Javanese gamelan," the "real 'authority over melody'"; it is what "directs the melodic motion" (p. 17). He finds evidence for such a melody in the habit many Javanese musicians have of humming melodies while they play or when they try to remember *gendhing* (p. 18).

The *rebab* part is often the part most similar to the inner melody (p. 72), but it is also sometimes more elaborate. Sumarsam illustrates this point by notating his version of the inner melody for a sixteen-beat passage from Ladrang Wilujeng *sléndro manyura* (1976:21).[4] The *rebab* line and the inner melody from this figure are reproduced in example 38. (The *bonang, gendèr,* and *gambang* parts for the first half of this passage can be seen in chapter 3, example 18.) The inner melody here is indeed very similar to the *rebab* line, though less rhythmically varied or active. At the fourth beat of this passage (the downbeat of the second measure), where the *balungan* sustains 3 |e+|, the inner melody, like the *rebab* (and the other "soft" *garap* parts), diverges, rising to 6 |a|. But at the eighth beat (the downbeat of the third measure), where the *balungan* cadences on 2 |d| and the *rebab*, anticipating the following phrase, already sounds 3 |e+|, the inner melody (along with the rest of the soft *garap* parts) holds to the *balungan*'s 2 |d|.

EXAMPLE 38. *Balungan, rebab,* and Sumarsam's "inner melody" for a passage from Ladrang Wilujeng *sléndro manyura.*

balungan

3   3   .   .   6   5   3   2   5   6   5   3   2   1   2   6̣

rebab

. 3 56.6. 6 6 .i. 3 1 2 232 3 5 3 566 . i̇65 5 6 6 .21 .62 1 6̣

"inner melody"

3   5 66   6 i̇ . 3 1 2 2 3 2 3 5 66 . 6i̇5 3 5 6 2 1 6̣ 2 1 6̣

Western staff trans-notation.

EXAMPLE 39. Two versions of *rebaban* for a phrase from Ladrang Wilujeng *sléndro manyura.*

balungan

3   3   .   .   6   5   3   2

rebaban A

.   3   5 6 . 6 .   6   6   . i .   3   1   2   2 3 2   3   5 etc.

rebaban B

.   6   i   ̇2   6   i   ̇2   i ̇2 ̇2   i ̇2632   1 6̣ 1   2   3   5 etc.

Western staff trans-notation.

The *rebab* part is also more variable than the inner melody. In the example from Ladrang Wilujeng given above, the *rebab* has an alternative *céngkok* for the phrase 33..6532. In example 39, version A corresponds to example 38, and version B is the alternative. For Sumarsam (10.v.82), version A is "fundamental" and follows the inner melody, while version B does not. This is clear if we compare the *rebab* and *balungan:* for *rebaban* A is a "closer" interpretation of 33..6532 than is *rebaban* B (19.v.92).

In any event, not merely the *rebab,* but *all* the instrumental parts, are "inspired" (p. 72) by the inner melody. Each player creates his part by adjusting his "conception of the inner melody" to the "range of his instrument and its performance technique" (p. 72). In the past, players of (for example) the *gendèr* might have constructed *gendèran* by following "the inner melody alone" (p. 25), but over time the effort to accommodate the inner melody to an instrument with a limited effective range might have produced the "standard patterns" (p. 25) used by *gendèr* players nowadays.

Sumarsam postulates a similar evolutionary trend in the case of the *balungan*. The *balungan* is "an abstraction of the inner melody felt by musicians" (p. 30). Although the inner melody is the primary source of the *balungan*, the latter must also take into account "the limitations of the *saron* range" (p. 30). Over time, the effort to balance these two (sometimes conflicting) demands has produced the relatively standardized *balungan* in use today. In some cases the standard *balungan* for a passage temporarily ignores the inner melody in order to create a melodic gesture that fits comfortably on the *saron;* divergence between *balungan* and *garap* is the result (p. 31).[5]

Sumarsam concludes that the "underlying feeling of *gendhing* is the essence of Javanese gamelan melody—the inner melody as felt by the musicians" (p. 71); it is the "spirit of the *gendhing* and the spirit of the Javanese gamelan" (p. 72).

Sumarsam presented his ideas at a formal discussion session at ASKI in 1978, where the atmosphere became "heated" (*ramé:* Supardi 25.v.93). Sumarsam managed to convince some of his colleagues, who subsequently acknowledged his ideas in their own work.[6] Others, however, found the inner melody problematic. One of them in particular, Supanggah, had certain specific criticisms of the idea and offered as an alternative his own concept of unplayed melody, the "essential *balungan*."

SUPANGGAH'S "ESSENTIAL *BALUNGAN*"

Supanggah, five years younger than Sumarsam, had followed a trajectory similar to that of his older colleague. He too attended ASKI (entering in 1967, a few years after Sumarsam) and was also appointed to the ASKI teaching staff upon graduation. Supanggah brought his intellectual and literary bent with him. As a child, even though his father was a *dhalang*, he wanted to progress *(maju):* he dreamed of becoming an engineer, architect, or author. In junior high school his short stories won several prizes (13.xi.91; 20.xi.91). Whereas Sumarsam was Martopangrawit's teaching assistant for his course, "Knowledge of *Karawitan*," Supanggah's relationship with Martopangrawit was initially more distant (13.xi.91). However, he took over responsibility for that course after Martopangrawit's death.

Supanggah mentioned two factors that led him to his formulation of the "essential *balungan*." The occasional "failure" of the *balungan*'s guidance function (which, as we have seen, motivated Sumarsam's search for the "source" of the *balungan*) also motivated Supanggah to look for the "real framework" of the composition (29.xii.86):

> After Supanggah could play various instruments, he realized their parts didn't always agree |*sesuai*| with the *balungan*. So he asked himself: What's the standard |*pathokan*|, the guide |*pedoman*|, the target |*ancer-ancer*| for the *rebab, gendèr,* and |the other *garap* parts|? What's the real framework of the *gendhing,* that really serves as the basis |*mendasari*| for the *gendhing?*

Supanggah also pointed to a specific experience as an inspiration for this idea. In 1979 he conducted a research project on the variety of *garap*. He recorded a number of musicians from varied backgrounds, some from the Solonese court tradition (such as Turahjo), but also many from the rural traditions transmitted in the families of *dhalang* (e.g., Gandasugeng of Klaten, Karnodihardjo of Gombang, etc.). He discovered much more variability in the interpretation of the same compositions than he had expected. The range of variation made him ask, What is the *balungan?* (20.x.91).

By 1979 Supanggah was doubtless already aware of Sumarsam's idea of inner melody, and to some extent his essential *balungan* may have been intended as an improvement upon it. As we have seen, Sumarsam conceived of the inner melody as "deeper" than the *balungan,* as the source or basis of the latter. It was precisely this claim that Supanggah found doubtful (25.ix.81). Is the inner melody created by the composer, he asked, or is it the musician's interpretation? Is there only one inner melody for each *gendhing?* Do all players have the same inner melody for, say, Gambirsawit? If the inner melody can vary among players, then it cannot be the basis of *(mendasari)* the *gendhing,* but must be an interpretation. The relationship between inner melody and *balungan* must be the opposite of the one postulated by Sumarsam. Far from being the source of the *balungan,* the inner melody is an interpretation *(penafsiran)* of the written *balungan,* which becomes *rebaban, gendèran,* etc., depending on the performer (4.vi.86). Hence the inner melody could not be prior to the *balungan* (1985:126–27):

> I feel thus that the inner melody is comparable |*pareil*| to the *balungan,* or represents one possible interpretation by the musician. The inner melody, a somewhat vague abstraction, would then depend conceptually on the *balungan.*

As for Sumarsam's claim that the musicians' hummings provide evidence for the existence of an inner melody, Supanggah noted (1983:5):

> I have observed that, when someone hums a *gendhing,* the humming usually depends on which melody instrument he is most familiar with

or has a background in, or else [it can be] a vocal melody developed from the *balungan*.

Supanggah concludes that the inner melody is either a musician's interpretation of the *balungan* (and thus on the same level [*sejajar*] with the *rebab, pesindhèn, gendèr*, or other parts) or else identical with the *balungan* (1983:6).

Supanggah introduced his own concept of unplayed melody, the essential *balungan*, in a paper he wrote in 1986.[7] Supanggah's aim in this paper is to remedy what he sees as a deficient understanding of the *balungan*, the framework of a *gendhing*, which is perhaps the most important factor in the practice of *karawitan* (1990:134; 1988:9). He first disposes of a few common misconceptions. Contrary to the opinion of some Western ethnomusicologists, the *balungan* is not the *saron* melody, since the former spans a range of more than two octaves, while the latter is limited to approximately one octave (1990:117; 1988:3). But neither is the *balungan* the multi-octave melody represented in *gendhing* notation. While this latter conception is relatively unproblematic for the routine tasks of teaching, performing, and documenting *karawitan*, it must be put in question when "more penetrating musical research" is at issue (1990:116; 1988:3).

Furthermore, the *balungan gendhing* is not the *gendhing*, though these two terms are often conflated in everyday life (1990:117; 1988:3). The *gendhing*—the sound of the entire ensemble—exists only in the moment of performance, or in the imagination of the musician. Because of the flexibility afforded by the oral tradition, any one performance of a *gendhing* may sound different from other performances of it. What makes the various performances recognizable as being of one and the same *gendhing* is the essence, core, or distillate of the *gendhing*, the *balungan gendhing*, which is not played by any one instrument. "Although the *gendhing* sounds different in each performance, the essence of the *gendhing* stays the same" (1990:119–20; 1988:4). The *balungan gendhing* is not identical with the *gendhing*, but it is inseparable from it. And as performances of a *gendhing* may differ according to place, time, and circumstance, so may the *balungan* that is distilled from the *gendhing* (1990:121; 1988:5).

The *balungan gendhing* itself is not played, but what is played and notated and called the *balungan* in everyday speech is a pseudo-*balungan* (*balungan semu*), a version of the real (*nyata*) *balungan* that has been modified so as to suit the idioms of various instruments (especially the *saron* family and the *bonang*: 1990:135; 1988:9).

In notation, Supanggah's "real" or "essential" *balungan* looks somewhat like Suhardi's *lagu*, as we can see by comparing the two. In example 40 I present the *balungan* for part of the first movement of Cucurbawuk,

EXAMPLE 40. The *balungan* of the first *gongan* (*ngelik*) of the first movement (*mérong*) of Gendhing Cucur-bawuk *sléndro manyura* (B) compared with two implicit melodies: Supanggah's "essential *balungan*" (P) and Suhardi's *lagu* (H). Source: Supanggah (1990:124), Suhardi (25.vii.86).

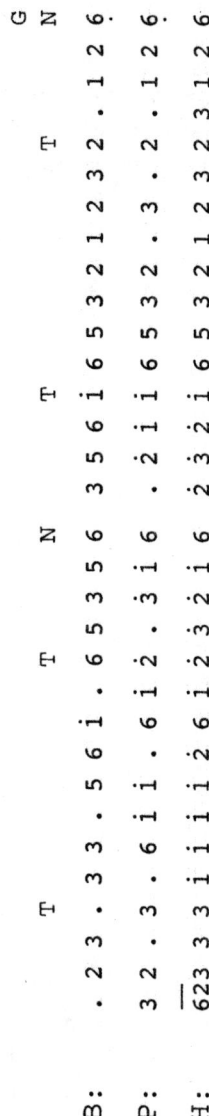

EXAMPLE 40. *(continued)* Western staff trans-notation.

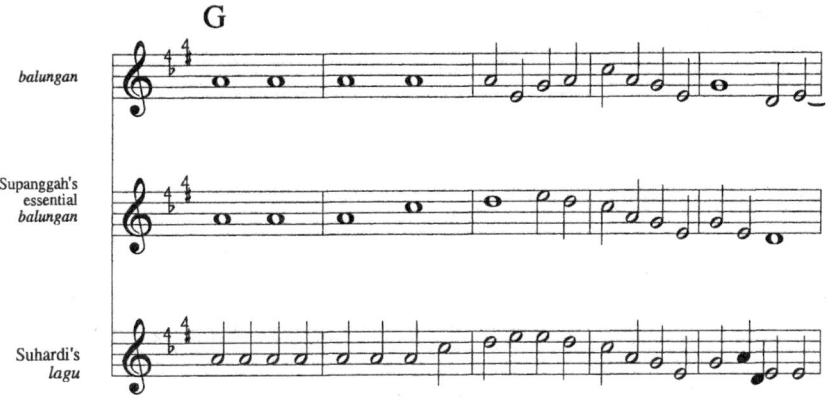

(continued)

a well-known *gendhing* with composition-specific divergence, along with Suhardi's *lagu* and Supanggah's essential *balungan*. Both of these un-played melodies hew closely to the elaborating parts when the latter di-verge from the *balungan* (as in the third *kenong*-phrase; compare the *re-bab* and *gendèr* parts given in chapter 3, example 21). However, Supanggah's implicit melody keeps somewhat closer to the idiom of the *balungan* than does Suhardi's. Notice that Suhardi's *lagu* employs no rests, while Supanggah's essential *balungan* does. This is characteristic: Suhardi notates his *lagu* at the density of *balungan mlaku*, i.e., four tones per *gatra*,

EXAMPLE 40. *(continued)*

and rarely indicates rests. Supanggah, by contrast, is willing to specify an essential *balungan* at the density of *balungan nibani* for pieces with *balungan nibani*. Indeed, in example 40, Supanggah even introduces a phrase of *balungan nibani* where the *balungan* has *balungan mlaku* (i.e., .3.2 instead of 1232).

THE IMPORTANCE OF CONGRUENCE

Thus, in attempting to improve upon the melodic guidance function in gamelan music, these three musicians postulated unplayed melodies. Their idealized guides serve a common cognitive need, introducing a degree of regularity into the web of interpart relations and reducing its apparent arbitrariness. They paint the heathertone texture of *balungan/garap* relations a uniform shade of congruence.

Several factors make the idea of an unplayed melody a plausible one: the contrast among different degrees of guidance, some clear, some obscure; the predominance of congruence over divergence; and the tendency of the "soft" parts to cluster together. It is especially important to understand the latter, as it is also the key to recognizing the limitations of all of the implicit-melody concepts.

In many cases of divergence, the actual *balungan* fails to guide the soft elaborating parts, but most of those parts are nevertheless *congruent with one another*. A sure sign that some aspect of a melodic part is not idiosyncratic is when other parts "walk together" with it, and the more parts that do so, the surer the sign. When the soft parts disregard the *balungan*'s guidance, but all disregard it in the same way, can they really be doing so independently of one another? Or are they perhaps following some other, hidden, guide?

Let us diagram possible interpart relations as I did in chapter 3 (example 41). I represent here one type of congruence and two types of divergence: in 41a we find the *balungan* congruent with all of the soft elaborating parts; in 41b the soft parts are congruent among themselves but diverge from the *balungan*; and in 41c there is no overall pattern: some of the soft parts are congruent with the *balungan*, but others diverge, and they diverge in different ways.

The scenario in example 41c is maximally irregular from the point of view of melodic guidance. Here the *balungan* is congruent with only one *garap* part; the other *garap* parts are congruent neither with the *balungan* nor with each other. Here the very idea of melodic guidance seems irrelevant; it explains very little of what is going on. If all of the divergence in Javanese music was of type 41c, there might be no reason to think that these cases of divergence could ever be understood as anything but arbitrary exceptions.

But divergence of type 41b is close enough to the scenario in 41a to suggest that perhaps the former can be understood in terms of the latter. In example 41b the soft *garap* parts diverge from the *balungan* but maintain congruence among themselves. This scenario is somewhat irregular from the point of view of the *balungan* as melodic guide, but it does not discredit the *idea* of guidance. For there is still a great degree of congruence in this picture. It is this scenario that offers support to the idea of an unplayed melodic guide. For if the overt, conventional guide—the *balungan*—cannot explain

EXAMPLE 41A. Schematic representation of a maximally congruent relationship among the melodic parts. The oval encircles parts that are congruent with one another. The vertical dotted line separates the *balungan* from the "soft" elaborating parts. In this example the *balungan* is congruent with all three of the soft elaborating parts listed.

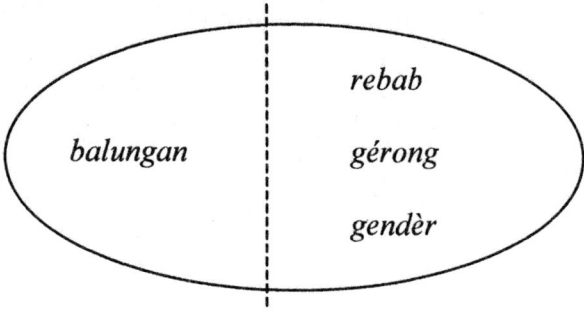

EXAMPLE 41B. Schematic representation of divergence between *balungan* and the "soft" elaborating parts (as found in Ladrang Ginonjing, or—minus the *gérong* part—Gendhing Cucurbawuk or Gendhing Lagu Dhempel). The elaborating parts are congruent with one another but diverge from the *balungan*.

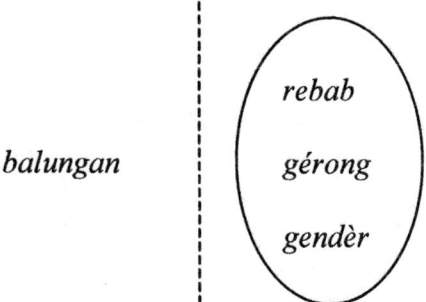

the congruence demonstrated here, perhaps there is some other, covert guide waiting to be discovered. And this suspicion could only be reinforced if the soft parts play identically in some other composition where the *balungan* is more congruent with them (or offers clearer guidance)—the situation described by Suhardi and depicted in example 37.

EXAMPLE 41C. Schematic representation of divergence both *between* the *balungan* and the "soft" elaborating parts and *within* the latter group (as found in Ladrang Siyem). The *balungan* and *gérong* parts are congruent; the *rebab* and *gendèr* parts are congruent neither with the *balungan* nor with each other.

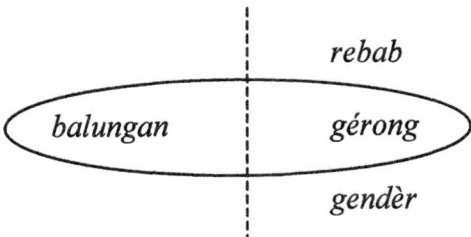

EXAMPLE 41D. Schematic representation of divergence between *balungan* and the "soft" elaborating parts. The *garap* parts are congruent with one another but diverge from the *balungan*. This suggests that the *garap* parts are in fact following the melodic guidance of a *balungan*, but not the *balungan* actually played (represented here by the dotted oval).

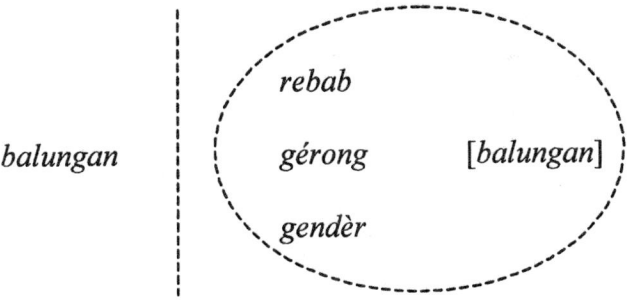

ANALOGICAL THINKING AND THE DIVERSITY OF SOURCES FOR THE IMPLICIT-MELODY CONCEPTS

But there is no unique way to idealize melodic guidance. There are two models available, the real-time, local guidance of the *rebab* and the conceptual guidance of the *balungan*. One could model the ideal guide on the *balungan* and rewrite the actual *balungan* with a *balungan*-like melody that conforms to or violates the *balungan* idiom to a greater or lesser degree. Or one could model the ideal guide on the *rebab*. Both of these solutions were proposed by my teachers; their concepts of implicit melody were consequently cast in very different melodic idioms. The dappled texture of Javanese music—congruence shot through with divergence—makes both idealizations plausible. It conjures the vision of a melodic guide more regular than either of the actual guides, but offers no unambiguous clues to its actual shape.

Suhardi and Supanggah, looking for a clearer melodic guide than the *balungan*, chose to postulate a clearer *balungan*. In constructing this hypothetical *balungan*, they make use of analogical thinking. I have represented this in 41d, where I recast the diagram in 41b along the lines of 41a. Since all of the soft elaborating parts are congruent, we need only postulate a virtual *balungan* that captures the melodic commonalities, on analogy with the actual *balungan* of example 41a. This is a type of within-domain analogy, remaining entirely within the realm of Javanese music; as such it could also be considered a type of conceptual extension, expanding the idea of guidance to include virtual as well as actual melodic lines.

Sumarsam used a different analogy. Rather than attempt to improve on the *balungan*, as Suhardi and Supanggah did, Sumarsam turned to the other major source of guidance in performance, and introduced his inner melody as a sort of idealized substitute for the *rebab* part. It makes sense that the role of the *balungan* should be taken precisely by a *rebab*-like part, since besides the *rebab*'s real-time leadership in the ensemble it also has an important mnemonic function.

Yet this is a somewhat more radical move. Sumarsam revised the presumption that the *balungan* is the object of *garap*, the stable substrate of interpretation. He demoted the *balungan*, as it were, in the conceptual hierarchy of *karawitan*, making it subordinate to a part modeled on one of the elaborating parts. There is a difficulty here. As an elaborating part, the *rebab*'s line must be variable: it will differ from one player to the next and even within a single performance. Such variability makes it an unlikely candidate for the "source" or "origin" of the somewhat more stable *balungan*. Hence the need for idealization: Sumarsam had to dismiss certain aspects of the actual *rebab* part (for example, the alternative *céngkok* in example 39) as irrelevant to the inner melody.

EXPLAINING DIVERGENCE

These unplayed melodies function cognitively to make the melodic texture of *karawitan* more coherent and its melodic guidance more consistent. Not only do they make the relationships among the parts more regular; they make divergence explicable. They allow Sumarsam and Supanggah to offer a general explanation for divergence, something never before attempted in Javanese music theory.

Divergence between the *balungan* and the *garap* parts is usually described as the deflection of the latter away from the former; in Martopangrawit's definition, it is elaboration that doesn't follow the course of the *balungan*. Martopangrawit explained this deflection in various ways. In some cases the soft parts diverge in order to protect the integrity of their melodic idioms; in other cases they diverge in merely ornamental fashion; and in cases of composition-specific divergence, Martopangrawit could offer no other explanation than the composer's arbitrary intention.

Sumarsam and Supanggah turn this assumption upside down: for them, the *balungan* diverges from the elaborating parts, not the reverse. To explain why the *balungan* sometimes wanders from the inner melody or essential *balungan* while the soft elaborating parts remain faithful to it, they appeal to the familiar imperative of idiomatic integrity, but applied now to the *balungan* rather than to a *garap* part: in these cases the *balungan* diverges in order to adjust its melody to the limited ambitus of the *saron*. Thus Sumarsam and Supanggah can explain otherwise arbitrary composition-specific divergence by applying a familiar aesthetic concept in a new way. They can specify the process of "derivation and complication" that leads from the ideal realm of the implicit melody to the actual world, and it is a principle well-attested throughout the music: that every part must "live its own life."

THE LIMITS OF IDEALIZATION:
THE CHALLENGE OF PIECEMEAL DIVERGENCE

Yet while the implicit-melody concepts smooth out irregularities of guidance, there are limits to such regularization. The nature of Javanese melodic practice makes perfect guidance impossible. Each concept of unplayed melody becomes indeterminate when it runs up against these limits. Each one can deal with a certain kind of divergence (when the *balungan* and *garap* parts separate into two large blocs). None of them can deal with the sort of piecemeal divergence that fractures the unity of the *garap* parts (as when the *rebab* and *gendèr*, or *rebab* and *gérong*, go separate ways) or with ambiguities of melodic guidance.

Consider first the idealized *balungan* of Suhardi and Supanggah. We saw in example 41b how situations in which the soft parts are congruent among themselves, but diverge from the *balungan*, make the idea of an unplayed *balungan* plausible. What, then, of those situations in which the elaborating parts diverge from the *balungan*, but are *not* congruent among themselves (as in example 41c)? As we saw in chapter 3, there are cases in which different elaborating parts approach the same cadential tone from opposite directions, and even cases in which the elaborating parts diverge in multiple directions at a cadential point. What sort of idealized *balungan* did Suhardi and Supanggah posit in such cases?

Significantly enough, they had difficulty specifying *any* implicit melody for such phrases, and they either chose one of several possibilities more or less arbitrarily or simply gave up the attempt.[8] Consider, for example, the passage from Ladrang Siyem *sléndro nem* we encountered in chapter 3 (example 17). In the first half of this passage the *gérongan* and *rebaban* converge on 2 |*d*| in the upper octave, but from opposite directions. This phrase was problematic for Suhardi. He had difficulty specifying a *lagu* for the *balungan* .3.2. Using a *balungan*-like shorthand to discuss this passage, Suhardi (21.xii.84) asked rhetorically: "The *gérongan* is 3352, the *rebaban* is 6122, and the *gendèran* is 3632, so what's the *lagu*?" Instead of choosing one of these possibilities, however, he abandoned the question: "The problem is, all |of the parts| diverge here" *(sudah misah semuanya, itu sulitnya).*

A similar kind of divergence, but at a goal-tone, created similar difficulties for Suhardi when he discussed *Ayak-ayakan manyura* (chapter 3, example 24). As we saw, the *rebab* uses the *puthut gelut céngkok*, just as it does in Ladrang Wilujeng at the *balungan* phrase 33..6532. In Wilujeng the *rebab* replaces the *balungan*'s sustained 3 |*e*+| with 6 |*a*|, and the *gendèr* and *gambang* follow the *rebab*. In *Ayak-ayakan*, however, although the *rebab* plays 6 |*a*| against the *balungan*'s 1 |*c*–|, it does so on its own: Suhardi felt the *gendèr* must either cadence on 1 |*c*–| as notated in example 24, or else perhaps cadence on 3 |*e*+|; but it should not cadence on 6 |*a*|. Where, then, is the *lagu*? "Hard to say" *(sulit)* was Suhardi's only reply (28.iv.84).

In other words, since the elaborating parts do not maintain the same degree of unanimity here as they do in Wilujeng, since they do not all diverge from the *balungan* in the same way, Suhardi was unable to construct an idealized *balungan* to restore congruence.

Thus these idealized *balungan* function to regularize the *balungan/garap* relationship, but can't entirely succeed. They attempt to recuperate the actual *balungan*'s "failures" of guidance, but they can do so only up to a point. The full range of *balungan/garap* relationships includes cases of divergence that cannot be captured by any idealizations.

THE LIMITS OF IDEALIZATION: THE AMBIGUITY OF GUIDANCE

As the examples above show, constructing an idealized *balungan* equally congruent with several of the soft elaborating parts can be an ambitious and sometimes impossible task. What of Sumarsam's idealized *rebab* line? As we saw in chapter 3, the *balungan* has a unique responsibility as a guide: it must be shaped in such a way that all of the melodic parts can interpret it according to their idioms. The *rebab* line is not held to this standard, and in fact Sumarsam did not try to summarize the melodic content of many *garap* parts in a single line. Hence in general the inner melody should be somewhat easier to construct than either of the other two implicit melodies. (This limitation of scope may have been one reason Supanggah described the inner melody as "on the same level with" the individual elaborating parts.) Yet even so, there are cases in which the inner melody, too, becomes indeterminate. This is because it is not always clear when the *rebab* part is in fact guiding—when the other parts must "walk together" with it—and when it is "living its own life." Only the former cases, not the latter, offer clues to the inner melody. Hence it is important to be able to tell them apart; whenever there is doubt on this matter, the shape of the inner melody should become correspondingly doubtful. This is in fact what we find.

Let's return to the *rebab*'s alternative *céngkok* in example 39. Recall that Sumarsam excluded this from the inner melody of Ladrang Wilujeng because it is too clearly an idiosyncrasy of the *rebab* part, too distant an interpretation of the *balungan*. But there are moments in many *gendhing* where the *rebab* plays a phrase type just as distant from the *balungan* as this *céngkok*, but where it has *no other options*. This is true of the *barang miring céngkok*. Remember that this distinctive phrase type uses specially lowered tones not available on the fixed-pitch instruments. But in some moments of certain compositions *barang miring* is an obligatory feature of the *rebab*'s performance practice, and there may be no obvious alternative for the inner melody. Consider, for example, a passage from the well-known Ladrang Diradameta *sléndro nem*. Here the *rebab* plays *barang miring* for a phrase of *balungan rangkep* (example 42).

Sumarsam was unwilling to consider this *céngkok* as a reflection of the inner melody, but neither did he find in the fast-moving *balungan* any indication of the inner melody. He analyzed this passage in two different ways at different times, but in neither case was he able to settle on a single, determinate shape for the inner melody. He first told me that the inner melody for this passage was simply "the feeling of melodic motion" (10.v.82). Eleven years later, he said that the *rebab* and *balungan* parts were two equally valid representations of the melodic essence of this passage (18.vi.93).

The *barang miring céngkok* is perhaps an extreme example of the indeterminacy of the inner melody, though it is quite common. It illustrates with especial clarity a general vulnerability of the inner melody. Since the inner melody could only be identified with the *rebab* part when the *rebab* line

EXAMPLE 42. A *balungan* phrase from Ladrang Diradameta *sléndro nem* and its *rebaban*, illustrating the use of *barang miring* (tones outside of the *sléndro* tuning system). A slash indicates a lowered tone. Source: Djumadi (1986:136).

balungan   .   .   2   3   5   6   i̇   .   6   i̇   5   6

rebab   .   2   5   6   .   6   i̇   2   2   3̸5̸2̇   i̇   6i̇5   6

Western staff trans-notation.

was not introducing its own "elaborations," it is important to be able to isolate the latter. But it is not always possible to tell when one of the melodic guides is "staying alive" and when it must be "walked together" with. We have seen this sort of ambiguity in the *balungan* (chapter 4, example 33). The same ambiguity is found in the relation of the *rebab* part to Sumarsam's inner melody. The *rebab* part functions as a guide only when it is not doing something simply to "stay alive." It is only the guiding content of the *rebab* part that reflects the inner melody; its idiomatic elaborations do not. But as with the *balungan*, it is not always possible to distinguish the *rebab*'s guidance from its idiosyncrasies. Given the identical *rebab* part, one musician might hear a *rambatan* where another musician hears a "fundamental" melody.[9]

Uncertainty over whether to consider a given *rebab* phrase to be a sign of the melody of the *gendhing* or merely something the *rebab* does to "live its own life" affected Suhardi as well, and it could produce doubts about the shape of his *lagu*. In example 43 I notate a simplified *rebab* part for a passage from Ladrang Krawitan *sléndro nem* along with Suhardi's *lagu* (28.xi.86).

There is no question of the *rebab*'s performance practice at the *kenong*-stroke (where I have bracketed Suhardi's *lagu*). The *rebab* plays to 5 |g|

EXAMPLE 43A: Simplified *rebab* notation for a passage from Ladrang Krawitan *sléndro nem* (Djumadi 1986:141). 43B: Suhardi's *lagu* for the same passage. The box indicates the segment of example 43b corresponding to the notation in 43a.

43a.

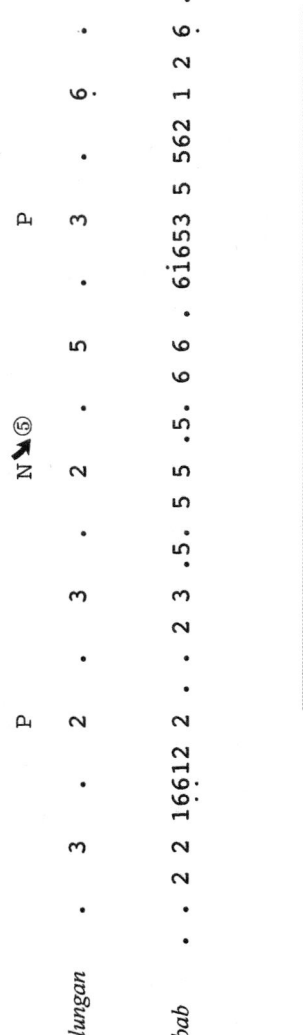

	P	N ⑤	P	G N
balungan	• 3 • 2	• 3 • 2	• 5 • 3	6. • 5.
rebab	• • 2 2 16612 2 • •	2 3 .5. 5 5 .5. 6 6 •	6i653 5 562 1 2 6.	• • 5.

43b.

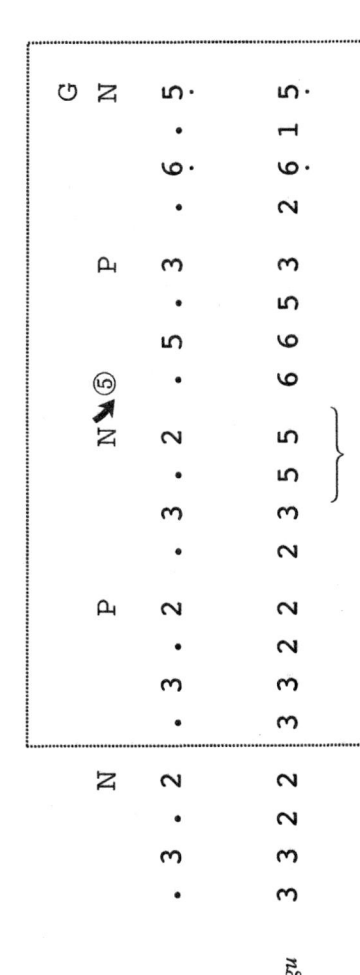

	N	P	N ➚ ⑤	P	G N
balungan	• 3 • 2	• 3 • 2	• 5 • 3	• 6. • 5.
Suhardi's *lagu*	3 3 2 2	2 3 5 5	6 6 5 3	2 6 1 5.

(continued)

EXAMPLE 43. *(continued)* Western staff trans-notation.

where the *balungan* cadences on 2 [*d*]. Some of the other *garap* parts "walk together" with the *rebab* here: the *kenong* "slips" to 5 [*g*], and so does the *pesindhèn*, but according to Suhardi the *gendèr* and *gambang* should cadence on 2 [*d*] (12.x.84). Hence here, as in example 24, we find divergence within the group of soft elaborating parts, and here (as there) Suhardi was doubtful about the *lagu*. This is very difficult, he said. The *rebab, kenong,* and *pesindhèn* all ignore the *balungan*'s 2 [*d*] in favor of 5 [*g*]. But why does the *rebab* play 5 [*g*]? Maybe it's because it needs to get in position for the following phrase (which cadences on 3 [*e+*]). Or perhaps it's because the

EXAMPLE 43. *(continued)*

phrase .3.2 occurs three times in a row here, and the *rebab* might be "bored" *(bosan)* with this constant cadencing on 2 [*d*] and want to try something different *(cari variasi)*. So perhaps the *lagu* cadences on 2 [*d*] here.

Thus Suhardi could not confidently deduce the *lagu* directly from the elaborating parts because he was not sure how to account for their behavior. The *kenong* and the *pesindhèn* would follow the *rebab*, as the melodic leader; but was the *rebab* embodying the melody of the composition or was it seeing to its own technical needs, preparing itself to play the next phrase? Or was it introducing a variation? This ambiguity is possible because the *rebab* is both a guide *(pedoman)* and a *garap* part. So it must be variable, but it must show the other parts what to play.

THE CONCEPTUAL ROLES OF IMPLICIT MELODY

The diversity of unplayed melodies is a diversity of idiom, but it is also more than this. Not only does the texture of gamelan music underdetermine the shape an implicit-melody concept must take, it similarly underdetermines the *role* such a concept might play. In some cases of divergence it is not difficult to construct an unplayed *balungan*, on analogy with the more congruent interpart relations found throughout the music. But once we have constructed it, how shall we use it? What conceptual role will it play? How shall we integrate this idea with our broader knowledge of the music? For example, will we allocate it an explanatory role within our mental model of the compositional process? What ontological status will we assign to it? How will it affect our idea of the identity of the musical composition?

As we have seen in chapter 1, the abstract entities we construct through analogical mappings can be put to many different uses and can be integrated into our conceptual networks in various ways. Similarly, the concept of an idealized melodic guide can function in several possible ways. It can be assigned primacy, as the source or essence of a *gendhing*, or regarded as simply an interpretation of it. We can attribute it to the mind of the performer, as a part of his or her conscious or unconscious knowledge of a composition. We can attribute it to the mind of the composer, as an aspect of the process of composition. On the other hand, we can treat it as an analytical abstraction, a construct that conveniently summarizes certain audible melodic relationships. Similarly, we can consider it as a pedagogical device, a teaching tool, that—whether or not it corresponds to anything in the composer's mind—can help the student learn *gendhing*.

The three implicit-melody concepts strikingly illustrate this underdetermination of conceptual role. For Sumarsam, Supanggah, and Suhardi made very different claims for their concepts of unplayed melody. Of the three, Sumarsam's and Supanggah's concepts, both of them theoretically oriented, contrast strongly with Suhardi's largely practical orientation.

For Sumarsam, the inner melody concept is an attempt to answer the question of the "origin of *gendhing*" (18.vi.93); it represents a "deep" understanding of a *gendhing*. The *balungan* is an abstraction of the inner melody, not merely conceptually but also chronologically: in *gendhing* where *garap* and *balungan* diverge, he felt that the composer creates the inner melody first, then derives the *balungan* from it (7.iv.82). Supanggah likewise felt that his essential *balungan* had priority over the *balungan*, since the latter was a modified version of the former (1990:122–23; 1988:5). Thus Sumarsam's inner melody and Supanggah's essential *balungan* were made to function within theories of the compositional process. Further, Sumarsam's statement that the inner melody is sung unconsciously by musicians implies a psychological theory of performance as well, so that the inner melody is both a theory of the performer's knowledge and a theory of the composer's activity. It describes both the musician's intuitive conception of *gendhing* melody and the source, origin, basis, or "spirit" of gamelan compositions—claiming, in effect, that these are identical. But this assumption is not self-evident, as Supanggah pointed out.

Sumarsam and Supanggah, by using the rhetoric of essence and origin, aimed at large explanatory goals, but encountered correspondingly difficult conceptual challenges. In particular, the variability of *garap* raises problems for any attempt to penetrate beyond the *balungan* to a "deeper" melodic essence. Insofar as implicit melodies track *garap* more closely than does the *balungan*, they are more sensitive to variations in performance practice. Furthermore, as we have seen, there are passages in some compositions for which musicians cannot specify any implicit melody with confidence. Finally, if implicit melodies can be obscure and can vary among musicians, how can any performer know if his or her idea of the implicit melody for a *gendhing* corresponds to the composer's?

That Supanggah in particular was concerned with this problem is evident from the terms of his critique of Sumarsam's inner melody: for him, the variability of the inner melody meant that it could not be the source of the *balungan*. But neither theory could escape this difficulty. Both Sumarsam and Supanggah stressed the originary, foundational unity of implicit melodies, though both also admitted their derivative, individual variability. Neither one explicitly articulated an account of implicit melody that could conceptually integrate both unity and variability.[10] Both men featured the shared, enduring, foundational role of their implicit melodies in their written expositions and acknowledged the potential for mutability and individual variation mostly in conversation. That is, they focused on different themes depending on the setting of the discourse and its level of generality or abstractness.

Thus, in his formal presentations of his ideas, Sumarsam clearly stated the foundational role of the inner melody: the *balungan* is "an abstraction of the inner melody" (1976:30). The inner melody is a common possession, "an implicit melody which each musician shares" (1995:314 n. 112). The inner melody lies at the originary moment of the compositional process: a composer works by creating an inner melody and deriving *balungan* from it (7.iv.82). Yet in conversation Sumarsam also admitted that the inner melody is "the result of interpretation"; it can change while the *balungan* remains the same, and it can differ between musicians (7.iv.82).

Supanggah likewise described his essential *balungan* in writing as the stable essence of *gendhing*, persisting unchanged through varying performances: "Although the *gendhing* sounds different in each performance, the essence of the *gendhing* stays the same" (1990:119–20; 1988:4). But in conversation he admitted that the essence of a *gendhing* can change, since "determining the essence of a *gendhing* is a kind of interpretation, too" (1.ii.87). Nor was this essence necessarily shared by all musicians. In answer to my question, if it was the "real" *balungan* that made a *gendhing* recognizable, he answered that the real *balungan (balungan sungguh)* of a piece is perhaps known only to its composer (20.xi.91).

Thus, despite their interest in finding the "source" and shared essence of compositions, both Sumarsam and Supanggah admitted that their implicit melodies might be variable, individual interpretations. A tension between explanatory reach and grasp is present in each theory. For example, Supanggah's concern to uncover the true "basis" of the *gendhing*, his refusal to content himself with mere individual interpretations of melodic essence, was one of the reasons he rejected Sumarsam's inner melody. The *balungan* is the common object of different musicians' interpretations. Someone searching for an unplayed but *shared* melody might consequently prefer to idealize the *balungan* rather than the *rebab* part. Yet even Supanggah's idealized *balungan* eventually recedes into the private consciousness of the composer, no more shareable or intersubjectively fundamental than Sumarsam's inner melody.

Neither Sumarsam nor Supanggah went on to formally articulate versions of their respective implicit-melody concepts that would reconcile their interest in essence and origin with the variability of musical practice. Sumarsam subsequently delved further into the question of origins, making a detailed study of the use of vocal models by composers (1995:161–237). However, in so doing he admittedly abandoned the performer's musical imagination, since many of the vocal prototypes he postulated for well-known *gendhing* were clearly not "sung in the heart" of the performer, whether consciously or unconsciously (4.iv.01). Thus his later work in effect sacrificed the unity of the inner melody concept, emphasizing the origins of *gendhing* at the expense of the performer's intuitive conception of melody.

But a musician can entertain a concept of implicit melody without making any theoretical claims for it or assigning it any explanatory role. Suhardi used the idea of the *lagu* neither to account for the compositional process nor to represent the performer's unconscious knowledge. He spent little time theorizing about it, but rather used it as a pedagogical tool in his daily teaching activities. He claimed only practical value for the *lagu,* calling knowledge of it a master key of *garap* (23.xi.84). On the issue of temporal priority in the compositional process, he simply refused to speculate. In general, Suhardi had much less interest in the compositional process than, say, Martopangrawit, and he saw little reason to talk about it. For example, he recognized that a composer could conceivably work in two ways, either devising a *balungan* and later fitting *garap* to it, or alternatively creating *garap* to which he would later fit *balungan.* But Suhardi (24.viii.84) chose to remain agnostic on this issue: "Which comes first, *garap* or *balungan?* We don't know." He similarly recognized the question of the relative priority of *balungan* and *lagu,* but consciously refused to consider it: "Which is composed first, *balungan* or *lagu?* People argue about it, and they'll probably never stop arguing" (31.i.86).

Suhardi's pragmatic orientation allowed him to recuse himself in similar fashion from speculation on the psychology of the performer. Where Sumarsam couched his theory of implicit melody in the vocabulary of interiority, using the term *batin* with all its resonances of spirituality, depth, and mysticism, Suhardi rarely used such language.[11]

Similarly, the indeterminacy of the *lagu* in cases of piecemeal divergence had no theoretical ramifications for Suhardi, since he did not use his implicit-melody concept as part of a larger explanatory project. Since for him the *lagu* did not represent any sort of "essence," the impossibility of determining the *lagu* for an especially divergent passage created a pedagogical glitch but not a theoretical embarrassment. When two or more of the major elaborating parts diverge, Suhardi became hesitant to assign any *lagu* to the passage, but no larger conceptual issues were at stake for him. At most, he would point to the practical consequences for him as a teacher, noting that in such cases of multiple divergence he had to teach the divergent parts separately (17.x.86). When the *rebab* and *gendèr* diverged from each other, he would ask rhetorically which one was the *lagu,* and answer pragmatically: "It's hard to say. You should know them both" (28.iv.84).

Finally, the possibility that different musicians might have different implicit melodies for the same composition did not trouble Suhardi. As something constructed—"this *balungan* that we make" (*yang kita buat:* 26.x.84)—the *lagu* could easily accommodate variability. Thus when Suhardi explained how a musician who played the *ayu kuning céngkok* for the *balungan* .2.1 could construct the *lagu* based on that *céngkok* (example 37), he casually added: "Of course, people who play different *garap* there will discover a different *lagu*" (26.x.84).

CONCLUSION

There is no such thing, it would appear, as *the* unplayed melody in *karawitan*. Implicit melody is not a single thing, but a variety of responses to the puzzle of melodic guidance—a puzzle that appears puzzling only when viewed from the distanced perspective of conscious reflection. The primacy of congruence, interrupted by sporadic moments of divergence, can inspire the thoughtful musician to mentally close the gaps; so, too, the way many cases of divergence respect the boundary between "soft" and "loud" parts can suggest the unheard presence of an alternative guide. Musicians who try to imagine the shape of that guide are not narrowly constrained; the puzzle has more than one solution—but no solution fits perfectly. There will always be some loose ends left untied. The deeply "nonclassical" nature of interpart relations defies all simple rules.

But just as interesting as the diversity of instrumental idioms in which these three musicians cast their implicit melodies is the diversity of uses to which they put them. The processes of analogical thinking seem to have generated these concepts of unplayed melody without earmarking them for any specific ends, making them available for whatever purposes most needed serving. Consequently, each musician incorporated them in his own projects, projects that naturally enough suited his own personal interests and the demands of his social situation. In the next chapter I will suggest how these interests and demands may have influenced the shapes assumed by the implicit-melody concepts.

7 Implicit-Melody Concepts in Perspective

Let us summarize the differences among the three implicit-melody concepts in a diagram (example 44). Two of them were modeled on the *balungan*, one on the *rebab* part; two of them—though a different two—were put to theoretical use, while one was largely a pedagogical device. All of them, as we have seen, idealized the concept of melodic guidance, replacing divergence with congruence, insofar as this is possible; but all encountered limitations in doing so. In this chapter I try to account for these similarities and differences.

Let us start with the similarities. It is clear that some common element in the experience of these three men suggested the idea of an unplayed melody. How else, after all, could we explain the independent postulation of implicit melodies by Suhardi and Sumarsam?

Perhaps that common element is something cultural. Perhaps the notion of an unstated melody occurred to them because it resonates with themes found in other domains of Javanese life. Sutton has argued along these lines that the inner melody and Suhardi's *lagu* are reflections of Javanese culture insofar as they embody Javanese attitudes toward interiority (1979:76–77). In performance a musician gives evidence of his or her knowledge of the implicit melody but never states it blatantly, just as in social life a person is admired who can maintain a composed outward demeanor regardless of the state of his or her inward feelings (1979:74).

Sutton's point is suggestive, though where he finds an analogue to the concealment of the inner self in social interaction I see the Javanese valuation of allusiveness and indirection as ideals of refinement. This is a pervasive theme in Javanese culture. In literature and the other arts, in mysticism, in the interpretation of dreams and omens, hidden meanings are valued over obvious ones, hints are valued over direct statements, the symbolic is

EXAMPLE 44. A schematic representation of three concepts of implicit melody, showing their conceptual dependencies on the two guiding parts (the *balungan* and the *rebab* part), as well as the contexts in which they were formulated.

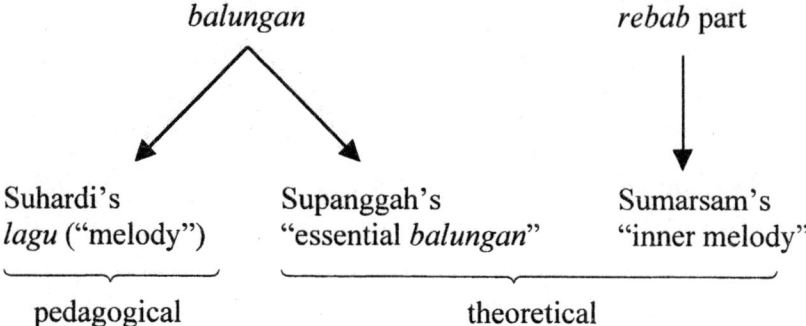

preferred to the literal, the abstract to the blatant, the oblique to the obvious. In these domains, the skilled and accomplished person is the one who can perceive the inconspicuous behind the conspicuous, who can read between the lines, who can take a hint *(tanggap ing sasmita)*. Indeed, it is possible to see one kind of conventional wordplay in everyday conversation and in song lyrics—the "indirect rhyme" *(wangsalan)*—as a playful tribute to this predilection. To appreciate the significance of the allusive and abstract in Javanese culture, and the value of the ability to interpret clues, we will need to examine at some length the role of indirection and symbolism in several cultural domains.

This theme is lexically encapsulated in the word *sasmita,* a rich and important term in Javanese aesthetics and spirituality. In its most concrete musical sense, it refers to the verbal and percussive cues given by the puppeteer to conduct the gamelan in a *wayang* performance (Heins 1970:103). In literature it refers to allusions and veiled references. It also names the supernatural hints or signs sought through meditation or asceticism. *Sasmita* is sometimes linked with *semu,* a term that usually refers to the appearance of something partially concealed, something that is neither clearly one thing nor another.[1]

Allusiveness is a key component of Javanese etiquette *(tatakrama).* Polite, refined conduct is indirect, leaving those who are sufficiently sensitive to figure out one's intentions by means of subtle clues. Becoming a refined person means being able to give, and take, hints, since "*alus* [refined] people often don't like to say what is on their minds" (Geertz 1960:244–45).

This indirectness is in fact built into the language. The "speech levels" of Javanese force speakers of the language to signal their social status and degree of intimacy relative to the person spoken to or spoken about. The ability to *mbasa*, to speak "high" Javanese, is in some respects like the ability to speak a second language, in that parents explicitly teach it to children when they reach a certain age. People think in ordinary ("low") Javanese— it is, one might say, their native language—but when they open their mouths they may have to perform obligatory acts of translation, suiting their speech to the social situation (Siegel 1986:15–33). Thus the experience of speaking polite Javanese constantly reminds the speaker of the distance between the inner *(batin)* realm of the subjective and the outer *(lair)* realm of interpersonal interaction.

Allusiveness of reference is one of the ways the Javanese language expresses deference (Errington 1988:174). People show respect for each other by referring to them, and to things in general, more vaguely and indeterminately (1988:192–93). This is not simply a matter of euphemism or circumlocution, but is built into the structure of the vocabulary. Polite Javanese often uses a single word where ordinary Javanese uses several; for example, *ngasta* is a common "high Javanese" term with many meanings, meanings that have their own distinct "low Javanese" terms. It can mean to hold *(nyekel)*, to carry *(nggawa)*, to make *(nggawé)*, or to have a job *(nyambut-gawé)*. There is no sense that one of these meanings is the basic one; different speakers, if pressed to specify one, choose different primary meanings (1988:172). In this way is the association of refinement with indirection encoded in the Javanese lexicon.

The linguistic delight in hints and indirection takes playful forms as well. We find it in a Javanese verbal genre based on indirect rhyme, called *wangsalan*. A *wangsalan* is built around two words similar in sound; usually one fully or partially rhymes with the other. But only one of these words actually appears in the *wangsalan*; the other is hinted at by means of a sort of crossword-puzzle clue. For example, I once ran into a Javanese acquaintance I had not seen for some time. She could have said, *Kadingarèn!* (What a surprise!), but instead she said, *Janur gunung!* (Mountain palm!). This is a conventional bit of indirect wordplay: the name of the mountain palm is *arèn*, which rhymes with *kadingarèn*.

Outside the domain of everyday social interaction, allusiveness takes deeper forms and demands the ability to interpret subtler clues. This is especially true in the spiritual and supernatural practices of divination and *kebatinan*. The latter term (literally, "concerning the inner") is sometimes used to mean the ability to control supernatural or psychic powers, sometimes the discipline of moral conduct and spiritual insight. In its most elaborate, rationalized form, *kebatinan* encompasses all of these: it is a complex of beliefs and practices that implicates ethics, aesthetics, interpretation, and power.[2]

Progress on the mystic path both requires and produces deep interpretive ability. The student of *kebatinan* must be able to learn from cryptic hints. For example, Howell (1977:93) presents a vivid instance of the expectation that spiritual teaching will be indirect. She reports the remarks of two students of the Solonese spiritual teacher Hardjanto:

> As Pak Tjipto put it, "everyday guidance" was in cryptic form: either metaphysical sayings and conundrums, or tasks, such as tilling the field, that forced the student to look beyond the commonplace meaning of forms and activities. One of Hardjanto's cantriks [students/apprentices], who was frustrated by my questions that presumed the guru's knowledge was communicated verbally or with other physical cues, put it to me that Hardjanto said nothing at all to him (of religious instruction) for the first several years of his tutelage. . . . At most, he said, Hardjanto injected some phrase in a conversation with someone else that he knew was directed at him because it satisfied some pressing need.

As one matures in the mystical practice, one becomes more sensitive to subtle signs in the speech and behavior of others, and indeed to the hints and clues *(sasmita)* that pervade the world. "All visible things are symbols," says the early-nineteenth-century *Serat Panitisastra* (Sudewa 1990:45). As one's desires cease to cloud one's perceptions, one becomes alert to these hidden meanings *(surasa)*. Only those who are free from the "distortion of perception implicit in self-interest" can detect the meanings inscribed in dreams and omens (Keeler 1987:249). Sensitivity to such clues has a practical function, in that it is thought to allow one to predict the future. In some Javanese practices of divination the hidden meanings are the ones most privileged. In oneiromancy, obscurity is equated with deep significance, and the dream images most difficult of interpretation are considered the most veridical (Keeler 1987:255).

Some of my teachers practiced divinatory interpretation to help them bet on the lottery, and it will be revealing to examine in detail the procedure one of them used for this purpose. Until its cancellation in the 1990s, the Indonesian national lottery was an ongoing preoccupation for large numbers of Javanese, including many musicians. At various times regional governments held their own lotteries. In his youth, one of my teachers (I will call him Pahing) bet regularly on a simple local lottery (17.x.86). It involved drawing numbers between 0 and 50. Like many of his friends, he used "prediction sheets" *(ramalan)*, sold widely.[3] These contained numbers and pictures, what Pahing called hints or signs *(sasmita)*. He relied on two of these sheets, sold under the titles "Tiger" and "Mount Kawi." Every issue of Tiger had a picture of a Chinese person. If it was a man, said Pahing, the winning number would be even; if a woman, it would be odd. Mount Kawi had a picture of a serpent with a dot above or below its head. If the dot was above, the winning number would be higher than 25; if below, the number would be lower. So it "made sense" *(masuk akal)*.

This allowed Pahing to narrow down the winning number to within a dozen possibilities. This information was enough to let him beat the odds by a small margin (though he often could not resist the temptation to place an additional bet, which always lost more money than he could win by following his system).

This story raises numerous questions: were the sheets really so reliable? How could they be? I shall not pretend to answer these questions, aside from repeating Pahing's own theory. He thought perhaps the prediction sheets were published by people who had attained clairvoyance through mystical insight *(ilmu kebatinan)*, but who were forbidden to profit *directly* from their knowledge of the future. For them, selling prediction sheets would be a way to make an indirect profit.

What is more important for our present purposes is that the prediction sheets, like the clairvoyants who are often asked for lottery predictions, indicated numbers indirectly, by *sasmita*. The bettor would have to solve *(memecahkan)* the resulting puzzle on his or her own. Furthermore, Pahing was never told the meaning of the "hints" embedded in the pictures: he figured them out by *nitèni*, by paying close attention, and interpreting them for himself *(menafsirkan sendiri)*.

Indirection and allusiveness are not only important in everyday life and mysticism, but in the arts as well. Indeed, when Humardhani (1923–1983), from 1975 director of the Music Academy in Solo, tried to characterize the traditional Javanese arts as a whole, he focused on their stylized aspect. They were not coarse or corporeal *(wadhag)*, he felt, but abstract *(tan-wadhag,* "non-*wadhag*": Rustopo 1990:138–40).

In literature, the need for interpretation is virtually a touchstone of aesthetic merit. Traditional Javanese literature is filled with symbols *(pralambang)* difficult of interpretation, "especially the writings of the *pujongga*," the master litterateurs (Padmosoekotjo 1960:84). Hence the reader will need to "read between the lines" *(maos ingkang boten kaserat ing sastra)*, to "peel away" *(ngoncèki)* the surface to discover the covert, figurative meaning (Arps 1992:352–61).

In the visual arts, stylizations are similarly preferred to lifelike representations. For example, the stylized birds depicted in batik patterns deliberately depart from realism; they are not meant to convey the feeling of birds in the "coarse" (material) world, the *alam kasar,* but "perfect" *(sampurna)* birds (Boow 1988:96). A good batik pattern is *semu:* "hinting," suggestive, ambiguous, hidden, abstract.

Javanese performers find these values exemplified in music as well. Martopangrawit (1.x.81; 21.iii.84) referred to Humardhani's ideas in discussing the cryptic titles of traditional compositions. He called these titles *abstrak* and *tan-wadhag* (interestingly, he said that there was no single Javanese term for this concept; the closest was *rasa,* "feeling"). Consider Gendhing Parigentang *pélog lima:* the title means "Pounding Rice." This is an odd name for an extremely large, dignified composition. Rice hulling was traditionally a noisy activity, with interlocking rhythms produced by the strokes of the pestles against the wooden trough. But nothing of this can be heard in the long, majestic phrases of this composition. Instead, what we find is the *feeling* of the farmer whose rice harvest has come in: he feels like a king.

The principle of indirect rhyme mentioned above *(wangsalan)* also serves as the foundation of many of the poems sung by gamelan vocalists. For example, many vocal texts are cast in four-line stanzas. This quatrain form is a variant of the *pantun* form found in many Indonesian languages, in which the first two lines make an impersonal statement (often a description of nature), while the last two lines, rhyming with the first couplet, contain the "contents" *(isi)* of the verse: they may make a personal statement or offer moral advice. But in the Javanese version, using the *wangsalan* principle, what is important is not the overt rhyme between the couplets, but the implied rhyme between the words *suggested* by the first couplet and the words that explicitly appear in the second couplet.

Here is an example, a quatrain commonly sung in musical contexts.[4]

Parabé Sang Smarabangun	Smarabangun's nickname
Sepat domba Kali Oya	The great fish in the Oya river
Aja dolan lan wong priya	Don't fool around with men
Nggeramèh nora prasaja	Misbehaving deviously

Only the last two lines represent the contents of the verse (in this case, a piece of moral advice for women). The first line contains the clue to a word in the third line, and the second line likewise suggests a word that rhymes

with something in the fourth line. Smarabangun is also known as Priyambada (in Javanese mythology, he is a son of Arjuna), and Priyambada suggests *wong priya* ("men") in the third line. The large *sepat* fish mentioned
in the second line is the *grameh;* as a verb, the same word means to misbe-
have, which we find in the fourth line.

Even when vocal texts do not use indirect rhyme, they may be allusive
in other ways. Harjito once wrote a Javanese verse in traditional poetic meter for one of his compositions, and as he planned to perform it in concert
he asked me to help him translate the stanza for the program notes. In fact
he had not quite finished with it; he had two alternatives for the last line,
and he thought out loud as he weighed their merits. In the end he rejected
the alternative that sounded too obvious: "There's nothing hidden there,"
he complained.

The addiction to insinuation, the evasion of plain speaking, and the love
of mysterious symbolism are features of the stereotype of the "inscrutable
Oriental," a stereotype that has been applied to many Asian societies. There
is therefore a danger of Orientalism in discussing the value of indirection
in Javanese society, the danger of positing indirection as a fixed trait of some
essentialized Javanese culture. We do well to remember, therefore, that indirection, allusion, symbolism, and abstraction are not equally prized in all
aspects of Javanese life, at all times, by Javanese of all ages, sexes, classes, or
religious tendencies. Not all compositions have cryptic titles, nor are all vocal texts equally obscure. (Indeed, in the modern genre of short, accessible
songs known as *kreasi baru* the language often approaches everyday Javanese.) I suspect that indirection and allusiveness tend to be most strongly
associated with the aspiration toward high-status *priyayi* beliefs and practices. But many of my teachers seemed to share such aspirations, and they
explicitly valued such things. Indeed, this was apparent in the first conversation I ever had with Martopangrawit.

Martopangrawit said little specifically about music during my first visit
to his house in 1981; rather, much to my surprise, he spent most of the time
delivering a long discourse on the words *setubuh* (Indonesian) and *carem*
(literary Javanese), "sexual intercourse." Whatever you do, he said, whatever instrument you play, you must unite with sexually. If I was learning
to play the *gendèr*, I must unite sexually with the *gendèr*. Speaking of himself, Martopangrawit (who was famous for his *gendèr*-playing) said, "The
gendèr is my wife."

He continued in this vein for quite a while, until—perhaps noticing the
bemused look on my face—he commented on the allegorical nature of his

talk, as if alerting me to the sort of thing I should expect to find during my stay in Java. "Here," he said, "there are many symbols" (21.vi.81).

To use Shore's terminology, we could say that indirection and allusiveness are foundational schemas in refined Central Javanese society; we find them spread across several different cultural domains, and it is quite plausible that we should find them in music as well. The sense that the world is full of hidden meanings, the idea that the most significant aspect of anything is its most obscure aspect, the association of indirection with refinement and status, the high value placed on the ability to read between the lines and to interpret hints *(sasmita)*—these are surely responsible for part of the appeal of the implicit-melody concepts. The idea that the true melodic essence of *karawitan* is never explicitly stated represents a powerful musical analogue to the role of allusion, suggestion, indirection, and abstraction in the other arts, in mysticism, and in everyday life.

But this cannot be the whole story, for it does not bring us into contact with the musical specificity of the unplayed melodies. There are many ways to find hidden meanings in gamelan music: one can find allegories in the shapes of the instruments, the number of tones in the scales, the names of pitches, or the sequence of *gendhing* in a medley (Perlman 1994:585–91). These sorts of interpretations are much more common than ideas of unplayed melody. Furthermore, the supposed general Javanese penchant for allusiveness does not explain why implicit-melody concepts were modeled on the *balungan* and *rebab* parts, but no others; it does not explain why each concept breaks down when it does. Nor does it explain why Sumarsam from the beginning described his postulated melody as something "inner," whereas Suhardi did not. We cannot understand the motivation for implicit-melody concepts only in terms of Javanese cultural ideals; something about the melodic texture of the music suggests the idea of an unplayed melody.

This suggestive something, I argue, is the almost-but-not-quite regularity of melodic guidance. Congruence is the predominant, "normal," central case of interpart relations. Moments of congruence teach the learner how one part can guide another. But moments of congruence are interwoven with moments of divergence; while guidance is often clear, it is not always so. Pockets of divergence and "failures" of guidance are scattered throughout the repertory. Culture-specific Javanese ideas of indirection or allusiveness will not of themselves prompt a musician to account for this situation by hypothesizing unplayed melodies. To understand the appeal of implicit-melody concepts, we need to study the details of interpart relations in the light of general cognitive principles.

The category of "relations between the melodic parts" cannot be characterized by any short definition or rule. It is not a "classical" category, like "odd number," but a congeries of "nonclassical" categories, like "bird" or "game" or "past tense form of a verb." For every generalization one would like to make about these categories there will be exceptions. Most birds have feathers and fly, but not all. Most English verbs form the past tense with the suffix *-ed*, but not all (and the ones that deviate from this pattern deviate in several different ways). Just so, the melodic parts usually coincide at every fourth *balungan* beat, but not always; and when they diverge, they do so in various ways. The musician's implicit knowledge accommodates this melange of regularity and irregularity, just as an English-speaker's implicit knowledge of her language embraces both the regular and irregular verbs. For the Javanese musician, just like the English-speaker, regularity seems to exert silent pressure on irregularity, and we sometimes find musicians normalizing moments of divergence, reconstructing them after the model of congruence that dominates the tradition (Perlman 1994:122–25). This type of change is comparable to analogical leveling in language (Campbell 1998:92–94), the process whereby strong ("irregular") past tense forms of verbs become weak ("regular"), as when people say *throwed* instead of *threw* or *strived* instead of *strove*.

We can think of these changes as the tribute that divergence pays to congruence. But this sort of change is piecemeal. Global ideas like the implicit-melody concepts can only arise once musicians construct explicit representations of the relations among the parts and view them in synoptic array, as it were; only then does the overall lack of uniformity in the pattern of interpart relations become noticeable. Only after musicians start to think of the nature of melodic guidance *as a whole* does its irregularity become evident, and only then can they feel the cognitive need to regularize it.

What gave Suhardi, Sumarsam, and Supanggah this panoramic view of interpart relations? In each case it seems to have been changes in the social and epistemic environment consequent to modernization, but the changes affected the three men differently. Sumarsam and Supanggah responded directly or indirectly to the stimulus of a transnational discourse of music theory in which the abstract question of the role of the *balungan* was an important issue. Suhardi did not participate in this theoretical dialogue, but his experiences as a teacher prompted him to think in explicit and general terms about the roles of congruence and divergence in his music—if only because he felt divergence was too hard for beginners. He preferred to start students out on *gendhing* that were largely congruent (the only musician I ever knew to make this his stated policy).

IMPLICIT-MELODY CONCEPTS IN HISTORICAL CONTEXT

Whatever it is in Javanese music that makes the idea of implicit melody plausible also severely underdetermines the particular form this idea must take: hence we have found a variety of unplayed melodies, as different from one another as the *rebab* and *balungan* parts. So far I have offered only a general explanation for this variety, arguing that it is due to the fact that the *rebab* and *balungan* both act as melodic guides in the ensemble. But can we say more than this? Can we explain the specific differences among these three accounts of implicit melody? Why did Suhardi and Supanggah choose to project the *balungan* idiom into an abstract realm, and why did Sumarsam rather choose the *rebab* idiom? Why did Sumarsam describe his unplayed melody as "inner"? Why did Sumarsam and Supanggah, but not Suhardi, make theoretical claims for their unplayed melody concepts?

Here I can only speculate. Explaining the unique aspects of historical events is always riskier than explaining common trends. I will, however, address these three questions, though I have more confidence in some of my answers than in others.

The first question is the most difficult. I have no clue as to why Sumarsam chose to idealize the *rebab* part while Suhardi and Supanggah focused on the *balungan* idiom instead. The *rebab* part, thanks to its mnemonic role, can be plausibly associated with notions of interiority. Perhaps Sumarsam had from the beginning thought of his quest as a search for something "inner," and this orientation made the *rebab* line somewhat more likely than the *balungan* as a candidate for idealization.

But why might Sumarsam have thought of his search in this way? This question at least admits of a slightly less speculative answer. Sumarsam may have turned to the language of interiority because he was well acquainted with traditional Javanese spiritual practices. During his years at the Music Academy Sumarsam lived in the house of his mentor, Bambang Sumodarmoko, from whom he learned much about mysticism *(kebatinan)* as well as art (20.iii.93). One of his fellow boarders was a *dukun* (a healer/clairvoyant), from whom he learned various prayers and practices (which could be used, for example, before taking exams). He also showed an interest in the spiritual aspects of music. In an early unpublished lecture, Sumarsam stressed the connections between Javanese music and spirituality *(kerochanian)*, citing various cases in which the gamelan promotes the relationship between humanity and the other world *(alam gaib).*[5] He contrasted listeners in search of mere entertainment to those who listened to *gendhing* as part of their efforts to bring themselves into relation with God.

But an interest in *kebatinan* cannot be a sufficient condition for the postulation of "inner" melodies, for Sumarsam was hardly unique in this respect. Martopangrawit was also deeply interested in mysticism, like many others; why was it only Sumarsam who coined the term "inner melody"? Perhaps it was Sumarsam's location in a postcolonial intellectual milieu, a theoretical tradition infused by first-world concepts.

On this interpretation, Sumarsam intentionally or unintentionally adapted a common conceptual strategy of anticolonialism. As he started to think about his music, Sumarsam found himself surrounded by an entrenched conceptual framework built over a period of decades under heavy Western influence. Faced with the need to "indigenize gamelan theory" (1995:10), to correct the "misinterpretation of indigenous concepts" fostered by the imposition of inappropriate Western musicological ideas (1995:144), he found inspiration in what Chatterjee has described as a fundamental strategy of anticolonialism in Asia and Africa: the partitioning of the social world into a material realm where Western power is unchallenged and a "spiritual" realm that functions as "an 'inner' domain bearing the 'essential' marks of cultural identity" (1993:6). Sumarsam likewise divided gamelan music into an "outer" realm of audible melodies—a realm explored with increasing thoroughness by Western ethnomusicologists over the past century—and the "inner" realm of the musician's intuition, a realm of essence untouched by the theories of Kunst and Hood. On this reading, Suhardi (who did not feel himself confronted by an established body of Western misinterpretations) had no need to clothe his concept of melody in the language of interiority or essence.[6]

I wish to make no inflated claims of plausibility for this interpretation. But I am somewhat more confident about my answer to the third question. Whether or not Sumarsam's situation within postcolonial academe influenced his turn to the rhetoric of interiority, it surely influenced his theoreticism. I pointed out above how the modesty of Suhardi's pragmatic claims contrasts with Sumarsam's and Supanggah's more theoretical orientation. Now, the latter two, unlike Suhardi, presented their implicit-melody concepts as written contributions in an ongoing academic enterprise. Is it possible that their theoretical orientation is a response to their academic context?

Certainly, Sumarsam's and Supanggah's talk of "essence" and their claims about the foundational status of their unplayed melodies suggest that their theoreticism is due to their participation in a transcultural, crossgenerational conversation with Western theorists of *karawitan*. Suhardi independently formulated a concept strikingly similar to Supanggah's, but because he was not in on the conversation, he had no need to present his concept as the answer to a theoretical problem.

CONCLUSION

I have argued in this chapter that implicit-melody concepts are creative responses to the irregularity of melodic guidance in Javanese music. They represent three attempts by three musicians to make sense of their music, three differing attempts to articulate their implicit knowledge and give it coherent and consistent form. I have suggested that the similarities among these concepts are due to the common problem that they try to solve; the differences may be due to differences in the historical contexts of their formulation.

The variety of implicit-melody concepts suggests that they are the result of creative thinking. My three teachers devised new ideas from old ones by conceptual extension or analogical thinking, projecting the image of the guiding parts into a subjunctive realm where they would be free from the idiosyncrasies of the actual parts. Working in different social and cognitive environments, they constructed different sorts of unplayed melodies. Sumarsam's "inner melody" is modeled on the *rebab* part; Suhardi's *lagu*, like Supanggah's "essential *balungan*," is modeled on the *balungan*. The choice of which part to project is not arbitrary; we can hardly imagine an implicit melody modeled on the *gendèr panerus* part. But both the *rebab* line and the *balungan* can serve well enough as blueprints for the construction of unplayed melodies.

These implicit-melody concepts thus serve to cognitively organize the texture of interpart relations, each in its own way unifying moments of congruence and divergence into a consistent pattern. But these concepts in turn can be integrated to varying degrees and in various ways into a larger mental picture of Javanese music. Suhardi was content to let his notion of *lagu* remain relatively disarticulated, using it only as a practical teaching aid, while Sumarsam and Supanggah situated their concepts at the core of the explanatory web of their theories, to address the deepest questions of *karawitan*'s origin and essence.

The study of implicit-melody concepts teaches us much about the nature of melodic practice in Javanese music. It focuses our attention on the dialectics of "staying alive" and "walking together" and on the multiformity and irregularity of melodic guidance. But I suggest that it also has implications for the general study of creative thinking about music. Since the cognitive processes of conceptual extension and intra-domain analogy are not limited to music but are common to many conceptual realms, we might find them at work in other traditions as well. The story of implicit-melody concepts in Java might be able to illuminate more than the specifics of Javanese music; it might offer ways we could study cognition in other music cultures. In my final chapter I turn to an entirely dissimilar musical tradition to test the cross-cultural fecundity of this approach.

8 Patterns of Conceptual Innovation in Music Theory

A Comparative Approach

To this point I have trafficked in the very specific and the very general. I have tried to understand a moment from the history of Javanese music theory by using psychological concepts of extremely broad application. The reader with exclusively musical interests might grant that in so doing I have provided the cognitive psychologist with useful data, but remain skeptical of the potential musical illumination to be had thereby. I suggest, however, that having observed these general features of musical cognition at work in Java, we can now look at creative thinking in other traditions with new eyes. In this chapter I illustrate this claim with case studies of innovative musical thought outside Java.

It is not yet possible to write a broad cross-cultural survey of the processes of conceptual innovation in music; the subject is too little studied. There is, however, one tradition for which it is well documented: European art music. In what follows, therefore, I will compare the processes of conceptual change described in this book with well-known cases of music-theoretic innovation in the West.

Historical case studies cannot, of course, provide the same type of ethnographic detail that was available to me in Java. When I wanted to know how Sumarsam arrived at his idea of inner melody, I asked him; I could not ask Lippius how he conceived the idea of the *trias harmonica*. Therefore I have had to infer cognitive processes from the written traces they left behind. Further, the court style of Central Javanese music changed relatively little during the years of my research, whereas European art music changed significantly during the period I cover in this chapter, and thus as the object of musicians' conceptualizations it represented a moving target. But the broad scope of historical studies offers insights of its own, and finding evidence of similar thought processes at work at different historical moments should strengthen the case for their generality.

NEAR AND FAR ANALOGIES IN WESTERN MUSIC THEORY

It is possible to find in the history of European art music examples of all of the creative strategies described in chapter 1: conceptual combination and differentiation, conceptual extension, and the various forms of metaphor and analogy. We will encounter all of these in the case studies that follow, but I pay special attention to the closely related processes of conceptual extension and within-domain analogy. This is intended not only to provide a counterpart to the discussion of these processes in Javanese music, but to complement recent research trends in the history of Western music theory.

Analogical thinking has lately received a great deal of attention from historians of theory, but the analogies studied have generally been distant ones between music and nonmusical domains. It is easy to see the reason for this. For some years now, the tendency of theorists to cultivate among themselves a highly technical conversation, seemingly esoteric and alienating to others (Burkholder 1993:14), has been countered by the attempt to demonstrate a link between high-level musical abstractions and broader aspects of human experience and culture. Sometimes this has been done by situating the history of theory within larger intellectual or cultural historiographies (Burnham 1993): finding traces of Cartesian mechanism, Newtonian experimentalism, or sensationalist psychology in Rameau's writings (Christensen 1993); revealing the influence upon Schenker of Goethe (Pastille 1985) or Hegel (Cherlin 1988); or showing the influence of the Pythagorean-Platonic metaphysics of unity on the theory and practice of organum (Cohen 1993). Sometimes this project uncovers the ideological aspects of music theory, such as Schenker's social conservatism and German chauvinism (Rothstein 1990:195–96), or the bourgeois subjectivity and fear of mass culture Robert Fink finds in Schenker's exaltation of musical "depth" (1999). It is in this spirit that scholars examine the use of metaphorical or analogical language, the "figurative underpinnings" of musical discourse, to elucidate the values and attitudes, the "fictions" and "myths," implicit in the practice of musical analysis (Guck 1994; Snarrenberg 1994). Drawing on cognitive linguistics, this approach can also explore the tangible, embodied roots of music-theoretic abstractions, stressing their dependence on image schemas derived from bodily experience (such as "source-path-goal": Saslaw 1996) or on cultural models (such as the static and dynamic models of musical form examined by Zbikowski 2002). In its attempts to break down the isolation of musical concepts and root them in a psychological, historical, or cultural context, this approach is one ethnomusicologists could find congenial.

Once we are alerted to the figurative aspects of theoretical discourse, once we recognize music theory's permanent debts to concepts and images taken from nonmusical domains, it is natural to look for the source of novel concepts in novel metaphors. Wide-reaching analogies between music and nonmusical phenomena have surely inspired many music-theoretic developments, and historians continue to uncover these—tracing, for example, the notion of harmonic progression back to Aristotelian physics (Cohen 2001b). Yet as we saw in chapter 1, from a cognitive point of view the same processes are responsible for metaphorical and nonmetaphorical thinking. Analogical reasoning, too, is fundamentally the same whether it functions within a domain or between domains, and in some contexts intra-domain analogy is by far the more common of the two.

Thus, while never forgetting how permeable music theory is to the concepts, themes, and cognitive styles of the culture surrounding it, we must not lose sight of the analogies musicians draw from close at hand. We are in no danger of sealing music theory back into its bubble, I feel, if alongside its most daring metaphors we appreciate the work analogical thinking does *within* the musical domain.

THE IMPORTANCE OF WITHIN-DOMAIN ANALOGIES

The history of Western music theory is full of examples of concepts with familiar musical senses being extended, applied analogically to other musical phenomena, for purposes of both analysis and composition. Consider three examples: the use of concepts properly applied to small time-scales (single measures or phrases, or small compositions) with reference to large time-scales (groups of phrases, entire movements, or large pieces); the use of terms for pitch relations (dissonance, modulation) to describe temporal relations (rhythm, meter, or tempo); and the extended use of concepts like "scale-step" and "passing tone" in Schenkerian analysis.

The idea that similar patterns, principles, or proportions govern both small and large musical units goes back at least to the eighteenth century. It first appeared in pedagogical contexts, where students were given recipes for expanding phrases by orders of magnitude. For example, Koch's *Versuch einer*

Anleitung zur Composition (1782–93) treats small forms like the minuet as "models in miniature of the larger compositions" (Sisman 1982:448). J. F. Daube's *Anleitung zur Erfindung der Melodie und ihrer Fortsetzung* of 1797 (Buelow 1979:186, 195) similarly explains how a composer can spin a one- or two-measure idea into a passage over a hundred measures long and turn a four-measure melodic idea into a symphonic movement. Theorists developed this idea for analytical purposes by comparing the relations between the durations of phrases and sections in a composition, on the one hand, with the relations between the durations of notes in a single phrase, on the other. Thus Koch in 1787 metaphorically applied the term for a pattern of note durations—"rhythm"—to the patterning of phrase lengths in a composition (1983:2). In 1832, Fétis used the term "phrase rhythm" (Arlin in press), a concept later taken up by Hanslick and described as "rhythm in the larger scale as the co-proportionality of a symmetrical structure" (1891:28). In the twentieth century, Lorenz introduced the idea of *potenzierte Formen*, in which small-scale forms can be "raised to a higher power" to become large-scale forms (for a convenient summary of his analysis of one act of *Die Walküre*, see Abraham 1964:122–29). Similarly, Cooper and Meyer (1960:61) found identical principles of rhythmic formation at lower and higher architectonic levels. Cone (1968:24–26), too, analogized musical form with rhythmic structure in his concepts of "extended upbeat" and "structural downbeat."[1]

The use of the vocabulary of pitch relations to describe time relations also goes back at least to Fétis.[2] In 1832, he speculated that music would someday acquire a rhythmic equivalent to the dominant seventh chord: a means of transition between meters comparable to its means of modulating between keys (Arlin in press). Soon afterward, in 1837, Berlioz insisted that "there are such things as rhythmic dissonances; there are rhythmic consonances; there are rhythmic modulations" (1837:338). Hauptmann's dialectical theory of harmony and meter postulated rhythmic equivalents to the intervals of the octave, fifth, and third (1853:189–94).

The projection of musical concepts from the domain of pitch to that of rhythm was a source not only of new theoretical insights, but of compositional ones as well. Cowell, for example, advocated "the building of ordered systems of harmony and counterpoint in rhythm, which have an exact relationship to tonal harmony and counterpoint" through "the application of overtone ratios" (1930:46, 50). He devised the rhythmic equivalent to a succession of different chords (1930:53) and suggested ways of combining meters into metrical harmonies (1930:67). Other composers have analogized temporal and pitch relations in other ways. The best-known example in twentieth-century music is surely the extension of serial procedures from pitch to rhythm as found in Babbitt's *Three Compositions for Piano* (1947) and Boulez's *Structures Ia* (1952). Tempo, too, was compared to pitch, most famously in Elliott Carter's practice of "metric modulation": "I thought that, in composing, it was possible to pass from one tempo to another, just as you go from one key to another" (1989:41). Stockhausen also employed this analogy (1989:41): "I use chromatic scales of tempi corresponding to pitch, between MM = 60 and MM = 120, which is a ratio of 1:2, like an octave on the keyboard."[3]

As a final example of conceptual extension, I must mention one of the major episodes in the history of Western music theory, though I cannot give it the detailed treatment it merits. Schenkerian analysis models large-scale complex musical textures on smaller, simpler ones. As Nicholas Cook observes, "Schenkerian analysis is based on a metaphor," comparing "the note-to-note structure of Fuxian counterpoint and the freely elaborated surface of real music" (Cook 1989:125). Other writers, too, have commented on Schenker's "expanded metaphors of strict counterpoint" (Littlefield and Neumeyer 1992:51) and on how the dissonant passing tone is for Schenker the "underlying model of all melodic motion" (Pastille 1990:82). Much of Schenker's originality can be traced to his creative expansion of several familiar concepts, such as "scale-step" or "melodic fluency." Dubiel has pointed out the crucial role played by Schenker's expansion of the notion of "passing": freed from the specificity of the passing tone by Schenker's "fantastic and profound extension of its scope" (1990:321), applied to much larger musical phenomena, the generalized notion of passing virtually entails the concept of structural levels (1990:318). Dubiel concludes (1990:327):

> Schenker uses the second-species passing tone essentially as a *metaphor* for the relation of one free-composition passage to another— a metaphor unlike what most theorists probably imagine under that name because it has no *extramusical* element: it compares the musical thing that it describes to another thing that is also music.[4]

Lest my purpose in citing these statements be misconstrued, let me remind the reader that I wish to trace the cognitive patterns of innovative thinking, not to judge the adequacy or validity of any particular theories. In some of the writings quoted above the point of describing Schenkerian statements as metaphorical is to deny them the cognitive status of objective truth-claims, as when Cohn favorably cites Cook's suggestion that "Schenkerian theory . . . should aim toward the suggestiveness of strong metaphors, rather than any more ultimate claims about truth or reality"

(1992:170). This is not my intention here; I have no interest in either impugning or affirming the epistemic claims of Schenkerian theory or analysis. My focus throughout is on processes of conceptual innovation that may well be common to both discovery and invention. Metaphor and analogy are useful for more than the creation of fictions; they have always played important roles in the history of discovery in the natural sciences. We can therefore point out their presence in a theorist's heuristics of discovery without deprecating the cognitive respectability of the theories she formulates as a result.

In the remainder of this chapter I explore in detail the origins of two concepts: the notions of chord root and harmonic progression. The story of the emergence of the root idea is useful to us, for it shows conceptual change operating over a long historical time span, and shows how a new concept can be framed in more than one way, through the extension of different source concepts. In examining the history of the idea of harmonic progression, I focus on one historical moment, Rameau's formulation of the *basse fondamentale*. This choice of focus allows us to see processes of conceptual extension at work in a larger context (richly described for us by Thomas Christensen). It also invites a surprisingly detailed comparison with the story of the Javanese implicit-melody concepts.

My survey of the idea of chord root is not meant to be comprehensive, but merely to illustrate the operation of conceptual extension in an unsuspected place. In these historical notes I pay close attention to the shifting terms for chord root, but it is not because I subscribe to a reflectionist theory of language—the assumption that a music culture's vocabulary directly mirrors its thought patterns—or to a naïve linguistic determinism, according to which the absence of a lexical item makes it impossible for people to think certain thoughts. I use these words simply as convenient entry points into the conceptual worlds of the people who used them. A theorist's choice of words for a concept can offer clues to the cognitive processes of extension or analogy that produced the concept, but those clues must always be validated by a close study of his arguments, the structure and sequence of his exposition, and so on.

As for my interest in theories that many would judge incoherent or deservedly forgotten, it is not purely antiquarian. There are methodological benefits to the study of ideas that to us may seem curious or confused. When we study ideas agreeable to our own, we are prone to suppose the fact of their formulation to be in need of no explanation; that they reflect reality (as we see it) sufficiently explains their genesis. Studying ideas that seem to us misguided has the advantage that we are more likely to see the processes that produced them *as* processes; we may more easily notice the cognitive work involved and the cognitive resources that were applied to the task.

BASS AND TONIC IN THE HISTORY
OF THE CONCEPT OF CHORD ROOT

The "triad," as it is understood in modern harmonic theory, is a relatively abstract thing. It is not a set of three pitches, but of three pitch-classes, which can be distributed in several ways among the octaves. The notion of the triad generalizes: it bundles together (for example) all of C-E-G, E-G-C, and G-C-E—three chords with very different functions in eighteenth-century music—as different versions (inversions, as we say) of "the same thing," a C major triad. But this abstract concept does not merely establish the equivalence of these three versions; it also discriminates among them. One of them—the "root position," the inversion that contains a perfect fifth between its lowest and highest pitches—is treated as primary; the others are derived.[5]

Each major or minor triad has a root, defined as the lowest pitch of the 5-3 (root) position. The notion of "root" is thus, like "triad" and "inversion," relatively abstract. It is not *very* abstract, but it is not as directly observable as the notion of "bass tone," the lowest-sounding tone of a chord. We can find the bass of a chord simply by noting the height of each chord tone and choosing the lowest one. To find the root, we need to do more: we need to measure the intervals between the chord tones, decide if the chord is in root position, invert it if it is not, and then choose the lowest tone.

Histories of music theory usually date the formulation of this complex of related abstractions (triad, inversion, root) to the seventeenth century. Some earlier musicians did indeed single out the 5-3 sonority for special treatment—Zarlino, for example, considered the combination of the fifth and third over the bass as "perfection in harmony" (1558:188)—but they did not necessarily think of a 5-3 chord on C and a 6-3 chord on E as in some sense the same entity. Zarlino, after praising the perfection of the 5-3 sonority, adds that the interval of a sixth can substitute for the fifth, but draws no connection between the two types of chords. From our point of view, Zarlino's concepts of the 5-3 and 6-3 sonorities were relatively disarticulated. This was presumably not because he was incapable of recognizing the commonality of pitch content between them. Indeed, we know of several musicians (at least in the seventeenth and early eighteenth centuries) who acknowledged the shared pitch content of such chords without, however, treating them as ontologically identical (Lester 1992:42, 54–55). This makes psychological sense; for without being integrated within a larger conceptual framework such observations about identity of pitch content would have had no clear significance. In the absence of such a framework, the fact that the same three pitches could form two different chords would be a mere curiosity, like the fact that the same three letters of the alphabet can spell both *cat* and *act*—an observation that might come in handy when playing a game of anagrams, but with no wider ramifications.

The idea of conceptually linking sonorities made up of identical pitch-classes, and singling out one of those pitch-classes as primary, developed over roughly two centuries. Musical composition was not static during that time, of course. A homophonic style took its place alongside the linear, imitative contrapuntal style. The prominence of strongly chordal, bass-dominated hymns and dance forms, and the rise of the thorough bass, presumably encouraged more attention to the so-called vertical dimension of pitch simultaneities, eventually even influencing the teaching of counterpoint itself (Rivera 1984:70–71; Christensen 1993:61–63). Of all the vertical sonorities, the 5-3 triad was clearly central to compositional, pedagogical, and notational practice. It could appear in the greatest variety of contexts. It was the only chord that could end a piece, and indeed it was obligatory at every full cadence. It was the first chord taught to the student. In figured bass notation it was the default chord, the *common cord* (Lampe 1737:14), the *harmonie ordinaire* (Masson 1699:102), the *Ordinar-Satz* (Werckmeister 1702:2). It was literally unmarked, to be understood whenever no other chord was explicitly called for.

The first major formulation of the triad/root/inversion complex is generally credited to the German theologian-theorist Johannes Lippius (1585–1612). Lippius described the triad *(trias harmonica)* as a *radix* ("root"), a key concept in his thinking. He seemed to use this term on analogy with the mathematical operation of *radicatio,* reducing a fraction to its simplest terms, and employed it as a metaphor for the primal source or form of any phenomenon.[6] God was the root of all things; the monochord was the root of all instruments. The seven pitch-names (what we might consider pitch-classes) were the "radical" *(radicalis)* tones of the gamut (Rivera 1980:63).

As the primal source or form of harmony, the triad provided for Lippius a unified basis for understanding the combination of consonances, one that had both a neoplatonic numerical justification and a Christian allegorical interpretation. He intended the notion of the *trias harmonica* to simplify and integrate the principles for combining intervals, for which "composers almost up to now have prescribed innumerable rules fraught with difficulty, or have proffered loosely scattered considerations that lack a true overall adhesive foundation" (Rivera 1980:225). He wanted to replace a thicket of unrelated compositional prescriptions with an arrangement of three notes, an arrangement he credited with vast explanatory power; with them he felt he could account for "all the most perfect and most complete harmonies that can exist in the world," even "thousands and millions" of them (1980:232). These three notes had a basis in the numerical proportions 4:5:6, and thus had the sanction of nature (1980:227). The order of these radical numbers, and the simplicity of their ratios, also provided an explanation of why certain chords sounded better than others (1980:229, 235; cf. 80). Finally, Lippius argued for the significance of the *trias harmonica* with a striking interdomain analogy: the fact that it requires only three sounds to form a full harmony corresponded to certain other threefold phenomena (the three letters of the root of the Hebrew word, the three terms of the syllogism) and represented "the semblance of that great mystery of the divine and solely adorable Tri-unity": God, "one in essence, but threefold in persons" (1980:227–28).

Lippius's theory is often described as revolutionary. But while his notion of *trias harmonica* is an ancestor of our triad/inversion/root constellation, the two differ considerably. Lippius's theory is not so much a theory of inversions and roots as a theory of the 5-3 sonority. It is this chord that he calls the *radix*, and this chord to which he devotes the most attention; indeed, he becomes quite rapturous in its praise. By contrast, while a distinct concept of chord root (in the modern sense) is present in Lippius, he devotes little attention to it. He did have several terms for the root *(basis, prima, infima)* as part of his complete nomenclature for the three component tones of the triad; some of these (including *basis*) he adopted from earlier writers (Rivera 1978:60). He also felt that the *basis* was the source of the other two tones, though this idea did not play a central role in his theory: he did not mention it in his *Disputatio musica tertia* of 1610, and in his *Synopsis musicae novae* (1612) he notes it only in passing (Rivera 1980:233). When he did try to justify the primacy of the *basis,* he did so allegorically. Using theological language, Lippius wrote that the fifth of the chord is "begotten" of the root *(ab illa genita),* and the third proceeds *(procedens)* from the cospiration *(conspirantes)* of the root and fifth—just as the Son is begotten of the Father *(genitum),* and the Holy Spirit proceeds from the Father and Son *(procedens)* in what can be called a spiration *(spiratio)* (Rivera 1980:122).

Lippius's claim to special insight, his boast of providing a "true overall adhesive foundation" for music, lies in the connections he draws, the way he weaves things together. These connections are of two sorts: he linked musical things with other musical things, but also with extramusical things. On the one hand, he gathered together all of the various possible sonorities by treating them as so many sprouts germinated from the 5-3 triad. In terms of Derrida's metaphysical exigency, this *radix* functioned as the simple origin from which manifold forms issue through processes of derivation and complication—which in this case are processes of octave displacement and doubling. On the other hand, Lippius connected chords to things extramusical, both the numerical ratios of *musica theorica* and the theological concept of triune divinity.

Lippius's account of the chord root relies explicitly on the latter sort of connection; his only overt analogy is an extramusical one. Nevertheless, his terminology suggests an internal connection as well. One of his terms for the root—*basis*—originally referred to the bass tone of a chord. It was used in this sense by Avianius (1581) and Burmeister (1606); for some writers it retained this sense well into the eighteenth century.[7] It was apparently Lippius's contemporary Harnisch who first used *basis* to refer to the root (in 1608: Rivera 1978:60). Thus Lippius and Harnisch adapted a term denoting the bass tone of any sonority and applied it to the bass tone of the 5-3 chord, allowing it to carry this designation whether it appeared in the bass or any other voice.

The dependence of the notion of chord root on the notion of chord bass is made much more explicit in contemporaneous English writers. Indeed, for most of the seventeenth century, English musicians who described what we would call a chord root did so in terms of the bass.

Thomas Campion's treatise of around 1613, *A New Way of Making Fowre Parts in Counterpoint*, instructs the student how to compose three parts above a bass line. He presents a mechanical procedure for setting octaves, fifths, and thirds above each tone of the bass; thus each bass note supports a 5-3 sonority. Campion then admits that certain bass tones (those that in our terms support sixth chords) cannot be given this treatment; in these cases he substitutes a sixth for the fifth. But in some cases not only is the fifth to be avoided, but so is the octave (i.e., the bass tone must not be doubled). This would seem to challenge the validity of Campion's procedure ("so that exception is to be taken against our rule of Counterpoint"). But he feels that these are not actually counterexamples to his rule of composition over the bass, for the bass tones in such cases are more apparent than real: "To which I answere thus, first, such Bases are not true Bases, for where a sixt is to be taken, either in F sharpe, or in E sharpe, or in B or in A, the true Base is a third lower, F sharp in D, E in C, B in G, A in F . . ." (1967:335). If we replace the sounded bass note with the "true Base," Campion's rules hold.

Here we see Campion using the notion of bass tone to represent what we would call a chord root. He separated bass tones that could be accounted for by a simple rule from those that could not; the former alone he considered real bass tones. To find the "true Base" of a chord that lacked one (say, the sixth chord F#-A-D), he presumably projected onto it the 5-3 chord composed of the same pitches. In this way the sixth chord could acquire a bass tone not actually present in its lowest voice.

In other words, Campion supplied the sixth chord with an unsounded, virtual bass, yet one in some sense *more real* than the sounded bass. It was more real because it was more regular. Campion used the notion of "true Base" to preserve his generalization—his "rule of Counterpoint"—against an apparent exception, and did so by positing an unplayed bass.

Campion's version of the concept of chord root is quite different from Lippius's, not least because he has no explicit concept that even approximates the notion of chord inversion. While he apparently understood the 6-3 sonority on the model of the 5-3 sonority, he does not posit an imagined act of transposition that produces the one from the other by shifting the bass upward by an octave. Thus he is not searching for a basic, ontologically prior sonority from which all other sonorities can be derived. The simplicity he posits is not a simplicity of sonority but of compositional procedure, his proposed new "rule of Counterpoint." But to preserve the simplicity of this rule he must create a new entity. He does so by means of conceptual differentiation, splitting off the concept of the "true" bass from the ordinary idea of the bass.

By the turn of the eighteenth century, the concept of chord root had become fairly well established, and the idea of chord inversion had taken on more of its now-familiar conceptual function.[8] For example, it seems to be Werckmeister who first distinguishes inversions (in the modern sense) from open-position spacings of the 5-3 triad (1702).

Werckmeister is also somewhat more explicit about the role of the chord root than Lippius. He borrowed one of Lippius's major terms, but reinterpreted it: instead of the *radix* being the entire triad, it was now the chord root (Rivera 1980:152). It is perhaps fitting that Werckmeister used Lippius's master term—in a way Lippius never did—to emphasize the generative role of the chord root. For he attached much more importance to the idea of this tone as the source of the others, relying on neoplatonic arguments about numerical proportions. The unison, represented by the number 1, contains in itself all the consonances (Christensen 1993:88); it is the root *(Wurtzel)* of the tree of harmony (Werckmeister 1687:77).

But Werckmeister also uses the idea of chord root to explain such practical matters as chord voicing. For example, in the "ordinary" chord of thorough bass (the 5-3 sonority) the bass tone is usually doubled at the octave. Werckmeister instructs the student not to double the bass tones of sixth chords; to justify this apparent exceptional treatment, he explains that such basses are "not the true roots [*radices*] of the harmonic triads" (Werckmeister 1698:15). Thus (somewhat like Campion) he uses the notion of chord root to relate an unusual practice to the norm.

The concepts discussed above were all used to bring order to a certain range of musical phenomena: to make sense of the relations between sonorities composed of the same pitch-classes, to simplify the rules of counterpoint, and to regularize the principles of chord voicing in a four-part texture. Rameau would dramatically extend the explanatory reach of such concepts, using them to account for chord progressions as well. He modified the set of phenomena to which the concept of root could be assumed to be relevant. But there were other theorists, before and after Rameau, who modified this set in other ways. They brought the idea of chord root into relation not just with the vertical structures of chords, but also with their position in the scale and their relation to the tonic. Speaking somewhat anachronistically, we can characterize these theorists as trying to provide an account of chord root that was also an account of tonality. Thus here we find a second model for the chord root: just as Campion tried to understand it in terms of the bass tone, some of these musicians tried to understand it in terms of the tonic (or, more generally, in terms of the idea of scale degree).

This is most clear in certain English writings, especially in the unpublished treatises of Roger North (1651?–1734), a lawyer and amateur viol and theorbo player. North has two ways of referring to a chord root. Like Campion, he adds a qualifying adjective to the word "bass." What Campion called a "true Base," North called a "proper base" or "reall base" (1990:79), and he distinguished it from "consort base notes," which were not roots (1990:141). But North also has a second way of referring to chord roots. He uses the term "key" or "key-note" to mean not only the tonic or tonal center ("the note . . . that leads the scale": p. 110), but also the "proper base" of a chord.

North introduces harmonic intervals and triads in terms of a scale. He defines "accords" (i.e., intervals) as "cosounding notes, according to their places in the scale, but more striktly referred to the key note" (1990:136).

He represents intervals in terms of scale degrees: thus with G as the tonic ("key"), G-B is a third, since B is the third tone in the scale of G. North admits that these intervals can be calculated between any two tones of the scale, "but generally in musicall accounts accords are taken from the lower note ascending with (unless the contrary is declared) the lower note as the leader of the scale, and the accords taken as derived upon that" (1990:136–37). Hence he argues that "all accords whatsoever (in truth) have for base the key of the scale." The tonic is not necessarily present in each chord, for it may happen that "the lower note of the accord usurps the place of the key; and is termed the base of that accord." But the "true base" is "the key note" (1990:141). In this way, the concept of a single tone governing a scale—a tonic—and that of a single tone governing a chord—a root—melt together in North's writing.

Thus North used the tonic as a model for a tone that represents a chord without necessarily being the bass of that chord. His attempt to coordinate in this way the domains of scale and harmony caused him some difficulties—he had some trouble formulating a definition of his idiosyncratic concept of "key" (1990:79–80)—but I am not concerned here to evaluate the cogency of his theory. I only wish to point out that North drew on two sources in conceptualizing the chord root: the idea of chord bass and the idea of a scale's tonal center.

This combination is one we find in other writers as well. The treatise by the Scottish mathematician, clergyman, and teacher Alexander Malcolm (1685–1763) uses language comparable to North's in some of these respects. He had no word for chord root, but like Campion and North qualified a familiar term to express the idea; unlike them, the familiar term he used was not "bass," but "key." Hence in describing the 6-4 chord G-C-E, Malcolm calls C (its root) the "true Key" (1721:277).

In German-language writings, the same two source concepts were also used to frame the notion of chord root, as we can see by reviewing the complex semantics of the terms *Grundton* and *Grundnote*. The combining form *Grund* (ground, bottom, base, foundation, basis, reason, cause) had several musical uses. In its most general sense it referred to something that served as the basis of something else.[9] This is in keeping with a common conceptual metaphor in European languages, that of the building constructed from the ground up (COMPLEX ABSTRACT SYSTEMS ARE BUILDINGS: Kövecses 1999:180). But it had long been given a musical sense related to the bass part, thanks no doubt to the conventional metaphor of pitch height according to which bass tones are deep or low *(tief)*. If a contrapuntal or harmonic texture is compared to a building, its foundation would be the bass part: thus the bass part could be called the *Grund-Stimme* (Printz 1696:35; Niedt 1710, chapter 10).

Throughout the eighteenth century, *Grundton* and *Grundnote* are accordingly used to refer to the bass tones. Walther, for example, describes *General-Bass* as a bass part that indicates the harmonies as well as the *Grund-Noten* (1732:268). Thus during this period we can never assume that *Grundton*, appearing *sans phrase*, refers to a chord root. But it was sometimes given special adjectival qualification to express unambiguously the idea of chord root.

Kirnberger, for example, consistently used *Grundton* by itself to mean the bass tone (as when he described the sixth chord as consisting of a *Grundton* with its third and sixth, and a six-four chord as a *Grundton* with its fourth and sixth; 1776–79:26). When he wished to describe a chord root he consistently referred to *der eigentliche Grundton* (1776–79:27; cf. also pp. 33, 50, 177) or *die wahren Grund-Töne* (cf. his concept of *Grund-Bass*: 1776–79:54).

Thus we can to some extent compare Kirnberger to Campion or North, who also expressed their concepts of chord root in terms of "true" or "real" bass notes. But there is another layer of complexity in the German case. For Kirnberger also uses *Grundton* to denote the principal tone of a mode or key (its finalis or tonic: 1776–79:3).[10] This fact does not seem very significant in Kirnberger's case, but it is also present—and very important—in the work of his contemporary Heinrich Koch.

For Koch (as for North and Malcolm), the idea of key inflects the bass/ root complex. He makes heavy use of the term *Grundton* but does not use it to mean chord root. As a term for a component of a chord it clearly means bass note, as it did in Kirnberger.[11] But Koch considers the strict meaning of *Grundton* to be the tonic of a key and only secondarily the bass tone of a chord (1802:705). This is perhaps consistent with the general tenor of his thought. For Koch is notable for his attempt to use a notion of tonality to resolve the debate over the priority of harmony versus melody: he derives both from the "primary matter of music" *(Urstoff der Musik)*, the tonal relations between pitches established through a mode or key (Baker 1988:16).

Kirnberger added a qualifying adjective *(eigentlich)* to *Grundton* to refer to the chord root, calling it in effect the true, real, or actual bass. Koch, too, distinguishes a category of *eigentlicher Grundton*, but unlike Kirnberger he does not use this expression to mean a chord root. In keeping with his ambition to account for tonality as well as chord structure, he intends it to describe only certain roots, those serving particular tonal roles.

Koch distinguishes two types of triads within a key. Those built on scale degrees 1, 4, and 5 he calls essential *(wesentlich)*; the others are unessential *(zufällig)*. The essential triads define the key, for their component tones include all of the tones of the scale (1782–93:I, 53). Koch's notion of "real *Grundton*" is defined in terms of this distinction. An *eigentlicher Grundton* is any of the bass tones of the key's three essential 5-3 triads; an *uneigentlicher Grundton* is the bass of an unessential 5-3 triad or of an inverted essential triad (1782–93:I, 239–40). A *Grundbass* is similarly a series of *eigentliche Grundtöne*. That is, it is a sequence of roots of the key-defining triads, scale degrees 1, 4, and 5 (1782–93:I, 259–62).

I will end my story in the early nineteenth century, when the semantic slippage of *Grundton* attracts comment and attempts are made to stabilize it. Gottfried Weber defines *Grundton* or *Grundnote* as chord root, and specifically insists on the need to distinguish it from the notion of the bass tone. Indeed, he complains that earlier writers have confounded these (1817:143).

The triad/root/inversion complex was a useful new way of thinking about music because it joined together previously disarticulated ideas. Behind the plethora of sonorities it found a simple 5-3 triad that itself could be represented by a single tone. To conceptualize this tone, however, musicians depended on existing notions of bass tone, tonic, or scale degree, extending them and applying them in new ways.[12] As we shall see, the same was true of Rameau. He, too, posited a world of simplicity behind music's surface complexities, but to picture the denizens of this world he relied on familiar musical ideas—in particular, the concept of the bass line.

RAMEAU'S FUNDAMENTAL BASS

As is apparent from Thomas Christensen's marvelous study of Rameau as a theorist, Rameau's creativity was due in large part to his skill at conceptual combination: "For such a revolutionary work, the *Traité de l'harmonie* contains surprisingly few individual components that can be said to be original to Rameau" (1993:43). His creative accomplishment lay rather in his synthesis of existing music-theoretical concepts.

Rameau found in thorough bass theory a tradition of conceptualizing a multipart texture as a series of discrete harmonic units, where voice-leading considerations sometimes became secondary or were even entirely absent (1993:47–51). Rameau's immediate predecessors classified the variety of cadences and recognized their occurrence in the midst of phrases as well as at their ends (1993:113–14). From the tradition of musical speculation known as *musica theorica* he absorbed an orientation toward the abstract properties of the basic materials of music, its tones, intervals, modes, or tuning systems (1993:29–31). In this tradition the intervals were typically derived from numerical proportions demonstrated on the monochord, proportions often interpreted in terms of a neoplatonic vision of cosmic harmony (1993:71–87). Moreover, Rameau was also inspired by the Cartesian ambition to discover a single clear and evident principle from which the details of musical practice could be deduced (1993:12),[13] and he was aware of contemporary attempts to understand the universe in mechanical terms, reducing all phenomena to patterns of colliding particles (1993:103–106).

Rameau's originality consists in large measure in his ability to combine these pre-existing musical concepts and relate them to the natural philosophy of his day. Like Lippius, Rameau made new sense of his music by drawing new connections, but Rameau's web of conceptual affiliation was much wider, encompassing the derivation of intervals from the monochord string, the triadic basis of harmony, chord inversion, the primacy of the bass line, and the taxonomy of cadences. Both musicians unified all of the consonant chords by deriving them from the 5-3 triad; both saw the root as the source and generator of the triad; but Rameau also made a strong claim of equivalence among all inversions of a triad (Christensen 1993:95) and reduced all dissonant chords to the dominant seventh (1993:98, 124). Further, he also posited a principle governing the succession of chords, deriving all progressions from the cadence (1993:120). Finally, he tried to unify chord structure and chord progression. He postulated a single set of intervals, generated by the division of the monochord string (or, in his later work, by the vibrations of the *corps sonore*), to govern both the construction of chords and their succession through time (1993:106).

Rameau was particularly proud of his unified treatment of voice-leading and criticized the disarticulated, piecemeal approach of earlier theorists, who gave "as many . . . different rules as there are different chords" (1722:82). They listed all of the allowable resolutions of dissonant intervals, not realizing that all exemplify a single principle. Where his predecessors dealt with each case separately, Rameau brought them together "to form a simple and intelligible entity."

This world of simplicity and intelligibility was governed by a bass line. It was distinct from the actual bass (the *basse continue*); in our terms it was largely made up of a succession of chord roots.[14] Nevertheless Rameau considered it to be a kind of bass part; he called it the fundamental bass *(basse fondamentale).*

It is natural that Rameau should have used the bass line to conceptualize what we now call a harmonic progression. The bass part had been considered paramount since Zarlino; it was "the foundation of harmony" (*fondamento dell'harmonia*: Zarlino 1561:239, 1558:179). The bass was the terminus from which all harmonic intervals were calculated, and upon which the other parts were said to be built; in the words of Thomas Campion, one "may view in it all the other parts in their originall essence" (1967:327). It was "the groundwork or foundation upon which all musical composition is to be erected" (Simpson 1667:19), "the base and foundation of the other parts, since one builds them upon it" (Masson 1699:31). Moreover, with the dominance of the thorough bass in the seventeenth and early eighteenth centuries the bass line and its associated figures became virtually identified with the teaching of harmony and composition.

Rameau's notion of the fundamental bass clearly grew from that of thorough bass and remained tied to it by a conceptual umbilical cord. Thorough bass practice was the "catalyst" that made Rameau's formulation of the fundamental bass possible; Christensen goes as far as to say that "Rameau's system of the fundamental bass is a theory of the thorough bass" (1993:51, 61). After all, the fundamental bass was, like the thorough bass, a bass line. Rameau notated the fundamental bass in the same way as the thorough bass (Keiler 1981:91). He used an existing notion—the bass line as the foundation of the composition—in a new way; we could say that the fundamental bass was a trope, a deliberate "misuse," a metaphoric extension, of the thorough bass.[15]

It may be difficult for us to perceive the conceptual kinship of the (ordinary) bass line with the fundamental bass, since we tend to view the latter notion through the lens of our own concept of harmonic progression, which makes no overt reference to the bass. Thus I suspect we mentally edit out all suggestion of a low-lying part when we hear the term "fundamental bass." But in the eighteenth century this suggestion could be very much alive.

For example, Roussier complained of a common misconception about Rameau's fundamental bass, which he attributed to the use of that expression in a different sense by Italian musicians, but also to the unsuitability of Rameau's term for the idea he wished to convey (1783). Roussier notes that the Italians used the term "fundamental bass" to describe the lowest bass part when more than one is written (as in polychoral music). But Rameau's fundamental bass is not always the lowest-sounding part in the texture. Roussier faults Rameau for using the word "bass," which is inappropriate for describing a primary tone that may appear in the upper parts as well as in the lowest; had Rameau avoided such language he would have rendered his system easier to understand and aided its dissemination.[16] Roussier claims that he himself prefers to speak of fundamental tones or chords so as to avoid the implication of a low-pitched part, which the word "bass" inevitably evokes—a preference shared by posterity, as our current usage indicates.

The idea of the fundamental bass reveals a world of great simplicity and regularity behind the variegated chord structures and bass progressions of the musical surface. In Rameau's mature theory it is an idea well integrated into a dense conceptual web. He motivates the processes of derivation and complication that connect this simplified world to the real one (he explains, that is, why the fundamental bass is not actually played): the *basse continue* deviates from the fundamental bass for variety's sake, but also because it must make "allowances for the progressions of the other parts written above it" (e.g., avoiding forbidden parallels) and because it should respect the "design," "affect," and "movement" of the melody it accompanies (1722:341). Rameau also has an explicit theory of the ear's power to detect the *basse fondamentale* when it is not the actual bass part but is only implied *(sous-entendu)*, and of course a theory of the source of the *basse fondamentale* in Nature as well as of the human ability to respond instinctually to that source (Cohen 2001a).

It is interesting to note that the idea of the fundamental bass was not always so well connected in Rameau's thinking, but was integrated to different degrees and in different ways into the conceptual web of his musical knowledge. As Christensen has noted, Rameau first conceived of the fundamental bass without the theoretical justification he later offered for it; the *basse fondamentale*, as an explanatory concept, grew out of a teaching device with no explanatory ambitions.

This is highly plausible, given that explanatory and nonexplanatory versions of a concept can coexist. Consider the history of one of the conceptual preconditions for the *basse fondamentale*, the notion of chord inversion. We traced the development of this idea above as the recognition of the identity of triadic sonorities made up of the same three pitch-classes, despite their differences in euphony and function. In Lippius the relationships among these sonorities are thought of as relations of derivation; the inversions grow out of the 5-3 position.

But alongside this understanding of chord inversion was a tradition of practical instruction in which the relations among sonorities were pointed out as an *aide-mémoire* for the student, without ontological implications; they were noted "to make some cords easie to your memory" (Godfrey Keller 1707, cited in Chenette 1967:237). In thorough bass practice the 5-3 chord was conceptually central, hence it is not surprising that some treatises gave the student ways to think about other chords in terms of the 5-3 triad. Michel de Saint-Lambert, for example, had the student associate certain figured bass signatures with triads built on a tone other than the bass tone. If the bass note C had a 6 above it, the student was to think of a 5-3 triad built on A. If the C had 6/4 above it, the student was to think of a triad built on F (Christensen 1993:50–51). These tips are offered for the cognitive economies they afford the student; they have no explanatory ambitions. Indeed, they are not even consistent with our notion of triadic inversion. In both of these examples, Saint-Lambert's method has the effect of picking out the root of the chord, but this is coincidental, as can be seen from his advice regarding the bass note C figured with a 7: to find this chord, the student should imagine a triad built on E. (For similar examples from Keller, see Lester 1992:54.)

It seems that Rameau first used the idea of the fundamental bass in a similar spirit. It occurred to him during his residence in Clermont-Ferrand (1715–22) as a heuristic device for teaching thorough bass and composition, without its later abstract interpretation. It came to Rameau without theoretical baggage, as a pedagogical convenience. It was a simplified scheme for realizing the dozens of figures and formulas in traditional figured-bass instruction. Hence it was a practical aid for the student of thorough bass, not a principle of scientific demonstration (Christensen 1993:23–26, 51–61). That emerged later, as Rameau discovered he could combine this handy rule of thumb with a mathematical derivation of all intervals from the unison, a mechanistic explanation of the succession of harmonies, and (eventually) the acoustic imprimatur of the overtone series. We could say that the fundamental bass was a relatively disarticulated idea at first, with no connections to Rameau's ideas of Nature or the abilities of the ear, with no explanatory role to play. It was at first a continuation of the "informal heuristics" of chord inversion taught by the thorough bass treatises; it shifted function, adding to its pedagogical role a theoretical one, when it was combined with the neoplatonic derivation of harmonies from the monochord string (Christensen 1993:90).

The development of Rameau's idea of the fundamental bass thus displayed all three of the features we found in the emergence of implicit-melody concepts in Java.[17] The fundamental bass, like the implicit melodies, regularized the multiform. It reduced the great variety of thorough bass movements to a simple cadential model. It was conceived by analogy to an existing musical part, the thorough bass, just as the three types of implicit melodies were modeled on existing melodic guides. Finally, the fundamental bass demonstrated a lability of conceptual role. Here the resemblance with the Javanese case is somewhat more abstract. The fundamental bass shifted roles over time, assuming different functions at different stages in the development of a single musician's thinking. By contrast, the implicit-melody concepts served different roles contemporaneously for different musicians.

Suhardi's *lagu* was, like Rameau's fundamental bass during his Clermont period, a pedagogical device, a practical tool to help his students. It was motivated by the demands of teaching, not theoretical passion or metaphysical proclivities. He had no interest in speculating about the *lagu*. It remained with him as it started, a convenience in the teaching process. Sumarsam and Supanggah, however, were faculty members at institutions of higher learning and research, familiar with the writings of foreign ethnomusicologists. Like the Rameau of the *Treatise*, they wanted to make abstract, general statements about their music's basic nature. They wanted to participate in the major theoretical debates of their time and engage the concerns of a wide intellectual community.[18]

CONCLUSION

All of the theorists discussed in this chapter tried to find simple explanations of their music's complex patterns; all constructed an ideal realm of regularity and used analogical thinking to populate it with abstract entities. They put this cognitive strategy to work in various ways, some modest, some ambitious. Lippius used the notion of the *trias harmonica* to provide a simple account of the "thousands and millions" of possible chords; Campion postulated a "true Base" to salvage the simplicity of his rule of counterpoint; Werckmeister used the idea of the chord root to explain the irregular doubling of the 6-3 chord; and Rameau, attempting—at least while he was wearing his Cartesian hat—to found musical practice on an "evident principle" (1722:xxxv), used the *basse fondamentale* to reduce the variety of chord progressions to a "simple and intelligible" regularity.

I have argued that this cognitive strategy is present as well in the story of Javanese implicit-melody concepts, but it is somewhat easier to notice in the European case. In part this is because of a difference in rhetoric, itself perhaps due to historical and cultural differences in discursive traditions:

the European writers explicitly thematize the value of simplicity and regularity. They affirm it as an explanatory virtue and use it to proclaim the merits of their own accounts. By contrast, even though the implicit melodies of Sumarsam and Supanggah regularize the irregular notion of melodic guidance, the two musicians do not argue their case on this basis. Though the search for a consistently congruent guiding part motivated their thinking, they did not feel the need to point out the regularity of their implicit melodies as recommendations for their theories. The fact that the European writers (Lippius and Rameau in particular) did praise the simplicity and regularity of their theories is probably due to the prestige of European models of intellectual inquiry (logic, mathematics, philosophy, science) in which these values were consciously affirmed. But while they were loudly advertised in the European case and went unmentioned in the Javanese case, they played a role in the cognitive processes involved in both.

I was inspired to undertake this comparative study of analogical thinking in two musical traditions by psychology's assurance that the cognitive processes of innovative thinking are quite general. Finding conceptual combination, differentiation, extension, and analogy at work in the history of both Javanese and Western music theory naturally raises the question of whether these processes might also be operative in other traditions. It is a question that deserves to be addressed in future studies. By examining cases of musical thinking in many other societies, we can estimate the prevalence of these cognitive processes, ascertain the conditions under which they are likely to fuel creative thinking, and perhaps discover other avenues of conceptual change.

Such studies will also be necessary to help refine the terms of analysis I have introduced here. As I noted in chapter 1, I have not tried to strictly demarcate the categories of cognitive process used in this book; I have been content to introduce them through examples rather than exact definitions. This is appropriate, given the relatively youthful state of the cognitive study of creative thinking, a field that does not yet have a unified, well-established theoretical framework. But we may hope that through a wide range of detailed case studies we will be able to bring these processes into ever-clearer focus. Elsewhere I undertake such an analysis in the context of a fuller historical account of the emergence of the concepts of chord root and fundamental bass (Perlman 2004). My intention in this chapter has been more modest. Showing how musicians in Europe put old concepts to new uses, I wished only to illustrate the potential of a cognitive approach to creative thinking in the study of traditions outside Java.

Still, this initial cross-cultural excursion suggests that the cognitive viewpoint may be useful in confronting even larger questions of music theory. Indeed, it may be able to clarify some of the largest questions, questions about the very nature of that theory. It may shed light on the elusive epistemological status of the claims we make when we talk about music— a possibility I explore in my conclusion.

Conclusion

Javanese gamelan melody is a landscape of congruences and divergences, where the parts work cooperatively while preserving their individual idioms. With its hints of hidden melody, it is a site of exploration for musicians. I have told here the stories of three especially articulate musicians to show how they arrived at new ideas about their music, ideas similar in outline but remarkably different in detail and purpose. In making sense of their music in late-twentieth-century postcolonial Java, Suhardi, Sumarsam, and Supanggah naturally used the schemas and models their culture provided them and responded to the opportunities and challenges their modernizing society—and the global reach of ethnomusicology—offered, but they also employed strategies of conceptual creativity that are neither specifically musical nor specifically Javanese and are probably common in all societies, at all times.

The study of Javanese musical thinking has much to contribute to our knowledge of *karawitan*, but also has the potential to illuminate the nature of musicians' thinking in general. In concluding I will reflect on some of these implications, then outline the wider ramifications of my cross-cultural methodology for ethnomusicology.

The approach I have used here—one that recognizes musicians' cognitive need for order, the cognitive usefulness of generalization, but in the context of the overall disarticulation of knowledge—focuses our attention on the complexity of melodic guidance; it encourages us to take equally seriously the regularity and irregularity of interpart relations. It reminds us that the musician's "effort after meaning" is just that—an effort, an activity of seeking pattern and relationship, a search for connections where connections may or may not be waiting to be found.

In this book I have used this perspective only with regard to the phenomenon of melodic guidance, but it might enrich our understanding of other aspects of Javanese music as well. I have mentioned two of them in passing: the system of *pathet* and of *irama*. In both cases we find regularity and irregularity mixed in varying proportions. Over the past century *pathet* has been an enduring conundrum for both Javanese musicians and Western ethnomusicologists (Kunst 1973:I, 72; Hood 1954; Becker 1980, 1981; Hastanto 1985; Walton 1987); Martopangrawit (1984:45) once claimed that the nature of *pathet* was a question always on his mind. These facts suggest that *pathet*, like melodic guidance, might be a nonclassical concept and could usefully be considered from the cognitive perspective offered here.[1]

The study of creative thinking about music enlarges our view of musicians' conceptualizations in general. Following the lead of John Baily, Timothy Rice, and Benjamin Brinner, I have tried to add nuance to our picture of musicians' knowledge. As we would expect, given what we know of the partially disarticulated nature of human cognition, musical knowledge is not one type of thing, but is internally heterogeneous. This insight has relevance for an issue that has long concerned ethnomusicologists, the relationship between "insider" and "outsider" accounts of music.

IMPLICIT, EXPLICIT, INSIDER, OUTSIDER

The surge of interest in "native" conceptualization that characterized ethnotheory assumed that the cultural "insider" had unproblematic access to authoritative knowledge about his or her music, knowledge that could be submerged or drowned out by the imposition of concepts imported from other cultures. Sumarsam, as we have seen, felt that indigenous Javanese musical concepts had been distorted and misinterpreted by the imposition of Western musicological ideas (1995:10, 144). But this anxiety—that Western theories can contaminate or overwhelm indigenous musical thought—is quite general. Nettl (1992b:393–94), for example, writes of the dilemma facing a Western ethnomusicologist trying to teach students from some distant society who "wish to do ethnomusicological work in their own backyards": "They characteristically want to learn Western-derived approaches and methods, but in doing so, they may simply become part of the army of Western investigators."

The assumption of "insider" epistemic authority was not uncontested: Nattiez, for example, vigorously argued that "the 'view from inside' is not necessarily more 'true' than the view from outside" (1990:195). But with the waning of the orthodox concept of culture, and the rising awareness of the amount of interpretive work undertaken by "insiders" to understand their own culture, the status of "native" knowledge was put in question. If "individuals operating within tradition continually appropriate their cultural practices [and] give them new meanings" (Rice 1994:6), if culture is no longer a place, no longer a secret grotto illuminated by a mystic light of self-evident meanings, is there any sense left to the distinction between insider and outsider viewpoints?

Once we recognize that knowledge is not a single thing, but comes in many varieties, we can see that the answer to this question cannot be a simple yes or no. As we saw in chapter 1, different sorts of concepts and knowledge coexist in the mind, sometimes well integrated, sometimes not. Implicit and explicit knowledge in particular can be dissociated, and when they are, we become mysteries to ourselves.

This does not, of course, completely solve the ethnomusicological problem of insider and outsider viewpoints. For that problem is also a problem of the authority of representations. It concerns the role of first-world analyses of third-world societies in "legitimating social inequality" and raises the question of the "authority of any nation, group, gender, or class to represent the experience of an-Other" (Shuman and Briggs 1993:114–15). This consciousness of the politics of scholarship brands as "neo-colonial arrogance" the outsider's claim to perceive something in a music culture that the musicians themselves do not verbalize (Becker and Becker 1983:10–11).

We do well to question the authority presumed by scholarly accounts; but it would be senseless to replace the absolute authority of the outsider's word with the absolute authority of the insider's word. Knowledge is too disparate, too disarticulated for that; as we saw in chapter 1, the insider's word may be cut off from his implicit knowledge. Nor is there any guaranteed safe passage from implicit knowledge to explicit knowledge: it is never possible to extract concepts directly from a musical practice. Formulating explicit knowledge is always a creative act, and it is grateful for whatever grain of sand it can find around which to shape its pearl.

However, to recognize the possibility that implicit knowledge may be dissociated from explicit knowledge is not to discount it altogether. Some of postcolonial theory's most rhetorically effective claims become disempowering if we leave implicit knowledge out of account. It would, for example, be possible to point to the role of Western thought or Western researchers in the growth of Sumarsam's ideas in order to argue that his insights into the nature of *karawitan* were not revelations of something indigenous but rather transcultural hybrid constructions. It is true that his ability to formulate (say) the distinction between the *saron* line and the multi-octave *balungan* came from his exposure to Mantle Hood's ideas, and in that sense his knowledge of it was a product of cross-cultural encounter. It is true that Sumarsam might never have formulated his theory of "inner melody" had he never met Vincent McDermott or had he never taught in America. But to emphasize this is to focus on explicit knowledge at the expense of implicit knowledge.

There is no royal road to explicitation, though as Sumarsam's experience demonstrates, dialogue between insider and outsider viewpoints can produce insights neither one could express alone. Insights can arise from the simple act of collation, when the outsider juxtaposes the understandings of insiders in new ways. At least this has been my hope in writing this book: if I have been able to shed light on *karawitan*, it is because I was able to bring together the thoughts of Sumarsam and Supanggah with those of Martopangrawit and Suhardi—a discussion group that (as far as I know) was never convened during the lifetimes of those remarkable men.

THE CROSS-CULTURAL STUDY OF COGNITIVE PROCESS: FURTHER PROSPECTS

I have focused on creative thinking about gamelan music to enrich our understanding of the multidimensionality of musicians' thinking, but also because I believe that an orientation to cognitive process rather than product is most fruitful in comparative research. Cross-cultural comparison has become an unpopular pursuit in ethnomusicology. In part this is because it is difficult, and many of the scholars who attempted it in the past seized upon superficial similarities they found in sketchy reports of musical practices from around the world. But there is also a suspicion that the only point of such comparisons is the search for universals, and whatever musical universals are to be found could only be vague, unfruitful generalities, airy nebulosities of little use for analysis (Powers 1992b:218).

As long as we confine ourselves to low-level comparisons of things, to comparative inventories of musical items or concepts, this pessimistic view may be warranted. But if we try to compare *processes*, as I have tried to do here, a new field of research opens before us. I have attempted to treat both Javanese and Western music theory not as static bodies of doctrine, but as dynamic trajectories; I am not interested in music theory at rest, so to speak, but music theory in action.

I have enlisted cognitive psychology and cognitive anthropology in this comparative venture. I am not the first to seek a cross-cultural bridge in psychological findings, of course; in a sense, all I have done here is apply to musicians' thinking about their music Harwood's suggestion that we seek universals in cognitive process, not cognitive content (Harwood 1976:522–23).

Ethnomusicology can borrow conceptual generality and breadth from the cognitive disciplines, though it should borrow in moderation; the cognitive approach could too easily become one of those exciting but vague research programs Geertz warns us against, one of those "general schemes which explain too much" (1995:127). But whether or not there are any interesting universals waiting to be discovered in this way, the act of cross-cultural comparison is valuable in itself for the way it enlarges our powers of observation. Comparison "broadens the boundaries of *what we are able to think*" (Turino 1993:6); according to the philosopher Charles Taylor, it can give us a "language of perspicuous contrast" that lets us see more in the most familiar things, the things we thought we already understood thoroughly (1985:125). It was because of my experience in Java that I went looking for evidence of analogical thinking in the history of Western music theory, and as a result I was led to the curious ancestry of the idea of chord root. In itself this finding may not be of great moment, but it illustrates how experience in one culture can give us new eyes with which to see our own.

In the 1980s, anthropologists started talking about "repatriating anthropology," bringing the results of anthropological research to bear on our understanding of ourselves. I am suggesting a way of repatriating ethnomusicology, using it to deepen our understanding of Western music theory by decentering it, by shifting the perspective: how different does it look if we try to view it from Java?

For example, an awareness of the cognitive processes of creative thinking might help us put aside presentist biases in studying the history of Western music theory. In tracing the history of current theoretical concepts it is often hard to avoid emphasizing those aspects of past concepts that resemble our own—even if the resemblance is only superficial. It is hard to avoid reading old texts anachronistically, in the light of our own notions. Too often our current ideas block the view of the older concepts from which they have descended, and it can be hard to pull the latter "out from behind" our current concepts (Bent 1996:xiii). In searching for the historical moments of origin of our concepts, it is tempting to treat them as moments of revolutionary eruption—the present breaking into the past. Noticing how a new theoretical concept can grow out of an old one by processes of extension and analogy, we may be better prepared to look for the gradual morphing of old into new.

I have emphasized in this book the multifunctionality of analogical think-ing, the many different cognitive roles an analogy can serve. This phe-nomenon, too, might be of heuristic value in thinking about the history of music theory. For example, the debate over the significance of rhetoric for our understanding of eighteenth-century music seems to turn on our un-certainty about the role of an analogy. The prestige of the art of rhetoric in the early modern period led to its application outside the domain of speech, to literature, painting, and music. Starting in the sixteenth century, theo-rists characterized musical practices and structures using technical terms bor-rowed from rhetoric or by coining new terms modeled after them (Bartel 1997:57–89). How are we to understand the role of these music/rhetoric analogies? Did they guide or shape the creative decisions of composers; were composers patterning their compositions after orations? Or were theorists drawing post hoc analogies with rhetoric to promote their views on how music should be created and understood? There is as yet no consensus among scholars on the issue (Hoyt 1994:129–30).

The multifunctionality of analogy is one expression of the general phe-nomenon of cognitive disarticulation. Because the components of any cog-nitive system are only loosely integrated, they can usually be brought into relation with one another in many different ways. As a result, any new ab-stract musical concept can often be linked in more than one way to our exist-ing concepts. The play or elasticity in the web of musical knowledge per-mits it to serve different roles. But just as disarticulation within the domain of musical knowledge makes multiple interpretations of musical concepts possible, the disarticulation of musical knowledge as a whole within the broader realm of human knowledge makes possible multiple interpretations of musical knowledge in general—and this multiplicity constitutes what we know as the debate over the nature of music theory.

Cognitively speaking, music-theoretic practice is an island of relative co-herence in the sea of disarticulated human knowledge. It is possible to spend a lifetime on this island; to vary the metaphor, it is possible to remain en-tirely within the circle of music-theoretic practice—to apply familiar meth-ods to the elucidation of new compositions, or to extend and refine those methods. But sometimes we step outside the circle to see how our practice fits into the larger scheme of things. Often our motivation for doing so comes from an interest in validation. When we begin to wonder how we know what we know—when we ask on what basis we can be sure that our claims are valid—we need to understand exactly what our claims are claiming, which means understanding the possible relations they can have with knowledge claims outside music theory. Are music-theoretic statements the sorts of thing that could be supported or disconfirmed by historical findings? Could psychological research render them more or less plausible? The various possible answers to these questions will construct links of various sorts between music theory and other cognitive domains, corresponding to various epistemological interpretations of music-theoretic statements.

We have already seen a concrete illustration of this variety in *karawitan*. The concept of implicit melody could bear several different interpretations: as a hypothesis about the composer's concept of the *gendhing*, a representation of the performer's unconscious knowledge, a pedagogical device, and so on.

A comparable multiplicity of interpretative possibilities is found in Western music theory. Music-analytical statements can be intended to make several possible claims (Sharpe 1993). They may be accounts of "the musical work itself." They may be accounts of the compositional process that produced the work. They may describe the stylistic knowledge of a competent listener. They may represent the way an individual theorist hears a particular piece. It may not always be clear which of these interpretations is intended in any given case. As Cook notes, the reader of theoretical writing on music may understand the specific claims it makes while remaining unsure "what sort of knowledge of music it gives us, what sort of truth it aspires to. . . . You can easily find yourself asking, without any clear sense of what the answer might be: is this theory about acoustic events or perceptions, about notational traces or ideal content? Sometimes one and sometimes another? Or several at once?" (Cook 2002:78–79). Indeed, theorists can produce very elaborate and subtle analyses without specifying (even to themselves) which of these possibilities they intend.

As scholars attempting to formulate insights about music with maximum clarity and precision, we may regard this multiplicity—which Cook calls "epistemological slippage"—as a fault. No one has campaigned against it with more passion or tenacity than Nattiez, for whom it represents a confusion of semiological levels (1990:30). When Western music theorists analyze a composition, they may intend (implicitly or explicitly) to elucidate it in terms of the creative process that produced it; in that case their statements would be on the poietic level. Alternatively, they may describe how it is heard, how it affects the listener; that is the esthesic level. (Of course, these may coincide to a greater or lesser extent in certain cases, but Nattiez insists that we can never assume this: 1990:212.) Analytical studies are frequently pulled between these semiological poles, and Nattiez proposes to introduce clarity into the enterprise of analysis by carefully separating these oft-confounded levels (1990:233, 237–38).

Cook, on the other hand, sees this epistemological slippage not as a defect, but as a defining characteristic of music theory (2002:102). Theorists appear to be in the embarrassing position of saying a great deal about music without being able to agree on just what it is they are talking about. For Cook, however, there is nothing to be embarrassed about. To be unsure what one is talking about is part of what it means to do music theory. To be caught between incommensurable epistemes (2002:99), between the descriptive and the prescriptive, is inherent in music theory—it is "the condition of its signification" (2002:102).

But the fact that we find cognitive tools in various musical traditions slipping easily between conceptual roles suggests we are dealing with a general phenomenon. Just as analogical thinking is not unique to music-theoretic cognition, neither is epistemological slippage. Even scientists can agree on a great many empirical findings but remain divided in their notion of what it is they are talking about. Indeed, the conceptual basis of an entire discipline can be the subject of long-term dispute.

Think of biological taxonomy, the Western tradition of classifying plants and animals into a hierarchical system of species, genera, families, and so on. Systematists do not all agree on the conceptual foundations of their activity. The evolutionary school of Simpson and Mayr views descent as the primary factor in classification: organisms and species descended from common ancestors should be categorized together. The numerical pheneticists, by contrast, classify organisms according to their overall similarity, regardless of their evolutionary past (Hull 1992:51–53).[2]

But for Cook, the epistemological slippage of music theory runs deeper than this. It may well be that scientists can agree in the accounts they give, while being unable to agree on what those accounts are accounts *of*. But at least in such cases there is a general consensus that these accounts are accounts *of something*. Music theorists, by contrast, do not have even this much common ground. Music-analytic statements may be intended as *accounts* of nothing at all, but rather as *creative responses* to a composition; not as descriptions of musical reality, but as "artistic statements, *in music, about music*" (as Benjamin 1981:160 claims for Schenkerian analyses). Or they may be intended as *invitations* to experience that composition in a new way, not assertions of fact but "performative injunctions (hear it *this* way!)"—an interpretation that Cook seems personally to favor (2002:95). It is this sort of radical disparity in interpretation that Cook refers to when he says that music theory speaks in "multiple epistemological registers"; it both "says how things are" and "suggests how you might hear things," and "each register merges imperceptibly into the next" (2002:102).

But even here music theorists are in good company, for we find the same type of disagreement in other disciplines. This is especially clear with regard to ethics, since there is an entire branch of philosophy, metaethics, whose business it is to figure out what we talk about when we talk about ethics. It is dedicated to questions of the meaning of moral statements, the nature of value, what moral knowledge is, and how we can have it. Philosophers who agree on many specific moral judgments can disagree over the nature of those judgments, over the meanings of the terms in which they are expressed, and over the sorts of argumentation necessary to support those judgments. Are moral judgments based on a special intuitive power that we have to discern an indefinable property we call goodness? When our moral judgments are true, are they universally and objectively true, or are they true only relative to the beliefs of an individual or the culture of a group? Or are there any true moral judgments—could it be that all of them are false?

But there are also metaethical positions comparable to the "performative" views about music theory that Cook urges on us. These so-called noncognitivist positions do not regard moral judgments as the sorts of things that can be true or false; rather, they see such judgments as expressions of a certain kind of feeling—feelings of approval or disapproval—or a special sort of preference, or as declarations of commitment on our part and invitations to others to make similar commitments (Arrington 1989:1–16; Darwall, Gibbard, and Railton 1992).

Here, as in music theory, the possibility of "epistemological slippage" arises when we try to link disarticulated conceptual domains, when we try to widen the circle of connection, when we try to relieve the isolation of moral thought by bringing it into relationship with other kinds of thinking. Metaethics is the attempt to bring morality "into some congruence with whatever else we hold in our going view of the world" (Darwall, Gibbard, and Railton 1992:126). It tries to place our moral ideas, feelings, and actions on a larger cognitive map, one that includes the claims of science. The diverse metaethical positions arise because moral thought and practice, as an island of cognitive coherence, can be connected in several different ways to the other islands in the sea of human knowledge.

Epistemological slippage may well be a defining characteristic of music theory, but it is not a distinctive characteristic. It is, rather, a typical result of the attempt to bring disarticulate concepts and practices into a larger unity.

If my readers are surprised to find, in a book about Javanese gamelan, visions of musical universals or a discussion of the debates over the nature of music theory, they could hardly be more surprised than I am myself. Just as I did not set out to apply cognitive anthropology to music, I did not live in Indonesia for seven years as part of a circuitous plan to contribute new ideas to Western music theory.

I would be the last to suggest that the only reason a European or American should study *karawitan* is to pursue cognitive universals or to defamiliarize Western music. There is a deep emotional truth in the claim that "to study someone's music merely to prove a theoretical point is . . . a crime, a sin, and a shame" (Benamou 1998:365). This book is only one aspect of a larger project on musical thinking in *karawitan*, one intended to build bridges of understanding between music cultures. But I did not want to neglect the wider implications of my findings, for to ignore the theoretical illumination potentially offered by a case study of one music is to squander an opportunity to find new ways to think about all music.

I started this project hoping to create sympathetic ears for Javanese music abroad. But it is gratifying to think that in doing so, as a side benefit, I may have a found a new and roundabout way of repatriating ethnomusicology. Ultimately, I hope that this book, by suggesting fruitful ways to study conceptual innovation, will inspire ethnomusicologists to pay close attention to the creative thinking of musicians in many other traditions. I like to imagine that my teachers, who so generously shared their insights with me, would be pleased to see the echoes of their ideas resonating widely around the world.

Notes

INTRODUCTION

1. This happens among the BaAka of the African equatorial forests (Arom 1976:491–92) and also to some extent in jazz drum solos (Berliner 1994:134). Perhaps the most famous example of a jazz drum solo that alludes to an un-played part is Max Roach's solo on "Blue Seven" (Sonny Rollins, *Saxophone Colossus*, 1956), which audibly traces the structure of the blues.

2. The Thai concept of *neua phleng* (literally, "meat of the composition") is more comparable in this respect to Javanese notions of implicit melody (Sum-rongthong and Sorrell 2000).

3. See Blacking (1981), Nattiez (1990:183–97), and Rice (1994:305–309), though, for three very different general discussions of musicians' conceptu-alizations of their music. Most ethnomusicological treatments of this topic focus on particular musical traditions; for the debate over the role of "local ideas" in understanding African rhythm, see Stone (1986) and Agawu (1992). Theorists of Western art music have also discussed the value of musicians' con-ceptualizations (as mediated by the historical record), though again usually with regard to particular repertories (e.g., Schubert 1994; see, however, Carter 1995).

4. As Jardine (2000) points out, the use of inappropriate concepts in the de-scription of a distant culture—ethnocentrism—is in some ways comparable to anachronism, the use of inappropriate concepts in the description of a tempo-rally distant culture. Both are examples of what he terms *anatropism*.

5. I use this term well aware that it does not appear in the programmatic statements or manifestos of the time. Moreover, the term may have been in-troduced or propagated by the movement's critics (cf. Nattiez 1990:186; Agawu 1992). As is often the case, "ethnotheory" as a coherent intellectual movement has perhaps been constituted retroactively—and as much by its detractors as by its proponents.

6. The earliest papers on ethnotheory were clearly inspired by ethnoscience, as is evident from their bibliographies. Zemp (1978) cites the work of Conklin,

Frake, Kay, and Tyler; Rice (1980) cites Black, Conklin, Frake, Goodenough, and Kay; Sakata (1983) cites Tyler. These works then functioned as references for subsequent ethnomusicological studies, supplanting the original anthropological writings. For example, Markoff (1986) cites Feld, Zemp, Rice, and Sakata.

7. I worked almost entirely with male musicians. This was natural, since women still occupied fairly restricted roles in *karawitan*. Since then, however, the work of Susan Walton (1996) and Sarah Weiss (1998) has greatly improved our knowledge of the female experience in Javanese music.

CHAPTER 1. COGNITIVE PRELIMINARIES

1. Some of my nonmusical examples are taken from language. Because there is a long history of applying linguistic concepts to music, the use of linguistic examples is dangerous; it may be read as committing me to a stronger view of the music/language relationship than I actually hold. In fact, I use language merely as a familiar and vivid example of a cultural tradition. I assume no structural or functional similarities between language and any music.

My use of examples from Western art music is an expository strategy and is not meant to suggest that Western music is aesthetically superior or worthier of attention, or to perpetuate its dominance in American institutions of higher education. To mitigate the abstractness of my argument, I need musical illustrations; to keep up the pace of exposition, I need familiar illustrations I can expect the reader to recognize and need not myself describe at length. Western art music serves me here—like jazz and popular music—as an approximation of a scholarly lingua franca.

2. I reluctantly follow this usage, though I prefer "generic knowledge" to "schema": the latter term, as a count noun, has unfortunate connotations that do not cling to "knowledge," which is a mass noun. When I think of "schemas" or "models" I find myself assuming them to be discrete, distinct, easily individuated entities—an assumption I do not, in general, want to make. (For surveys and critiques of the schema concept in various domains of psychology and linguistics, see Alba and Hasher 1983; Edwards and Middleton 1986; Fiske and Linville 1980; Tannen 1993; Whitney, Budd, Bramucci, and Crane 1995.)

D'Andrade (1995:152) proposed a distinction between the terms "schema" and "model," reserving the latter term for the most complex schemas. However, since there is no consensus on how to draw the line between them (Strauss and Quinn 1997:264 n. 4), I use the terms more or less interchangeably here.

3. In each of these cases, the profession of individualistic values can coexist with a strong respect for group norms and behavior. Cf. the discussion of cognitive compartmentalization *infra*.

4. For examples of how a single mind can accommodate conflicting schemas through unconscious compromise, ambivalence, or compartmentalization, see Strauss and Quinn (1997:213–15).

Note that inconsistency is only one case of disarticulation, though a particularly striking case. If we have two ideas, goals, or values, A and B, to say they are disarticulated means that the relationship between them is not present to the mind, that thinking of one does not tend to suggest the other, and that they are not integrated within a larger complex of ideas, goals, or values. It may be possible to integrate them; perhaps A is similar to B in some respects, or is an instance of B, or can be explained by B. But as long as A and B remain disarticulated, we do not notice these potential connections. Inconsistency is an extreme form of disarticulation: for not only are A and B unintegrated, they *can't* be integrated, since they are in some way at odds with each other.

5. This section is based on Barsalou (1992:18–31); Medin and Coley (1998); Medin and Heit (1999); Medin, Lynch, and Solomon (2000); and Pinker (1999:270–75). Zbikowski (2002) refers to my "classical" categories as Type 2 and my "nonclassical" categories as Type 1.

The terms "concept" and "category" are sometimes used interchangeably in the literature; some writers reserve "concept" for mental representations and "category" for the entities in the world referred to by a concept. I do not distinguish rigorously between them here.

6. Talk of embodiment here is a dangerous metaphor: a psychological schema can't be injected into external forms, at least not in such a way that anyone exposed to those forms would be certain to internalize the same schema. We can't read off the contents of individual minds from public forms (Strauss and Quinn 1997:117, 136).

7. The terms "implicit" and "explicit" do not necessarily describe a dichotomy: there can be degrees of explicitness (Karmiloff-Smith 1992; Dienes and Perner 1999; Strauss and Quinn 1997:184; Comaroff and Comaroff 1991:29).

In general, there is a great deal of diversity and complexity in psychological typologies of knowledge and learning, complexity I have not been able to treat adequately here. Researchers use a number of criteria to distinguish types of knowledge (conscious, explicit, accessible, voluntary, declarative; implicit, inaccessible, unverbalizable, procedural), and the relations among them are not always clear. Thus it should not be surprising that ethnomusicologists seeking inspiration in cognitive psychology borrow these distinctions in different ways. Brinner (1995b:34–39, 48–60), for example, contrasts "intuitive" and "explicit" knowledge, and also "procedural" and "declarative" knowledge, but seems to use these concepts in a slightly different sense than that meant here.

8. It is probably misleading to talk of "making" the implicit explicit, as if we could transform the one into the other. Implicit and explicit knowledge are not different states of an identical substance: we cannot pour our fluid, hard-to-grasp implicit knowledge into ice-cube molds and put it in an epistemic freezer, to retrieve it later as solid, explicit knowledge. Explicitation is a creative act. It does not shrink-wrap the unspoken in words; it requires creative thinking.

9. This experimental demonstration of "everyday structuralism" depends on certain conditions. The students must not have background knowledge relevant to the task, and the stimuli must all be presented together, so that the students can compare each one with all of the others simultaneously. When the

students are encouraged to compare *pairs* of stimuli, or when they have background knowledge that mitigates the arbitrariness of the stimuli and explains why they take the forms they do, this experimental effect is less likely to be found (Regehr and Brooks 1995; Spalding and Murphy 1996).

10. This prohibition, implicit in Fux's four rules, was explicitly formulated as the key rule by later authors such as Padre Martini (Mann, in Fux 1965:22).

11. When later theorists examined the actual use of parallel fifths, they recognized both gradations of goodness and the contextual mitigation of otherwise objectionable parallels. See, for example, August Ambros's *Zur Lehre vom Quinten-Verbote* of 1859 (Laudon 1992:49–50).

12. For a useful illustration of various "illusory" parallel fifths and octaves, see Salzer and Schachter (1989:222–23). As Benjamin (1981:163) has noted, the middleground is not in fact generally more conformant to the rules of counterpoint than is the surface; parallel fifths and octaves occur in the middleground as well. Schenker does not address this inconsistency, however.

13. The reader might notice with some frustration that all of these processes serve to explain the creation of something new in terms of the transformation of something old, and thus render seemingly mechanical the miraculous power of creativity. I do not claim that these processes offer an exhaustive explanation of creativity, only that they do seem to be operative in many cases of musical and music-theoretic creativity.

14. Ward calls this phenomenon, whereby new ideas are heavily structured in predictable ways by the properties of existing concepts, *structured imagination* (Ward 1995). He emphasizes how structured imagination can constrain novelty as well as generate it. For example, the engineers who built the first railway cars modeled them on the stagecoach, even though such a design made for unsafe working conditions for the conductor.

Critics of the application to popular music of Schenkerian analysis (or other analytical methods designed for Western art music) can be understood as making a point similar to Ward's. Their insistence that musicologists must deconstruct their inherited theoretical tools (McClary and Walser 1990:281) rests, in effect, on a claim that the use of a pre-existing model of music-analytic understanding can blind the analyst to important aspects of the piece she is analyzing. For example, in constructing a voice-leading graph for a Jimi Hendrix song, the analyst is led to bracket off, as "extraneous features," everything else that is going on in the music (McClary 2000:137). (I am grateful to Marcus Zagorski for this point.)

15. Following the convention of cognitive linguistics, I represent conceptual metaphors using small capitals.

16. The status of conceptual metaphor is controversial. The strongest claim—that metaphors actually *constitute* our understanding of abstract concepts—has been questioned by Naomi Quinn; cf. Strauss and Quinn (1997:141–54) and the replies by Gibbs (1994:202–206) and Kövecses (1999). See also the exchange between Murphy and Gibbs (Murphy 1996, Gibbs 1996, Murphy 1997). Lakoff's

claims about the psychology of metaphor have been criticized as well. Gentner et al. (2001) provide evidence that only novel metaphors involve the mapping of whole domains; conventional metaphors do not.

17. The key points of divergence are the following. Where conceptual metaphor theory speaks of large conceptual domains (such as those of space or pitch), blending theory speaks of "mental spaces," temporary cognitive representations or scenarios. Where conceptual metaphor theory speaks of stable one-way mappings from source to target, blending theory speaks of the integration of mental spaces through processes of composition, completion, and elaboration whereby the blended space may acquire emergent content not present in either of the input spaces (Grady, Oakley, and Coulson 1999).

18. In one of the very few ethnographic studies of analogical thinking in scientific discovery, Dunbar investigated how biologists at four molecular biology laboratories came up with new ideas at their lab meetings. They often used analogies, but usually close analogies, staying within the domain of biology: analogizing one virus to another, for example. Less than 2 percent of their analogies compared a biological phenomenon to a nonbiological one (Dunbar 1997).

19. Indeed, Hofstadter makes the same point with relation to analogy that Grady, Oakley, and Coulson make with regard to metaphor, that the mind's application of existing concepts to new experiences is a kind of mapping:

> The triggering of prior mental categories by some kind of input—whether sensory or more abstract—is, I insist, an act of analogy-making. Why is this? Because whenever a set of incoming stimuli activates one or more mental categories, some amount of slippage must occur (no instance of a category ever being precisely identical to a prior instance). . . . The process of inexact matching between prior categories and new things being perceived . . . is analogy-making par excellence. . . . It is the mental mapping onto each other of two entities—one old and sound asleep in the recesses of long-term memory, the other new and gaily dancing on the mind's center stage—that in fact differ from each other in a myriad of ways. (2001:503–504)

CHAPTER 2. A BRIEF INTRODUCTION TO *KARAWITAN*

1. The topics introduced succinctly in this chapter are treated at much greater length in a manuscript I am preparing, *Making Sense in Javanese Music*.

2. I deliberately speak of the punctuating and framework *instruments* but of the elaborating *parts*, since the latter group also includes singers, and in many compositions the voices function in the same way as the elaborating instruments.

3. Not all compositions are metric in this way. There are a relatively small number of nonmetric compositions, but they are played by a subset of the en-

semble. For a discussion of the performance practice of these pieces, see Brinner (1995b).

4. The exceptions are the chorus of male singers, *gérong,* and the mixed chorus that sings in pieces that accompany the *bedhaya* and *srimpi* dances.

5. There are also a relatively small number of compositions whose introductions are played by other instruments, mostly the *gendèr barung* or the *kendhang.*

6. For further discussion of interaction and leadership, see Brinner (1995b: 208–34).

7. While the *saron* part often preserves its contour when a *gendhing* is transferred from *sléndro* to *pélog* (as in example 4), there are also certain *saron* phrases that typically change contour.

8. Here I am adapting a metaphor Martopangrawit used to describe the melodic idiom of the *balungan* (17.iv.84).

9. The parts are all notated in the same register, even though they are spread throughout a four-octave range; this will be explained in the next section, on the ranges of the parts. Also, the *gambang* part, played in parallel octaves, is reduced here to a single line.

10. For detailed studies of some of these instruments, see Sutton (1993:121–25, 130–32), Brinner (1993), and Marsudi (1988).

11. The reader seeking more details about the idiomatic characteristics of the elaborating parts will find Sutton (1993:88–137) helpful.

12. The range given for the *saron* family is the one most common, but some gamelan lack the low 6 but have an additional high tone, 2.

13. There is a tradition in Western scholarship of treating the *gatra* as a melodic formula, a tradition criticized by Sumarsam (1995:229–30). I treat the *gatra* here as essentially a metric unit.

14. Suhardi used *mlaku* as an antonym of "slipping," and when I pressed Harjito and Sumarsam to find a term that would serve as the antonym of "hanging," they independently suggested *mlaku* as well. Therefore I have adopted it as a general label for this unmarked category. This term already has a technical sense in music: when applied to *balungan,* it refers to the idiom in which tones can appear on all four beats of the *gatra.* Since this seems to be the most conceptually basic type of *balungan,* it seems likely that *mlaku* is a basic Javanese metaphor for the feeling of a melody as something travelling through pitch space (just as "motion" is in English).

15. The *irama* of this example (and subsequent ones in this section) is *irama dadi.* See chapter 3 for an explanation of *irama* density-ratios.

16. *Céngkok* is also used to mean a melodically distinct *gong*-phrase as well as metrically free vocal ornamentation. As a verb, it can mean "to imitate" or "to be melodic." For a detailed survey of the senses of *céngkok,* see Perlman (1994:570–74).

17. There has, however, been some controversy over the appropriateness of the term "improvisation" as a description of the *garap* of the elaborating parts (Sutton 1998).

CHAPTER 3. *KARAWITAN* AS A MULTIPART MUSIC

1. Musicologists eager to trace the origins of polyphony saw the "heterophony" of various Asian ensemble musics as a sort of wild counterpoint, inchoate and unregulated. Guido Adler called it "polyphony without rules, with cohesion being left largely to chance" (Adler 1908:628). In a similar spirit, one early Dutch observer contrasted the "heterophonic" texture of Javanese gamelan with "rational" Western counterpoint (Brandts Buys 1921:5): "The Javanese . . . are in possession of an old, alogical, irrational multipart music, a heterophonic polyphony."

Curt Sachs wrote in 1958 that heterophony is one of the most confused concepts in musicology *(MGG),* and Peter Cooke (in the *New Grove*) admits that the term cuts an enormous swath through the world's music, ranging from "minute discrepancies in unison singing or playing . . . to the most complex of contrapuntal writing" (Cooke 1980:537).

2. For example, differences between two parts that are caused by differences in range are not always identified as divergence. As we have seen, the effective ranges of the melodic parts vary from about one octave to over two octaves. Consider a *saron* part—one of the narrowest—trying to "track" a part with wider ambitus: when the latter uses tones unavailable on the *saron*, the *saron* will transpose the melody back into its own range. This is not usually considered to detract from the degree of congruence between those parts, however.

3. I will provide a detailed discussion of the types of congruence in *Making Sense in Javanese Music.*

4. This is the sort of divergence found in Gendhing Majemuk *sléndro nem,* Gendhing Rondhon and Lagu Dhempel (both *sléndro sanga*), and Gendhing Merak Kasimpir and Cucurbawuk (both *sléndro manyura*).

5. Here I follow Suhardi's practice. I have in fact heard other musicians play to 6 [*a*] at this point on the *gendèr,* though rarely.

6. While no instrumental or vocal part is assigned the task of presenting this multi-octave *balungan,* some instruments in fact do occasionally play it, though briefly. When the tempo of a *gendhing* is fast enough to make melodic elaboration sound fussy, the *bonang barung* and *rebab* can play the *balungan* for short passages. This often happens at the start of a *gendhing,* immediately after the *buka.*

CHAPTER 4. THE *BALUNGAN* AS MELODIC GUIDE

1. Although he used different examples, the point could also be illustrated by the variety of vocal parts used for identical *balungan* phrases in examples 20, 25, and 26 (chapter 3).

2. In everyday Javanese, *ijoan* means "oral" as opposed to "written" (predicated, for example, of an invitation). Mitropradongga likened *ijoan* to the dancer's *garingan* (practicing a dance without its accompanying music).

3. The extent of the *rebab*'s range seems to be the issue here, though it is

in fact only part of the story. Martopangrawit admitted (20.viii.85) that the *gambang* also has the "full melody" of the piece; indeed, the *rebab* and *gambang* are the only parts that have it, not excepting the *pesindhèn* and *gérong.* "The *gambang* is basically [*dasarnya*] the same as the *rebab,* but its technique differs." Yet I never heard anyone suggest the *gambang* part as a memory-aid.

4. It should be remembered, though, that a musician can associate the *rebab* with *lagu,* and can compose *gendhing* starting with *lagu,* and yet still find the *rebab* less than ideal as a way to memorize *gendhing.* This seems to be the case with Darsono, who told me (8.xi.84) that he considered the *bonang* and *slenthem* parts best *(paling kuat)* for memorizing *gendhing;* by comparison, the *rebab* part is inferior *(lemah),* since a *rebab* player can learn to play a piece simply by analogy with other pieces: "This *gatra* is like [the identical passage] in Gambirsawit, that *gatra* is like [the identical passage] in Clunthang, etc."

5. Javanese musicians use a type of oral notation or rhythmic solfège in which different drums strokes are represented by nonlexical syllables.

6. Several examples of this can be found in Perlman (1994:555–77): for example, the overlapping senses of *wiletan* and *sekaran* for some speakers, or of *luk* and *céngkok.* For an example of historical change in terminology, note that in Yogyakarta, the term *wilet* seems to have been replaced by *balungan* (Perlman 1994:560).

7. For example, Mitropradongga told me to "learn the *gendhing* first, then the *garap*"; similarly, Mloyowidodo (2.iv.87) said that the masters used to say, "Learn the *gendhing* first; once you know it, then study the *rebab* and *gendèr.*" Sutton (1982:37) gives *gendhing* as an older Yogyanese term for *balungan.*

8. *Céngkok* has long meant a melodically distinct *gong*-phrase within a *gendhing* (Perlman 1994:570–71). We know that in the cognate Yogyanese tradition the word *wilet* was used in this sense (Kunst 1973:I, 334). Yogyakarta also used *wilet* for the *balungan,* as is clear from early Yogyanese books of notation (including the Pakem Wirama: Perlman 1994:557–58, 560). Brandts Buys (1921:64 n. 15) also mentions *wilet* as a Yogyanese term for the *balungan.* Given the fact that Surakarta sometimes uses the term *céngkok* where Yogyakarta uses *wilet,* it is possible that *céngkok* once meant *balungan* in Surakarta, just as *wilet* once meant *balungan* in Yogyakarta; see Kunst (1973:I, 127 n. 2).

9. This passage, difficult to interpret precisely, reads as follows: *Demung dumunung irama / Mangungkung céngkok ngugeri* (Canto 2, stanza 5). The first line clearly reads, "The *demung* is the place of the *irama,*" but the second could be translated either as "[It] sounds and sets the *céngkok*" or "Sounding the *céngkok* [it sets] the rule." Alan Feinstein, in his manuscript translation of this passage, finds an enjambment here: "The demung helps to steady the tempo, / Its melodies laying a base for / The saron barung, which interposes its high note."

10. Note, however, that the text seems to use *céngkok* and *lagu* interchangeably in some contexts. For example, it refers to the melody of certain *sulukan* as both *céngkok* (in the case of Sendhon Tloloran; Canto III, Asmaradana, stanza 6) and *lagu* (Sendhon Sastradatan, stanza 8). Also, Tondhakusuma may

use *céngkok* in the modern sense, referring to the basic forms of the elaborating parts' stock phrases.

11. Nor is it likely that Dutch assumptions about melody/accompaniment textures inspired the Javanese to notate a single melodic line. First, while Becker is probably correct in assuming that the kind of Western music most familiar to late-nineteenth-century Dutch in Indonesia would have had a single melody with harmonic accompaniment, the Western staff can notate other textures equally well, as the vast body of notated contrapuntal compositions attests. Indeed, at least some interested Dutch observers tried to encourage the Javanese musicians to produce full scores of gamelan music and were disappointed when musicians persisted in notating a single melodic line: the *balungan*. (For an account of the 1923 notation competition sponsored by the Java Institute, which unsuccessfully attempted to stimulate interest in full scores, see Brandts Buys 1924.)

12. This is the case, for example, with Ladrang Éling-éling kasmaran, played in *sléndro sanga* and *pélog barang*. Although there are also cases in which the *balungan* too changes with change of *laras*, the changes are usually small and predictable: for example, *sléndro*'s 2126 becomes 2756 in *pélog barang*.

13. When a *gendhing* falls out of the mainstream repertory but is preserved in Sekatèn (as seems to have happened with Ladrang Rangsang *sléndro nem;* Mloyowidodo 30.vi.94), hearing it performed gives no clue to the *garap* or even the multi-octave *balungan*. Thus, for example, Martopangrawit was familiar with Gendhing Kembang Dara *pélog nem* only from Sekatèn (19.ii.85). So he had to figure out the *garap* for it when I asked him to teach it to me.

CHAPTER 5. THEORIZING MELODIC GUIDANCE

1. The quotation about buried iron is from a manuscript version of the *Serat Sastramiruda* dated 1897 (LOr 6389B, p. 88, as cited in Feinstein 1995). The phrase "for the general good" can also be found in this manuscript, as well as on the title page of the first issue of the Radya Pustaka's journal *Sasadara*, in the textbook of the first public gamelan course (*Komisi Pasinaon* 1924:3), and numerous other places. It may be a Javanese translation of the motto of the first colonial-period learned society, the Bataviaasch Genootschap van Kunsten en Wetenschappen onder de zinspreuk "Tot nut van 't Algemeen" (Batavian Society for Arts and Sciences, with the motto "For the General Good"), founded in 1778 (*ENI* 1921, art. "Vereenigingen").

2. The earliest writings on *karawitan* published in Surakarta that I have been able to discover are samples of vocal notation in the journal *Sasadara* (vol. 2, no. 3, pp. 103–105; Rabingulakir AJ 1831 [= 1901]). In 1904, the same journal published R. M. Suwita's "historical" survey of the gamelan. For a study of later sources, see Sumarsam (1995).

3. I was told this in 1984 by Rustopo (then acting director of the Academy). Almost all of the most prominent Academy graduates were born some distance

from Solo. Supanggah, as of present writing the director of the Indonesian College of the Arts, was born in Klégo, forty kilometers north of Solo. The previous director, Sri Hastanto, is from Sragen (a county thirty to forty kilometers east of Solo). Sumarsam and Harjito came from even farther afield; they are from Bojonegara and Trenggalek (respectively), both small towns in East Java.

4. But see Kunst (1937:5) for evidence that he was aware of the multi-octave nature of the *balungan*.

5. In his later publications, Hood changed his terminology somewhat but did not apparently alter the substance of his views. He came to call the *saron* melody the "Fixed Melody" and to reserve the term *balungan* for the part of the *bonang panembung* (Hood and Susilo 1967:22). This, at least, is my own conclusion from Hood's usage; he does not point out the change in his terminology. Possibly Hood is following Yogyanese usage here (cf. Sutton 1982:79 n. 4). In any event, the *bonang panembung* is a specifically Yogyanese instrument, virtually unknown in Solo; one tradition attributes its invention to Hamengkubuwana I (r. 1755–1792), founder of Yogyakarta (Jayadipura 1921:104).

But for Hood the *saron* melody of a piece—the Fixed Melody—is still "the specific 'tune' that makes it different from all other pieces" (1971:238) and still "provides the melodic basis for orchestral improvisation" (Hood and Susilo 1967:15; cf. also Hood 1975:28).

6. "The particular disposition of the principal melody within the one-octave range of the saron causes these |cadential| scale passages, in effect, to assume a slightly different shape for each patet" (1954:122). Hood suggests that the disposition of steps and skips in each *pathet*'s cadential formula contributes to

> the climactic build-up, from calm to more excitement to the most
> excitement, which characterizes the sequence of the three periods
> of the wayang night. . . . A simple descending scale passage of four
> tones is typical for the first wayang period. As melodic movement
> this creates a minimum tension, suitable to the relatively quiet mood
> of the opening period. In the second period the typical pattern sug-
> gests a classic rule of disjunct movement in a melodic line: two steps
> descending, a wide leap up and the melody turns back on itself again
> in a descending step. This pattern produces more melodic tension
> than a simple scale passage but also lessens the effect produced
> in the wide leap, by the final step-wise movement. . . . The typical
> cadence of the third period . . . generates the most tension: three
> descending steps and a wide leap up, which is not resolved at all.
> (1954:129)

7. McDermott and Sumarsam here argue as if the preferability of conjunct over disjunct motion is the main argument for distinguishing the *saron* part from the *balungan*. As we have seen in chapter 3, the fact that the multi-octave *balungan* is more "well-behaved" melodically than the single-octave *balungan* is only one factor motivating the distinction.

8. "I believe the preference for a one-octave saron as the instrument to be

entrusted with the nuclear theme is directly attributable to a desire, conscious or otherwise, to preserve the melodic contour or *shape*, if you will, of the principal melody—the melodic *shape*, I repeat, of the all-important cadential formula which closes the three critical sections, which serves as the framework of the whole gendhing, which, in short, is one of the strongest features in the identification and, consequently, the very preservation of the pathet concept itself" (1954:242).

9. I have not otherwise encountered this idea—which Sumarsam himself later (19.xii.92) characterized as a "desperate effort to answer the question"—during my research. When I explained this idea to Harjito (18.xii.92), he replied that he never felt that 21 on the *saron barung* continues with 65 on the *demung*.

10. The ASKI staff may have accepted Sumarsam's idea because it resonated with their implicit knowledge of *karawitan*, or possibly they had already articulated the concept for themselves. Supanggah recalled (20.x.84) that "since 1973 or 1974, all of us at ASKI agreed that the *balungan* isn't the *saron* part."

CHAPTER 6. THREE CONCEPTS OF UNPLAYED MELODY

1. He was eventually offered a chance to teach at one of the state conservatories, but he refused. The reason he gave me was that students needed junior high school or high school diplomas to enter those institutions, and he preferred to make his knowledge available to anyone, regardless of their formal educational qualifications.

2. Sumarsam also mentioned a third reason: the *balungan* of certain pieces displays paradoxical motion, e.g., "descending" to reach the upper register. This phenomenon, which I elsewhere call melodic aporia (Perlman 1994:303–11), also represents a "failure" of the *balungan*'s guidance function.

3. This was Hastanto's immediate reaction when I asked him about the cases of divergence I have called melodic aporias (Perlman 1994:312).

4. When this figure was reprinted in Becker and Feinstein's *Source Readings* collection (1984:265), its caption was changed to "the author's hypothetical version of the inner melody."

5. Here Sumarsam refers particularly to the type of divergence I have called aporetic (Perlman 1994:303–12).

6. For example, Sri Hastanto commented in his dissertation that "Sumarsam rightly points out that the *balungan gendhing* is an abstraction of a more elaborate, pre-existent melody which he calls the 'inner melody'" (1985:40).

7. Supanggah's Indonesian version of his paper was published in 1990; meanwhile, however, my translation had already appeared (1988). I discussed the translation with Supanggah in great detail; as a result of my questions, he made a few revisions. I incorporated these without comment in my translation. When his original was published, however, I noticed that these revisions had not been made. The most significant discrepancy concerns figure 4 (1990:124; 1988:5).

8. In what follows I give examples from my interviews with Suhardi. For a similar example from Supanggah, see Perlman (1994:500–501).

9. Indeed, it is even possible for a single musician to alternate between these two interpretations. See, for example, Sumarsam's uncertainty in trying to decide whether the middle-octave *rebab* part for the *balungan* phrase 2235 in Gendhing Mégamendhung *sléndro nem* reflects the *gendhing* melody (Perlman 1994:496–99).

10. In his later work on the compositional process, Sumarsam (1995:234) admitted a degree of heterogeneity and multiplicity in the origins of *gendhing*. However, as I describe below, this later theory differs in important ways from his "inner melody" theory.

11. When Suhardi did use the rhetoric of interiority, he may have done so as a result of his perception of my interests. Over the months of our conversations, Suhardi adjusted his terminology to communicate with me, sometimes adopting words or images he heard me use. (For example, Suhardi disliked the effect of adjacent pitches played simultaneously. In one of our conversations on this subject I used the term "collision" |*tabrakan*| to describe this unpleasant effect, and Suhardi picked up this image and used it in our subsequent discussions.) This may have happened in our conversations about the *lagu*. To judge from Sutton (1979), Suhardi never explicitly described his *lagu* as something inward during his conversations with Sutton in the 1970s. The same was true for the first four months of my conversations with him. At that point, however, I told him about Sumarsam's term "inner melody" *(lagu batin)*. Unfortunately, I did not take notes on my own explanation of the idea, and so I do not know now whether I went into much detail about it; in any event, Suhardi apparently concluded that Sumarsam's idea was the same as his own, commenting only that "everyone discovers it for himself" (21.vii.84). Soon afterward (3.viii.84) he started using the term in passing, sometimes explicitly marking it as borrowed by calling it "Sumarsam's inner melody," and equating it with his own *lagu* (23.xi.84). He then dropped Sumarsam's term in favor of his own coinage— "inner *balungan*" *(balungan batin)*—as an alternative way to refer to the *lagu* (14.xii.84). But this term, too, he used only intermittently; I didn't hear it again for nine months (13.ix.85).

Suhardi's use of "inner *balungan*" did not, however, imply a fully worked-out theoretical position as to the presence of the *lagu* in the musical imagination. Years later I brought up the subject again, asking him if his *lagu* was something he heard in his *batin*. He had apparently never considered the question, and it seemed to throw him into confusion; over a period of months he struggled with it, offering vacillating answers. He eventually concluded that he did *not* hear the *lagu* in his mind's ear (Perlman 1994:523–24).

CHAPTER 7. IMPLICIT-MELODY CONCEPTS IN PERSPECTIVE

1. These uses of *sasmita* have long histories. The use of *sasmita* to describe cues in the *wayang* is found in the earliest written-out *wayang* texts; e.g.,

Kusumadilaga (1930:59) and Te Mechelen (1882:11). For the early use of *sasmita* in literary criticism, see the *Serat Cabolèk* (a nineteenth-century text with possible origins in the eighteenth century), where the Old Javanese writings *Bima Suci* and *Arjunawiwaha* are described as containing "many allusions" (*kèh sasmitané:* Ricklefs 1998:149). For *sasmita* as supernatural sign, see, e.g., Sastrasoewignja (1932).

On *semu*, see Florida (1995:275–76). *Abang semu ireng,* "dark red," is not pure red but red tinged with black (*ireng:* Suhardi 22.ii.85). Words "tinged with anger" (*semu duka*) are not angry words, but anger can be felt behind them. For an example linking *sasmita* and *semu,* see Florida (1995:290 n. 8).

Semu has musical uses as well. Wahyopangrawit (1.v.85) used it to describe a *gong*-stroke placed slightly behind the beat, and also the *rebab's* nonobligatory use of the *barang miring* conventional melodic gesture.

2. This exposition of *kebatinan* draws upon Stange 1984, Errington 1984, Keeler 1987, and remarks by Mloyowidodo.

3. For some examples of prediction sheets and an interpretation of Javanese betting strategies, see Siegel (1986:149–57).

4. It is a verse from Ketawang Puspagiwang; the text is by Mangkunagara IV (1934:IV, 170).

5. Lecture delivered to the staff of the provincial office of the Department of Education and Culture, 22 July 1971.

6. Yet the imagery of the *batin* is so highly respected in Javanese culture that once introduced into a universe of discourse, it can quickly spread. As stated in chapter 6, after I introduced Suhardi to Sumarsam's term "inner melody," he easily adapted it for his own use, occasionally referring to his *lagu* as an "inner *balungan.*"

However, we should not assume from their usage of a common term that Suhardi and Sumarsam meant the same thing by it. When a term radiates through society it may not carry all of its meaning along with it. The language of interiority is so widely recognized in Javanese society that its terminology has easy entrée to many semantic domains. But ease of access does not imply stability of meaning. Once it arrives in a new domain, the concept of the "inner" can assume new connotations.

CHAPTER 8. PATTERNS OF CONCEPTUAL
INNOVATION IN MUSIC THEORY

1. It would be interesting to know if such micro/macro analogies are found in other traditions. I know of only two. For example, the prominent Irish fiddler Martin Hayes tries to give his concert programs a definite shape through his choice and sequencing of tunes. The shape he aims at is, he feels, a projection into a larger time-span of the kind of shape he detects within individual tunes. Specifically, he speaks of the traditional tunes as containing structures of "call and response," "resolution," and "climaxes," which he tries to build into "more

of a meta kind of structure for the whole show." (I am indebted to Orla Heni-han for bringing this example to my attention. Hayes made these statements in an interview with her on 6 August 1998.)

Oddly enough, musicians in Java (where large compositional forms often project the patterns of small forms) almost never make such comparisons. The only example I know of is Supanggah (1994), which compares the four-beat *gatra* unit with a *gong*-cycle consisting of four *kenong*-units.

2. I am grateful to Richard Cohn for first suggesting the extension of pitch concepts into the temporal realm as an example of intra-domain analogical thinking.

3. The translation of pitch intervals into ratios of tempo had already been anticipated by Cowell (1930:91): "Considered in terms of tone, accelerated or diminished tempo would . . . represent a sliding tone going upwards or down-wards in the scale" (1930:94). For other examples of pitch metaphors of tem-poral relations, see Krebs (1999:3–21).

4. In view of the close kinship of conceptual extension and within-domain analogy noted in chapter 1, it is significant that Dubiel describes Schenker's transformation of the idea of the passing tone as *both* a sort of extension *and* a kind of metaphor.

5. In generalizing, we establish the equivalence of the three inversions by focusing on their common pitch-class content, ignoring their diverse functions and sonority. In discriminating between them, we appeal to some evaluative prin-ciple or posit a derivational sequence. (The principles and derivations used for this purpose have historically tended to be mathematical ones, according to which the fifths and thirds of the root position are prior to, and more perfect than, the sixths and fourths of the other inversions.) As Rivera points out (1984:67), theorists have differed in the relative emphasis they put on each of these two conceptual operations.

6. Of course, behind this mathematical source we can discern a botanical conceptual metaphor, COMPLEX SYSTEMS ARE PLANTS (Kövecses 1999).

7. Mattheson (1721:556), for example, labels the bass of a sixth chord its *ba-sis*; Heinichen too uses *basis* to mean bass tone (1728:623).

8. Printz (1696:52–54), for example, uses Lippius's term *basis*, drawing as well on Baryphonus's development of Lippius's ideas.

9. For example, Heinichen (1728:558) used *Grund-Stimmen* and *Radical-Stimmen* (somewhat in the spirit of Lippius) to refer to the distinct voices of a chord, minus octave doublings.

10. Note that Kirnberger also uses *Grundton* to mean the lower tone of any interval, but this sense seems clearly related to its sense as bass tone.

11. This is obvious from his explanation of why the bass of a sixth chord should not be doubled (Koch 1811:65): "Der Grundton des Sextenakkordes wird eigentlich nicht verdoppelt, weil er die Terz des Dreyklanges ist."

12. This is not to deny the role of conceptual metaphors; as we have seen, cross-domain mappings from the worlds of plants and buildings were impor-tant sources for some of the terms we surveyed. But in each case these distal

mappings were mediated by a proximate intra-domain mapping from one musical element to another: *basis* was used metaphorically to refer to the bass tone, and only then was it applied to the chord root; *radix* came to mean chord root only after it had been used to mean the 5-3 triad.

13. As Christensen points out, though, Rameau's method was not an exclusively rationalistic one, any more than was Descartes's (1993:33–35).

14. Largely, but not exclusively, since Rameau occasionally included in the *basse fondamentale* tones that were not roots of any of the sonorities present in the texture, but whose presence was in some sense implied—a practice explored more fully by later theorists, such as Kirnberger and Schulz (Grant 1977).

15. Keiler (1981) calls it metalinguistic, but he too seems to assume that it is a trope. Technically, a metalinguistic statement is one that refers to linguistic expressions, such as "'John is easy to please' and 'To please John is easy' are paraphrases of each other." Keiler does not compare the fundamental bass to a statement of this sort. Rather, he calls a statement like "To please John is easy" metalinguistic, even though this statement has no overt reference to linguistic entities. Keiler says such a statement "can also *function* metalinguistically when it is offered as a paraphrase" of "John is easy to please" (1981:91, emphasis added)—in other words, it is not in itself metalinguistic, but it can be put to metalinguistic *use*. Presumably, then, Rameau's fundamental bass is like this: not in itself metalinguistic, it is *used* metalinguistically.

But such extended usages are tropes. We commonly use sentences to mean things they do not literally mean. We say "Do you know what time it is?" to mean "Tell me what time it is"; we say "Nice day!" to mean "The weather is horrible." These are instances of nonliteral usage: one is an indirect speech act, the other is ironic. They are deliberate misuses, tropes. Similarly, under certain circumstances it might be possible to say "To please John is easy" and mean "'John is easy to please' and 'To please John is easy' are paraphrases of each other." But such a use would be equally nonliteral. It, too, would be a deliberate misuse, a trope. If the fundamental bass represents a metalinguistic use of music, it does so because it also represents a musical trope.

16. Thus, for example, Roussier holds that the term *basse fondamentale* "ne pouvoit exprimer que très improprement le son ou l'accord primitif, que dans son systême, il appelle fondamentale, puisque ce son ou cet accord n'occupe pas toujours le lieu le plus grave dans une harmonie donnée" (1783:332).

17. Of course, Rameau's thinking also employed strategies not found in the Javanese examples. Notably, he legitimized the fundamental bass by relating it to a prestigious inherited body of thought *(musica theorica)*; there is no Javanese equivalent to the canonist tradition of deriving the intervals and scales of music from monochord divisions (Christensen 1993:29–31, 71–77).

18. Differently put, we could say that the contrast between Rameau and the Javanese case is a contrast between diachronic lability and synchronic lability. Perhaps as a result, there is another disanalogy between the fundamental bass and the implicit melody concepts. Rameau did not abandon his earlier pedagogical intentions for the fundamental bass when he expanded his theoretical

ambitions; rather, he added the latter to the former. By contrast, Sumarsam and Supanggah never attempted to use their implicit melody concepts in the practical business of teaching.

CONCLUSION

1. Brinner has indeed pointed out how *pathet* has graded structure, one of the marks of a nonclassical concept (1995b:61–62).

2. These differences of interpretation have no practical effects as long as we remain on the level of isolated, disarticulated observations—when we try to classify relatively small populations of organisms in one place over short periods of evolutionary time (that is, the situation in which most members of most societies find themselves most of the time). It is only when we try to enlarge the picture, when we try to integrate these observations into a coherent whole—when we look at an entire species of organisms in its global distribution or when we look at larger taxonomic categories—that these disagreements become significant.

Glossary

More extensive notes and examples of usage for some of these terms (e.g., *céngkok, wilet,* etc.) can be found in Perlman 1994, Appendix I.

ada-ada:	A type of *suluk,* performed by *dhalang* (or other singer), *gendèr barung, kendhang, kempul, kenong,* and *gong.* Unlike other varieties of *suluk,* its rhythm is strongly pulsed.
ayak-ayakan:	A *gendhing* form associated with the *wayang* (shadow-puppet play).
ayu kuning:	Name of a certain *céngkok.*
barang:	Name of one of the *pathet* in the *pélog* tuning system.
barang miring:	Also called *miring* or *mineer.* Melodic patterns for the *rebab* and *pesindhèn,* which are played in *sléndro* but use tones not found on the fixed-pitch *sléndro* instruments.
bawa:	A lengthy male vocal solo, used to introduce a composition instead of its *buka.*
bedhayan:	(Of a *gendhing*) performed as it would be to accompany the court dances *bedhaya* and *srimpi.*
bonangan:	What the *bonang* plays.
buka:	The introduction to a gamelan composition, usually played by *rebab, bonang, gendèr, kendhang,* or (rarely) *gambang.*
céngkok:	(1) A conventional melodic phrase for an elaborating part, one or two *gatra* long. (2) A melodically distinct *gong*-phrase.

ciblon:	A type of *kendhang* (drum) used to accompany dance.
dadi:	An *irama* level between *tanggung* and *wilet*.
dua lolo:	Name of a certain *céngkok*.
gantungan:	Lit. "hanging." Melodic stasis; the sustaining or repetition of a tone.
garap:	Lit. "to make, to do." (1) Any particular instrumental technique. (2) Performance practice in general. (3) The elaborating parts *(ricikan garap)*. (4) The musician's activity of interpreting a *gendhing* by performing one of the elaborating parts.
garapan:	That which is produced by the act of *garap*ing, i.e., an interpretation or treatment. More broadly, a person's playing or performance practice.
gatra:	A melodic phrase of four *balungan* beats.
gembyang:	The musical interval formed by two tones separated by five scale degrees; acoustically comparable to an octave.
gembyangan:	The playing of *gembyang* ("octave") simultaneities, especially on the *bonang*.
gendèran:	What the *gendèr* plays.
gendhing:	(1) The most general term for fixed-meter gamelan compositions. (2) The largest group of compositional forms, larger than *ladrang* and containing at least two movements, each of which can be repeated.
gérongan:	A choral vocal part, sung by men (the *gérong* or *penggérong*).
gongan:	A musical passage occupying the time interval between two *gong*-strokes.
imbal-imbalan or *imbal:*	A playing technique used on the *bonang*, whereby the *bonang barung* plays repeated patterns of two tones each, interlocking with one or two tones played on the *bonang panerus*.
inggah:	The second movement of a *gendhing*.
irama:	(1) Tempo. (2) A concept of melodic tempo describing the ratio between the fastest pulse of the elaborating parts and the beat of the basic melody. The names of the five main levels of

irama used here are *lancar, tanggung, dadi, wilet, rangkep.*

karawitan: (1) The instrumental and vocal music of Central Java, especially the highly developed music of the gamelan. (2) (As used in the Indonesian educational system) traditional Indonesian music.

kempyung: The musical interval formed by two tones separated by three scale degrees; acoustically comparable to a fifth.

kenongan: A musical passage ending on a *kenong*-stroke.

ketawang: A compositional form whose *gongan* consists of sixteen *balungan* beats divided into two *kenongan.*

kinanthi: A variety of *macapat* verse form (six lines of eight syllables each); a common poetic meter for *gérongan* texts.

klenèngan: Music performed on its own, not accompanying dance or *wayang;* (of a *gendhing*) performed as it would be on its own, not as an accompaniment.

ladrang: A compositional form whose *gongan* consists of thirty-two *balungan* beats divided into four *kenongan.*

lancaran: A compositional form whose *gongan* consists of eight *balungan* beats divided into four *kenongan.*

laras: (1) Tone. (2) One of two tuning systems, *sléndro* and *pélog.*

lima: Name of one of the *pathet* in the *pélog* tuning system.

macapat: A class of sung verse forms, each with its own poetic meter and set of melodies.

manyura: Name of one of the *pathet* in the *sléndro* tuning system.

mérong: The first movement of a *gendhing.*

mlaku: Lit. "walking, moving." One type of rhythmic idiom for the *balungan.*

nem: (1) Name of one of the *pathet* in the *sléndro* tuning system. (2) Name of one of the *pathet* in the *pélog* tuning system.

ngelik:	(1) Placed in the upper register. (2) The upper-register section of a composition.
nibani:	A relatively sparse rhythmic idiom for the *balungan,* highly constrained both rhythmically and melodically.
ompak:	(1) A transitional section in a *gendhing,* linking the (repeatable) *mérong* to the (repeatable) *inggah,* but which itself cannot be repeated. (2) In smaller compositional forms, the initial *gongan* of a piece, as distinct from the *ngelik* section. (3) A metrically regular passage in a *suluk.*
pathet:	(1) One of six (or seven) "modes" in *sléndro* and *pélog.* (2) *Pathetan.*
pathetan:	A variety of *suluk,* performed by *dhalang* (or other singer), *rebab, gendèr barung, gambang, suling, kendhang,* and *gong.* Also used outside *wayang* performances, in which case the vocal part, *kendhang,* and *gong* are omitted. *Pathetan* are played after all *gendhing* that end slowly (except for *gendhing bonang*) and can be played before a *gendhing* in order to signal a change of *pathet* or to introduce a *bawa.*
pipilan:	A playing technique used on the *bonang.*
plèsèdan:	Lit. "slipping." A term denoting a type of performance practice on the *kenong, kempul,* or *garap* parts. (1) For the *kenong* or *kempul:* when the *kenong* or *kempul* does not play the tone of the *balungan* stroke simultaneous with it, but anticipates a melody tone yet to be played. (2) For the *garap* parts: when a part arrives at a goal-tone and then immediately shifts to another tone, anticipating the future course of the melody.
puthut gelut:	Name of a certain melodic pattern *(céngkok).*
rambatan:	Lit. "trellis for a creeping plant." A phrase that serves as a transition (often between registers).
rangkep:	(1) The *irama* level beyond *wilet.* (2) "Doubled," of *irama* or playing technique. (3) The densest rhythmic idiom of the *balungan.*
rebaban:	What the *rebab* plays.
sanga:	Name of one of the *pathet* in the *sléndro* tuning system.

Santiswaran:	A genre of vocal music, accompanied by *terbang* frame drums and *kendhang.* Some of these unison songs seem to be versions of eponymous gamelan compositions.
sekaran:	Also called *kembangan.* (1) A playing technique used on the *bonang* in conjunction with *imbal-imbalan.* (2) Certain patterns played on the *ciblon* drum.
sèlèh:	Lit. "settled." The goal-tone or cadential pitch of a phrase.
sendhon:	A variety of *suluk,* performed by *dhalang* (or other singer), *gendèr barung, gambang,* and *suling.*
sesegan:	Also called *sabetan.* The third movement of certain *gendhing,* customarily played loudly in fast tempo.
sindhènan:	What the *pesindhèn* sings.
sindhènan bedhayan:	The choral vocal part, sung by male and female voices, used to accompany *bedhaya* and *srimpi* dances.
suluk:	Also *sulukan.* Songs sung by a *dhalang* (puppeteer of a shadow-puppet play or narrator of a dance-drama) accompanied by a small group of instruments.
suwuk:	The end of a performance of a *gendhing,* usually marked by decelerating tempo.
suwukan:	(1) A special passage played in certain *gendhing* only when the piece is ending. (2) A vertically suspended gong, smaller (and higher-pitched) than the *gong ageng* but larger (and lower-pitched) than the *kempul.*
tanggung:	An *irama* level between *lancar* and *dadi.*
wayangan:	(Of a *gendhing*) performed as it would be to accompany a shadow-puppet play.
wilet:	The *irama* level between *dadi* and *rangkep.*

References Cited

MANUSCRIPT SOURCES

Serat Gulang Yarya (1870). Author: R. M. H. Tondhakusuma. Reksa Pustaka MS
A21. Istana Mangkunagaran, Surakarta.
Wileting Gendhing Pradongga (1932). Also called *Pakem Wirama*. National Li-
brary, Jakarta, no. Dj 59.

PUBLISHED SOURCES

Abbate, Carolyn. 1981. *"Tristan* in the Composition of *Pelléas." 19th Century
Music* 5:117–41.
Abraham, Gerald. 1964. *A Hundred Years of Music.* Chicago: Aldine.
Adler, Guido. 1908 [1985]. "Heterophony." Pp. 624–33 in Donald Mitchell, *Gus-
tav Mahler: Songs and Symphonies of Life and Death.* Berkeley: University
of California Press.
Agawu, V. Kofi. 1992. "Representing African Music." *Critical Inquiry* 18:245–66.
Ahn, Woo-Kyoung, and Douglas Medin. 1992. "A Two-Stage Model of Cate-
gory Construction." *Cognitive Science* 16:81–121.
Alba, Joseph, and Lynn Hasher. 1983. "Is Memory Schematic?" *Psychological
Bulletin* 93:203–31.
Arlin, Mary. In press. "Metric Mutation and Modulation: The Nineteenth-
Century Speculations of F.-J. Fétis." *Journal of Music Theory.*
Arom, Simha. 1976. "The Use of Play-Back Techniques in the Study of Oral
Polyphonies." *Ethnomusicology* 20:483–520.
———. 1991. *African Polyphony and Polyrhythm.* Cambridge: Cambridge Uni-
versity Press.
Arps, Bernard. 1992. *Tembang in Two Traditions: Performance and Interpreta-
tion of Javanese Literature.* Dissertation, Leiden University.
Arrington, Robert. 1989. *Rationalism, Realism, and Relativism.* Ithaca, N.Y.:
Cornell University Press.
Atran, Scott, and Dan Sperber. 1991. "Learning without Teaching: Its Place in

Culture." Pp. 39–55 in L. T. Landsmann, ed., *Culture, Schooling, and Psychological Development*. Norwood, N.J.: Ablex.

Baily, John. 1988. "Anthropological and Psychological Approaches to the Study of Music Theory and Musical Cognition." *Yearbook for Traditional Music* 20:114–24.

Baker, James. 1990. "Voice-Leading in Post-Tonal Music: Suggestions for Extending Schenker's Theory." *Music Analysis* 9:177–200.

Baker, Nancy Kovaleff. 1988. "*Der Urstoff der Musik:* Implications for Harmony and Melody in the Theory of Heinrich Koch." *Music Analysis* 7:3–30.

Bamberger, Jeanne. 1991. *The Mind behind the Musical Ear: How Children Develop Musical Intelligence*. Cambridge, Mass.: Harvard University Press.

Barsalou, L. W. 1992. *Cognitive Psychology: An Overview for Cognitive Scientists*. Hillsdale, N.J.: L. Erlbaum.

Bartel, Dietrich. 1997. *Musica Poetica: Musical-Rhetorical Figures in German Baroque Music*. Lincoln: University of Nebraska Press.

Bartlett, Frederic. 1932. *Remembering: A Study in Experimental and Social Psychology*. Cambridge: Cambridge University Press.

Beatty, Andrew. 1999. *Varieties of Javanese Religion*. Cambridge: Cambridge University Press.

Becker, Judith. 1980. *Traditional Music in Modern Java*. Honolulu: University of Hawaii Press.

———. 1981. "Some Thoughts about *Pathet*." Pp. 530–35 in D. Heartz and B. Wade, eds., *Proceedings of the International Musicological Society, Berkeley 1977*.

———. 1984. "Preface." In Judith Becker and Alan Feinstein 1984.

———. 1988. "Introduction" to Appendix 2. Pp. 49–58 in Judith Becker and Alan Feinstein 1988.

Becker, Judith, and A. L. Becker. 1983. "A Reconsideration in the Form of a Dialogue." *Asian Music* 14(1):9–16.

Becker, Judith, and Alan Feinstein, eds. 1984. *Karawitan: Source Readings in Javanese Gamelan and Vocal Music*. Vol. 1. Ann Arbor: University of Michigan Center for South and Southeast Asian Studies. Michigan Papers on South and Southeast Asia, no. 23.

———. 1987. *Karawitan: Source Readings in Javanese Gamelan and Vocal Music*. Vol. 2. Ann Arbor: University of Michigan Center for South and Southeast Asian Studies. Michigan Papers on South and Southeast Asia, no. 30.

———. 1988. *Karawitan: Source Readings in Javanese Gamelan and Vocal Music*. Vol. 3. Ann Arbor: University of Michigan Center for South and Southeast Asian Studies. Michigan Papers on South and Southeast Asia, no. 31.

Benamou, Marc. 1998. "Rasa in Javanese Musical Aesthetics." Ph.D. dissertation, University of Michigan.

Benjamin, William. 1981. "Schenker's Theory and the Future of Music." *Journal of Music Theory* 25:155–73.

Bent, Ian. 1992. "History of Music Theory: Margin or Center?" *Theoria* 6(1):1–21.

———. 1996. "Preface." Pp. xi–xiv in *Music Theory in the Age of Romanticism*. Cambridge: Cambridge University Press.

Berliner, Paul. 1994. *Thinking in Jazz*. Chicago: University of Chicago Press.

Berlioz, Hector. 1837 [1969]. "Berlioz on the Future of Rhythm." Pp. 336–39 in J. Barzun, ed., *Berlioz and the Romantic Century*. Vol. 2. New York: Columbia University Press.

Blacking, John. 1971. "Deep and Surface Structures in Venda Music." *Yearbook of the International Folk Music Council* 3:91–108.

———. 1973. *How Musical Is Man?* Seattle: University of Washington Press.

———. 1981. "The Problem of 'Ethnic' Perceptions in the Semiotics of Music." In Wendy Steiner, ed., *The Sign in Music and Literature*. Austin: University of Texas Press.

Boden, Margaret. 1994. "What Is Creativity?" Pp. 75–117 in M. A. Boden, ed., *Dimensions of Creativity*. Cambridge, Mass.: MIT Press.

Boow, Justine. 1988. *Symbol and Status in Javanese Batik*. Monograph Series no. 7. Nedlands: Asian Studies Center, University of Western Australia.

Bourdieu, Pierre. 1977. *Outline of a Theory of Practice*. Cambridge: Cambridge University Press.

———. 1990a. *The Logic of Practice*. Stanford: Stanford University Press.

———. 1990b. *In Other Words*. Stanford: Stanford University Press.

Brandts Buys, J. 1921. "Over de ontwikkelingsmogelijkheden van de muziek op Java." *Djawa* 1 (Prae-adviezen 2):1–90.

———. 1924. "Uitslag van de Prijsvraag inzake een Javaansch Muziekschrift." *Djawa* 4:1–17.

Brinner, Benjamin. 1993. "Freedom and Formularity in the *Suling* Playing of Bapak Tarnopangrawit." *Asian Music* 24(2):1–38.

———. 1995a. "Cultural Matrices and the Shaping of Innovation in Central Javanese Performing Arts." *Ethnomusicology* 39(3):433–56.

———. 1995b. *Knowing Music, Making Music*. Chicago: University of Chicago Press.

Bruner, Jerome. 1957. "On Perceptual Readiness." *Psychological Review* 64:123–52.

Buelow, George. 1979. "The Concept of 'Melodielehre': A Key to Classic Style." Pp. 182–95 in *Mozart-Jahrbuch 1978/79*.

Burkholder, J. Peter. 1993. "Music Theory and Musicology." *Journal of Musicology* 11:11–23.

Burnham, Scott. 1993. "Musical and Intellectual Values: Interpreting the History of Tonal Theory." *Current Musicology* 53:76–88.

Cadwallader, Allen, and William Pastille. 1992. "Schenker's High-Level Motives." *Journal of Music Theory* 36:117–48.

Campbell, Donald T. 1988. *Methodology and Epistemology for Social Science: Selected Papers*. Edited by E. Samuel Overman. Chicago: University of Chicago Press.

Campbell, Lyle. 1998. *Historical Linguistics: An Introduction*. Cambridge, Mass.: MIT Press.

Campion, Thomas. 1967. *The Works of Thomas Campion*. Edited by Walter R. Davis. Garden City, N.Y.: Doubleday & Co.

Carter, Elliott. 1989. *Elliott Carter: In Conversation with Enzo Restagno for Settembre Musica 1989*. I.S.A.M. Monographs no. 32. New York: Institute for

Studies in American Music, Conservatory of Music, Brooklyn College of the City University of New York.

Carter, Tim. 1995. Review of *Music Theory and the Exploration of the Past*. *Music Analysis* 14(1):105–11.

Centhini. 1985–. *Serat Centhini Latin*. Yogyakarta: Yayasan Centhini.

Chater, Nick, and Mike Oaksford. 1999. "Ten Years of the Rational Analysis of Cognition." *Trends in Cognitive Sciences* 3(2):57–65.

Chatterjee, Partha. 1986. *Nationalist Thought and the Colonial World: A Derivative Discourse?* London: Zed Books.

———. 1993. *The Nation and Its Fragments*. Princeton: Princeton University Press.

Chenette, Louis F. 1967. "Music Theory in the British Isles during the Enlightenment." Ph.D. dissertation, Ohio State University.

Cherlin, Michael. 1988. "Hauptmann and Schenker: Two Adaptations of Hegelian Dialectics." *Theory and Practice* 13:115–31.

Christensen, Thomas. 1993. *Rameau and Musical Thought in the Enlightenment*. Cambridge: Cambridge University Press.

Cohen, David E. 1993. "Metaphysics, Ideology, Discipline: Consonance, Dissonance, and the Foundations of Western Polyphony." *Theoria* 7:1–85.

———. 2001a. "The 'Gift of Nature': Musical 'Instinct' and Musical Cognition in Rameau." Pp. 68–92 in Suzannah Clark and Alexander Rehding, eds., *Music Theory and Natural Order from the Renaissance to the Early Twentieth Century*. Cambridge: Cambridge University Press.

———. 2001b. "'The Imperfect Seeks Its Perfection': Harmonic Progression, Directed Motion, and Aristotelian Physics." *Music Theory Spectrum* 23(2): 139–69.

Cohn, Richard. 1992. "The Autonomy of Motives in Schenkerian Accounts of Tonal Music." *Music Theory Spectrum* 14(2):150–70.

Collins, H. M. 1990. *Artificial Experts: Social Knowledge and Intelligent Machines*. Cambridge, Mass.: MIT Press.

Comaroff, Jean, and John Comaroff. 1991. *Of Revelation and Revolution*. Vol. 1. Chicago: University of Chicago Press.

Cone, Edward T. 1968. *Musical Form and Musical Performance*. New York: W. W. Norton.

Cook, Nicholas. 1989. "Music Theory and 'Good Comparison': A Viennese Perspective." *Journal of Music Theory* 33:117–41.

———. 2002. "Epistemologies of Music Theory." Pp. 78–105 in Thomas Christensen, ed., *The Cambridge History of Western Music Theory*. New York: Cambridge University Press.

Cook, Nicholas, and Mark Everist, eds. 1999. *Rethinking Music*. New York: Oxford University Press.

Cooke, Peter. 1980. "Heterophony." *New Grove Dictionary of Music and Musicians*. London: Macmillan.

Cooper, Grosvenor, and Leonard B. Meyer. 1960. *The Rhythmic Structure of Music*. Chicago: University of Chicago Press.

Coulson, Seana, and Todd Oakley. 2000. "Blending Basics." *Cognitive Linguistics* 11:175–96.

Cowell, Henry. 1930 [1996]. *New Musical Resources*. Cambridge: Cambridge University Press.

Crafts, Susan, Daniel Cavicchi, and Charles Keil, eds. 1993. *My Music*. Hanover, N.H.: Wesleyan University Press.

D'Andrade, Roy. 1981. "The Cultural Part of Cognition." *Cognitive Science* 5:179–95.

———. 1990. "Some Propositions about the Relations between Culture and Human Cognition." In James W. Stigler, R. Shweder, and G. Herdt, eds., *Cultural Psychology: Essays on Comparative Human Development*. Cambridge: Cambridge University Press.

———. 1995. *The Development of Cognitive Anthropology*. Cambridge: Cambridge University Press.

Darwall, Stephen, Allan Gibbard, and Peter Railton. 1992. "Toward *Fin de siècle* Ethics: Some Trends." *Philosophical Review* 101:115–89.

Derrida, Jacques. 1977 [1988]. "Limited Inc a b c . . ." Pp. 29–110 in *Limited Inc*. Evanston: Northwestern University Press.

———. 1978. "Structure, Sign and Play in the Discourse of the Human Sciences." Pp. 278–93 in *Writing and Difference*. Chicago: University of Chicago Press.

Dewantara, Ki Hadjar. 1930 [1964]. *Serat Sari Swara*. Djilid 1. Djakarta: Pradnjaparamita.

———. 1941. "Metode 'Sari-Swara' dan Bedanja dengan Kepatihanschrift." *Poesara* 11(4):2–7.

———. 1957. "Rantjangan, wewatoning kawruh tuwin pasinaon gendhing Djawi." In *Mardawa Lagu Djawa*. Solo: Sadu-Budi.

Dienes, Zoltan, and Josef Perner. 1999. "A Theory of Implicit and Explicit Knowledge." *Behavioral and Brain Sciences* 22:735–808.

Djumadi. 1975. *Titilaras Rebaban*. Vol. 3. Surakarta: Akademi Seni Karawitan Indonesia.

———. 1986. *Titilaras Rebaban II*. Surakarta: Taman Budaya Surakarta.

Drabkin, William. 1991. Review of Agawu, *Playing With Signs*. *Music Analysis* 10(3):381–87.

Dubiel, Joseph. 1990. "'When You Are a Beethoven': Kinds of Rules in Schenker's *Counterpoint*." *Journal of Music Theory* 34:291–340.

Dunbar, Kevin. 1997. "How Scientists Think: On-Line Creativity and Conceptual Change in Science." Pp. 461–93 in T. B. Ward, S. M. Smith, and J. Vaid, eds., *Creative Thought*. Washington, D.C.: American Psychological Association.

Edwards, Derek, and David Middleton. 1986. "Conversation with Bartlett." *Quarterly Newsletter of the Laboratory of Comparative Human Cognition* 8(3):79–89.

ENI. 1921. *Encyclopaedie van Nederlandsch-Indie*. 2nd edition. The Hague: M. Nijhoff.

Errington, Joseph. 1982. "Speech in the Royal Presence: Javanese Palace Language." *Indonesia* 34:89–101.

———. 1984. "Self and Self-Conduct among the Javanese *Priyayi* Elite." *American Ethnologist* 11:275–90.

―――. 1988. *Structure and Style in Javanese*. Philadelphia: University of Pennsylvania Press.

Everett, William. 1987. "Text-Painting in the Foreground and Middleground of Paul McCartney's Beatle Song, *She's Leaving Home:* A Musical Study of Psychological Conflict." *In Theory Only* 9(7):5–21.

Feinstein, Alan. 1995. "Construction of Javanese Tradition." Paper presented at the First Conference of the European Association for South-East Asian Studies, Leiden.

Feld, Steven. 1974. "Linguistic Models in Ethnomusicology." *Ethnomusicology* 18:197–217.

―――. 1981. "'Flow Like a Waterfall': The Metaphors of Kaluli Musical Theory." *Yearbook for Traditional Music* 13:22–47.

―――. 1984 [1994]. "Communication, Music, and Speech about Music." *Yearbook for Traditional Music* 16:1–18. Reprinted as pp. 77–95 of Keil and Feld 1994.

―――. 1988 [1994]. "Aesthetics as Iconicity of Style, or 'Lift-up-over-sounding': Getting into the Kaluli Groove." *Yearbook for Traditional Music* 20:74–113. Reprinted as pp. 109–50 of Keil and Feld 1994.

Fink, Robert. 1999. "Going Flat: Post-Hierarchical Music Theory and the Musical Surface." Pp. 102–37 in Cook and Everist 1999.

Fiske, Susan, and Patricia Linville. 1980. "What Does the Schema Concept Buy Us?" *Personality and Social Psychology Bulletin* 6(4):543–57.

Florida, Nancy. 1995. *Writing the Past, Inscribing the Future*. Durham: Duke University Press.

Fux, Johann Joseph. 1965. *The Study of Counterpoint*. Translated and edited by Alfred Mann. Revised edition. New York: W. W. Norton.

―――. 1992. "*Gradus ad Parnassum* (1725): Concluding Chapters." Translated and introduced by Susan Wollenberg. *Music Analysis* 11:209–43.

Gay, Leslie C., Jr. 1998. "Acting Up, Talking Tech: New York Rock Musicians and Their Metaphors of Technology." *Ethnomusicology* 42:81–98.

Geertz, Clifford. 1960. *The Religion of Java*. Chicago: University of Chicago Press.

―――. 1983. "'From the Native's Point of View': On the Nature of Anthropological Understanding." Pp. 55–70 in *Local Knowledge: Further Essays in Interpretive Anthropology*. New York: Basic Books.

―――. 1995. *After the Fact: Two Countries, Four Decades, One Anthropologist*. Cambridge, Mass.: Harvard University Press.

Gentner, Dedre, Brian Bowdle, Philip Wolff, and Consuelo Boronat. 2001. "Metaphor Is Like Analogy." Pp. 199–253 in D. Gentner, K. Holyoak, and B. Kokinov, eds., *The Analogical Mind*. Cambridge, Mass.: MIT Press.

Gessele, Cynthia. 1989. "The Institutionalization of Music Theory in France: 1764–1802." Ph.D. dissertation, Princeton University.

Gibbs, Raymond W., Jr. 1994. *The Poetics of Mind: Figurative Thought, Language, and Understanding*. Cambridge: Cambridge University Press.

―――. 1996. "Why Many Concepts Are Metaphorical." *Cognition* 61:309–19.

―――. 1997. "How Language Reflects the Embodied Nature of Creative Cognition." Pp. 351–73 in Ward, Smith, and Vaid 1997.

Gilbert, Stephen E. 1995. *The Music of Gershwin.* New Haven: Yale University Press.

Gjerdingen, Robert. 1988. *A Classic Turn of Phrase.* Philadelphia: University of Pennsylvania Press.

Grady, Joseph, Todd Oakley, and Seana Coulson. 1999. "Blending and Metaphor." Pp. 101–24 in G. Steen and R. Gibbs, eds., *Metaphor in Cognitive Linguistics.* Philadelphia: John Benjamins.

Grant, Cecil Powell. 1977. "The Real Relationship between Kirnberger's and Rameau's Concept of the Fundamental Bass." *Journal of Music Theory* 21:324–38.

Guck, Marion. 1994. "Analytical Fictions." *Music Theory Spectrum* 16:217–30.

Hanslick, Eduard. 1891 [1986]. *On the Musically Beautiful.* Translated and edited by Geoffrey Payzant. Indianapolis: Hackett.

Harwood, Dane. 1976. "Universals in Music: A Perspective from Cognitive Psychology." *Ethnomusicology* 20:521–33.

Hastanto, Sri. 1985. "The Concept of Pathet in Central Javanese Gamelan Music." Ph.D. dissertation, University of Durham.

Hatch, Christopher, and David W. Bernstein. 1993. *Music Theory and the Exploration of the Past.* Chicago: University of Chicago Press.

Hauptmann, Moritz. 1853 [1888]. *The Nature of Harmony and Meter.* Translated and edited by W. E. Heathcote. London: Swan Sonnenschein.

Heinichen, Johann David. 1728 [1994]. *Der Generalbass in der Komposition.* Hildesheim: Georg Olms.

Heins, E. L. 1970. "Cueing the Gamelan in Javanese Wayang Performance." *Indonesia* 9:101–28.

Hirschfeld, Lawrence, and Susan Gelman, eds. 1994. *Mapping the Mind.* Cambridge: Cambridge University Press.

Hofstadter, Douglas. 2001. "Analogy as the Core of Cognition." Pp. 499–538 in D. Gentner, K. Holyoak, and B. Kokinov, eds., *The Analogical Mind.* Cambridge, Mass.: MIT Press.

Holyoak, Keith, and Paul Thagard. 1995. *Mental Leaps: Analogy in Creative Thought.* Cambridge, Mass.: MIT Press.

Hood, Mantle. 1954. *The Nuclear Theme as a Determinant of Patet in Javanese Music.* Groningen: J. Wolters.

———. 1971. *The Ethnomusicologist.* New York: McGraw-Hill.

———. 1975. "Improvisation in the Stratified Ensembles of Southeast Asia." *Selected Reports in Ethnomusicology* 2(2):25–33.

———. 1980. *Music of the Roaring Sea.* Wilhelmshaven: Heinrichshofen.

———. 1988. *Paragon of the Roaring Sea: The Evolution of Javanese Gamelan, Book III.* Wilhelmshaven: Noetzel.

Hood, Mantle, and Hardja Susilo. 1967. Text accompanying the LP recording *Music of the Venerable Dark Cloud.* Los Angeles: Institute of Ethnomusicology, UCLA. IE Records IER 7501.

Howell, Julia D. 1977. "Vehicles for the Kalki Avatar: The Experiments of a Javanese Guru in Rationalizing Ecstatic Religion." Ph.D. dissertation, Stanford University.

Hoyt, Peter. 1994. Review of Mark Evan Bonds, *Wordless Rhetoric*. *Journal of Music Theory* 38:123–43.

Hull, David. 1992. "Biological Species: An Inductivist's Nightmare." Pp. 42–68 in Mary Douglas and David Hull, eds., *How Classification Works*. Edinburgh: Edinburgh University Press.

Jardine, Nick. 2000. "Uses and Abuses of Anachronism in the History of the Sciences." *History of Science* 38:251–70.

Jayadipura, R. M. T. 1921. "Katranganing bab gongsa." *Djawa* 1 (Prae-adviezen 2):91–108.

Karmiloff-Smith, A. 1992. *Beyond Modularity*. Cambridge, Mass.: MIT Press.

Keeler, Ward. 1987. *Javanese Shadow Plays, Javanese Selves*. Princeton: Princeton University Press.

Keil, Charles, and Steven Feld. 1994a. *Music Grooves*. Chicago: University of Chicago Press.

———. 1994b. "Dialogue 2: Grooving on Participation." Pp. 151–80 in Keil and Feld 1994a.

Keiler, Allan. 1981. "Music as Metalanguage: Rameau's Fundamental Bass." Pp. 83–100 in Richmond Browne, ed., *Music Theory: Special Topics*. New York: Academic Press.

Keller, Gottfried. 1707. *A Compleat Method for Attaining to Play a Thorough-Bass upon either Organ, Harpsichord, or Theorbo Lute*. London: John Cullen.

Kirnberger, Johann Philipp. 1776–79 [1968]. *Die Kunst des reinen Satzes in der Musik*. Vol. II. Berlin: C. F. Voss. Reprinted: Hildesheim: G. Ohms.

———. 1982. *The Art of Strict Musical Composition*. Translated by David Beach and Jurgen Thym. New Haven: Yale University Press.

Koch, Heinrich Christoph. 1782–93. *Versuch einer Anleitung zur Komposition*. 3 vols. Leipzig, A. F. Böhme.

———. 1802 [1964]. *Musikalisches Lexicon*. Hildesheim: G. Olms.

———. 1811. *Handbuch bey dem Studium der Harmonie*. Leipzig: Hartknoch.

———. 1983. *Introductory Essay on Composition: The Mechanical Rules of Melody, Sections 3 and 4*. Translated by Nancy Kovaleff Baker. New Haven: Yale University Press.

Komisi Pasinaon Nabuh Gamelan ing Paheman Radya Pustaka. 1924. *Buku piwulang nabuh gamelan*. Vol. 1. Surakarta: Swastika.

Korsyn, Kevin. 1988. "Schenker and Kantian Epistemology." *Theoria* 3:44–50.

Koskoff, Ellen. 1982. "The Music Network." *Ethnomusicology* 26:353–70.

Kövecses, Zoltán. 1999. "Metaphor: Does It Constitute or Reflect Cultural Models?" Pp. 167–88 in G. Steen and R. Gibbs, eds., *Metaphor in Cognitive Linguistics*. Philadelphia: John Benjamins.

Krebs, Harald. 1999. *Fantasy Pieces: Metrical Dissonance in the Music of Robert Schumann*. New York: Oxford University Press.

Kunst, Jaap. 1937. *The Music of Java*. Koninklijke Vereeniging "Koloniaal Instituut" Mededeeling no. 43 Afd. Volkenkunde no. 10. Amsterdam: [Koloniaal Instituut].

———. 1973. *Music in Java*. 2 vols. 3rd, enlarged edition. Edited by Ernst Heins. The Hague: M. Nijhoff.

Kursus. 1959. "Kursus Menabuh Gamelan." *Hudan Mas* 1(1):28–30.

Kusumadilaga, K. P. A. 1930. *Serat Sastramiruda.* Solo: Bliksem.

Lakoff, George. 1987. *Women, Fire, and Dangerous Things: What Categories Reveal about the Mind.* Chicago: University of Chicago Press.

———. 1993. "The Contemporary Theory of Metaphor." Pp. 202–51 in Andrew Ortony, ed., *Metaphor and Thought.* 2nd edition. New York: Cambridge University Press.

Lakoff, George, and Mark Johnson. 1980. *Metaphors We Live By.* Chicago: University of Chicago Press.

Lampe, John Frederick. 1737 [1969]. *A Plain and Compendious Method of Teaching Thorough Bass.* New York: Broude Brothers.

Landy, Joshua. 1997. *The Cruel Gift: Lucid Self-Delusion in French Literature and German Philosophy, 1851–1914.* Ph.D. dissertation, Princeton University.

Laudon, Robert. 1992. "The Debate about Consecutive Fifths." *Music and Letters* 73:48–61.

Lawler, Robert. 1981. "The Progressive Construction of Mind." *Cognitive Science* 5:1–30.

Lerdahl, Fred, and Ray Jackendoff. 1983. *A Generative Theory of Tonal Music.* Cambridge, Mass.: MIT Press.

Lester, Joel. 1992. *Compositional Theory in the Eighteenth Century.* Cambridge, Mass.: Harvard University Press.

Lindsay, Jennifer. 1985. "Klasik, Kitsch, or Contemporary: A Study of the Javanese Performing Arts." Ph.D. dissertation, University of Sydney (Australia).

Littlefield, Richard, and David Neumeyer. 1992. "Rewriting Schenker: Narrative—History—Ideology." *Music Theory Spectrum* 14(1):38–65.

McClary, Susan. 1987. "The Blasphemy of Talking Politics during Bach Year." In Richard Leppert and Susan McClary, eds., *Music and Society: The Politics of Composition, Performance, and Reception.* Cambridge: Cambridge University Press.

———. 2000. *Conventional Wisdom: The Content of Musical Form.* Berkeley: University of California Press.

McClary, Susan, and Robert Walser. 1990. "Start Making Sense! Musicology Wrestles with Rock." Pp. 277–92 in Simon Frith and Andrew Goodwin, eds., *On Record.* New York: Pantheon.

McDermott, Vincent, and Sumarsam. 1975. "Central Javanese Music: The Patet of Laras Slendro and the Gender Barung." *Ethnomusicology* 19:233–44.

Malcolm, Alexander. 1721 [1970]. *A Treatise of Musick, Speculative, Practical, and Historical.* New York: Da Capo.

Mangkunagara IV, K. G. P. A. A. 1934. *Serat-serat anggitan-dalem Kangjeng Gusti Pangéran Adipati Ariya Mangkunagara IV.* Vol. 4. Surakarta: Java Instituut.

Marcus, Scott. 1989. "Arab Music Theory in the Modern Period." Ph.D. dissertation, UCLA.

Markoff, Irene. 1986. "Musical Theory, Performance and the Contemporary Baglama Specialist in Turkey." Ph.D. dissertation, University of Washington.

Marsudi. 1988. "An introduction to the slendro gender panerus including cengkok notation." *Balungan* 3(2):24–35.

Martopangrawit, R. Ng. 1968. *Buku: Gojègan ro Kancané.* Typescript.

———. 1972. *Titilaras Kendangan.* Surakarta: Bagian Research, Konservatori Karawitan Indonesia.

———. 1973. *Titiraras Cengkok-cengkok Genderan dengan Wiletannya.* Vol. 1. Surakarta: Akademi Seni Karawitan Indonesia.

———. 1975. *Catatan-catatan Pengetahuan Karawitan.* 2 vols. Surakarta: Akademi Seni Karawitan Indonesia.

———. 1976. *Data-data Sindenan Bedaya dan Srimpi Kraton Surakarta.* Surakarta: Akademi Seni Karawitan Indonesia.

———. 1983. *Gending-gending Martopangrawit.* Surakarta: Akademi Seni Karawitan Indonesia.

———. 1984. "*Catatan-catatan Pengetahuan Karawitan* [Notes on Knowledge of Gamelan Music]." Translated by Martin F. Hatch. In Becker and Feinstein 1984.

———. 1988. *Dibuang Sayang.* Surakarta: Seti-Aji and Akademi Seni Karawitan Indonesia.

Masson, Charles. 1699 [1967]. *Nouveau traité des regles pour la composition de la musique.* New York: Da Capo.

Mattheson, Johann. 1721 [1976]. *Das Forschende Orchestre.* Hildesheim: G. Olms.

Mechelen, Ch. te. 1882. "Drie Teksten van Tooneelstukken uit de Wayang Poerwa." *Verhandelingen van het Koninklijk Bataviaasch Genootschap voor Kunsten en Wetenschappen* 43.

Medin, Douglas, and John Coley. 1998. "Concepts and Categorization." Pp. 403–39 in J. Hochberg, ed., *Perception and Cognition at Century's End.* San Diego: Academic Press.

Medin, Douglas, and Evan Heit. 1999. "Categorization." Pp. 99–143 in B. M. Bly and D. E. Rumelhart, eds., *Cognitive Science.* San Diego: Academic Press.

Medin, Douglas L., E. B. Lynch, and K. O. Solomon. 2000. "Are There Kinds of Concepts?" *Annual Review of Psychology* 51:121–47.

Meyer, Leonard B. 1989. *Style and Music.* Philadelphia: University of Pennsylvania Press.

Mitchell, William J. 1970. "The Prologue to Orlando di Lasso's Prophetiae Sibylarum." *Music Forum* 2:264–73.

Mloyowidodo, S. 1976. *Gending-gending Jawa Gaya Surakarta.* 2 vols. Surakarta: Akademi Seni Karawitan Indonesia.

Monson, Ingrid. 1997. *Saying Something: Jazz Improvisation and Interaction.* Chicago: University of Chicago Press.

———. 1998. "Oh Freedom: George Russell, John Coltrane, and Modal Jazz." Pp. 149–68 in Bruno Nettl and Melinda Russell, eds., *In the Course of Performance.* Chicago: University of Chicago Press.

Morgan, Robert P. 1976. "Dissonant Prolongation: Theoretical and Compositional Precedents." *Journal of Music Theory* 20:49–91.

———. 1978. "Schenker and the Theoretical Tradition: The Concept of Musical Reduction." *College Music Symposium* 18:72–96.

Murphy, Gregory. 1996. "On Metaphoric Representation." *Cognition* 60: 173–204.

———. 1997. "Reasons to Doubt the Present Evidence for Metaphoric Representation." *Cognition* 62:99–108.

Nattiez, Jean-Jacques. 1990. *Music and Discourse: Toward a Semiology of Music.* Princeton: Princeton University Press.

Nawa Windu. 1960. *Nawa Windu Paheman Radyapustaka.* Yogyakarta: Taman Siswa.

Nettl, Bruno. 1974. "Thoughts on Improvisation." *Musical Quarterly* 60:1–19.

———. 1992a. *The Radif of Persian Music.* Revised edition. Champaign, Ill.: Elephant & Cat.

———. 1992b. "Recent Directions in Ethnomusicology." Pp. 375–99 in Myers 1992.

Nettl, Bruno, and Melinda Russell, eds. 1998. *In the Course of Performance.* Chicago: University of Chicago Press.

Newman, William S. 1983. *The Sonata in the Classic Era.* 3rd edition. New York: W. W. Norton.

Niedt, Friedrich Erhardt. 1710. *Musikalische Handleitung oder gründlicher Unterricht.* Hamburg: Benjamin Schillern.

Nooshin, Laudan. 1998. "The Song of the Nightingale: Processes of Improvisation in *dastgah Segah* (Iranian Classical Music)." *British Journal of Ethnomusicology* 7:69–116.

North, Roger. 1990. *Roger North's The Musicall Grammarian: 1728.* Edited by Mary Chan and Jamie Kassler. Cambridge: Cambridge University Press.

Padmosoekotjo, S. 1960. *Ngéngréngan Kasusastran Djawa.* Vol. 2. Yogyakarta: Hien Hoo Sing.

Pastille, William. 1985. "*Ursatz:* The Musical Philosophy of Heinrich Schenker." Ph.D. dissertation, Cornell University.

———. 1990. "The Development of the *Ursatz* in Schenker's Published Works." Pp. 71–85 in Allen Cadwallader, ed., *Trends in Schenkerian Research.* New York: Schirmer.

Perlman, Marc. 1976. "Learning Behavior in the Javanese *Gamelan* as Reflected in the Autobiographies of Three Musicians." MS.

———. 1994. "Unplayed Melodies: Music Theory in Postcolonial Java." Ph.D. dissertation, Wesleyan University.

———. 1997. "Conflicting Interpretations: Indigenous Analysis and Historical Change in Central Javanese Music." *Asian Music* 28(1):115–40.

———. 1998. "The Social Meanings of Modal Practices: Status, Gender, History and *Pathet* in Central Javanese Music." *Ethnomusicology* 42(1):45–80.

———. 1999. "The Traditional Javanese Performing Arts in the Twilight of the New Order: Two Letters from Solo." *Indonesia* no. 68, pp. 1–37.

———. 2001. "Mode V, 4: South-East Asian *Pathet.*" *New Grove Dictionary of Music and Musicians.* 2nd edition. Vol. 16, pp. 844–52. (A revision and expansion of the original entry by Harold S. Powers.)

———. 2004. "The Emergence of the Concept of Chord Root: A Case Study in the Genesis of Music-Theoretic Ideas." *Journal of Music Theory* (forthcoming).

Pinker, Steven. 1999. *Words and Rules: The Ingredients of Language*. New York: Basic Books.

Porter, James, and Ali Jihad Racy. 1988. "Introduction." *Selected Reports in Ethnomusicology* 7:vii–xvii.

Powers, Harold S. 1980. "Language Models and Musical Analysis." *Ethnomusicology* 24:1–60.

———. 1992a. "Is Mode Real? Pietro Aron, the Octenary System, and Polyphony." *Basler Jahrbuch für Historische Musikpraxis* 16:9–52.

———. 1992b. "Modality as a European Cultural Construct." Pp. 207–19 in Rossana Dalmonte and Mario Baroni, eds., *Secondo Convegno Europeo di Analisi Musicale*. Trento: Università degli Studi di Trento.

———. 1992c. "Reinterpretations of Tradition in Hindustani Music: Omkarnath Thakur contra Vishnu Narayan Bhatkhande." Pp. 9–51 in Jonathan Katz, ed., *The Traditional Indian Theory and Practice of Music and Dance*. Panels of the 7th World Sanskrit Conference, vol. 11. Leiden: E. J. Brill.

Pressing, Jeff. 1988. "Improvisation: Methods and Models." Pp. 129–78 in J. Sloboda, ed., *Generative Processes in Music*. Oxford: Clarendon.

Printz, Wolfgang Caspar. 1696. *Phrynis Mitilenaeus*. Dresden: Mieth & Zimmermann.

Rameau, Jean-Philippe. 1722 [1971]. *Treatise on Harmony*. Translated by Philip Gossett. New York: Dover.

Rankin, Susan. 1994. "Carolingian Music." In R. McKitterick, ed., *Carolingian Culture: Emulation and Innovation*. Cambridge: Cambridge University Press.

Reck, David. 1983. "A Musician's Tool-Kit." Ph.D. dissertation, Wesleyan University.

Regehr, G., and L. R. Brooks. 1995. "Category Organization in Free Classification: The Organizing Effect of an Array of Stimuli." *Journal of Experimental Psychology: Learning, Memory and Cognition* 21:347–63.

Rice, Timothy. 1980. "Aspects of Bulgarian Musical Thought." *Yearbook of the International Folk Music Council* 12:43–67.

———. 1994. *May It Fill Your Soul: Experiencing Bulgarian Music*. Chicago: University of Chicago Press.

Ricklefs, M. C. 1998. *The Seen and Unseen Worlds in Java, 1726–1749*. Honolulu: University of Hawaii Press.

Rivera, Benito. 1978. "The *Isagoge* (1581) of Johannes Avianius: An Early Formulation of Triadic Theory." *Journal of Music Theory* 22:43–64.

———. 1980. *German Music Theory in the Early 17th Century: The Treatises of Johannes Lippius*. Ann Arbor, Mich.: UMI Research Press.

———. 1984. "The Seventeenth-Century Theory of Triadic Generation and Invertibility and Its Application in Contemporaneous Rules of Composition." *Music Theory Spectrum* 6:63–78.

Rothstein, William. 1990. "The Americanization of Heinrich Schenker." Pp. 193–203 in H. Siegel, ed., *Schenker Studies*. Cambridge: Cambridge University Press.

Roussier, Pierre-Joseph. 1783. "Lettre aux auteurs de ce Journal, sur l'acception des mots Basse fondamentale, dans le sens des Italiens & dans le sens de Rameau." *Journal Encyclopédique* 56:330–36 (September 1783).

Rustopo. 1990. "Gendhon Humardhani (1923–1983): Arsitek dan Pelaksana Pembangunan Kehidupan Seni Tradisi Jawa yang Modern Mengindonesia." Thesis (S-2), History and the Humanities. Yogyakarta: Gadjah Mada University.

Sakata, Hiromi Lorraine. 1983. *Music in the Mind*. Kent, Ohio: Kent State University Press.

Salzer, Felix. 1967. "Tonality in Early Medieval Polyphony: Towards a History of Tonality." *Music Forum* 1:35–98.

Salzer, Felix, and Carl Schachter. 1989. *Counterpoint in Composition*. New York: Columbia University Press.

Saslaw, Janna. 1996. "Forces, Containers, and Paths: The Role of Body-Derived Image Schemas in the Conceptualization of Music." *Journal of Music Theory* 40:217–43.

Sastrasoewignja, S. 1932. "Het Wondergraf van Kjai Tjakarma." *Djawa* 12: 313–14.

Schacter, Daniel. 1996. *Searching for Memory*. New York: Basic Books.

Schubert, Peter. 1994. "Authentic Analysis." *Journal of Musicology* 12(1):3–18.

Schwarz, K. Robert. 1993. "Nadja Salerno-Sonnenberg: Tough-Talking Bad Girl of the Violin." *Stereo Review* 58(7):78–80 (July 1993).

Sharpe, R. A. 1993. "What Is the Object of Musical Analysis?" *Music Review* 54:63–72.

Shore, Bradd. 1996. *Culture in Mind*. New York: Oxford University Press.

Shuman, Amy, and Charles Briggs. 1993. "Introduction: Theorizing Folklore." *Western Folklore* 52:109–34.

Siegel, James. 1986. *Solo in the New Order*. Princeton: Princeton University Press.

Simpson, Christopher. 1667 [1970]. *A Compendium of Practical Music in Five Parts*. Edited by Phillip J. Lord. Oxford: Basil Blackwell.

Sisman, Elaine. 1982. "Small and Expanded Forms: Koch's Model and Haydn's Music." *Musical Quarterly* 68:444–75.

Sloboda, John. 1985. *The Musical Mind*. Oxford: Clarendon.

Sloman, Steven. 1996. "The Empirical Case for Two Systems of Reasoning." *Psychological Bulletin* 119:3–22.

Small, Christopher. 1998. *Musicking: The Meanings of Performing and Listening*. Hanover, N.H.: Wesleyan University Press.

Smith, Carol, Susan Carey, and Marianne Wiser. 1985. "On Differentiation: A Case Study of the Development of the Concepts of Size, Weight, and Density." *Cognition* 21:177–237.

Snarrenberg, Robert. 1994. "Competing Myths." Pp. 29–56 in A. Pople, ed., *Theory, Analysis and Meaning in Music*. Cambridge: Cambridge University Press.

Soelardi, R. 1918. *Serat Pradongga*. Weltevreden: Widya Pustaka.

———. 1923. "Ajengipun kagunan Jawi." *Pusaka Jawi* 1(9):134–36.

Solie, Ruth. 1980. "The Living Work: Organicism and Musical Analysis." *19th-Century Music* 4:147–56.

Soorjo Poetro, R. M. 1920. "Van de Javaansche muziek en hare verhouding tot andere Aziatische en tot Europeesche muziek." *Nederlandsch Indië, Oud en Nieuw* 5:44–52.

Spalding, Thomas, and Gregory Murphy. 1996. "Effects of Background Knowledge on Category Construction." *Journal of Experimental Psychology: Learning, Memory, and Cognition* 22:525–38.

Stange, Paul. 1984. "The Logic of Rasa in Java." *Indonesia* 38:113–34.

Stock, Jonathan. 1993. "The Application of Schenkerian Analysis to Ethnomusicology: Problems and Possibilities." *Music Analysis* 12:215–40.

Stockhausen, Karlheinz. 1989. *Stockhausen on Music.* London: Marion Boyars.

Stone, Ruth. 1986. "The Value of Local Ideas in Understanding West African Rhythm." *Ethnomusicology* 30:54–57.

Strauss, Claudia, and Naomi Quinn. 1997. *A Cognitive Theory of Cultural Meaning.* Cambridge: Cambridge University Press.

Sudewa, Alexander. 1990. *Serat Panitisastra: Tradisi, Resepsi, dan Transformasi.* Yogyakarta: Duta Wacana University Press.

Sumarsam. 1975. "Inner Melody in Javanese Gamelan Music." *Asian Music* 7(1):3–13.

———. 1976. "Inner Melody in Javanese Gamelan." Master's thesis, Wesleyan University.

———. 1978. "Inner Melody in Javanese Gamelan." Lecture delivered to the students and staff of ASKI Surakarta, 17 February 1978. Typescript.

———. 1984. "Inner Melody in Javanese Gamelan." In Becker and Feinstein 1984.

———. 1995. *Gamelan: Cultural Interaction and Musical Development in Central Java.* Chicago: University of Chicago Press.

Sumrongthong, Bussakorn, and Neil Sorrell. 2000. "Melodic Paradoxes in the Music of the Thai Pi-Phat and Javanese Gamelan." *Yearbook for Traditional Music* 32:67–80.

Supanggah, Rahayu. 1983. "Pokok-pokok Pikiran tentang Garap." Colloquium paper, ASKI Surakarta. September 1983.

———. 1985. "Introduction aux Styles d'Interprétation dans la Musique Javanaise." Thèse redigée en vue de l'obtention de Doctorat de troisième cycle, Université de Paris VII.

———. 1988. "Balungan." Translated by Marc Perlman. *Balungan* 3(2):2–10.

———. 1990. "Balungan." *Seni Pertunjukan Indonesia: Jurnal Masyarakat Musikologi Indonesia* 1(1):115–36.

———. 1994. "Gatra, Inti dari Konsep Gendhing Tradisi Jawa." *Wiled: Jurnal Seni Sekolah Tinggi Seni Indonesia (STSI) Surakarta* 1:13–26.

Suroso Daladi. N.d. *Titilaras Balungan dan Gerongan.* 5 vols. Surakarta.

Sutton, R. Anderson. 1975. "The Javanese Gambang and Its Music." Master's thesis, University of Hawaii.

———. 1978. "Notes Toward a Grammar of Variation in Javanese *Gender* Playing." *Ethnomusicology* 22:275–96.

———. 1979. "Concept and Treatment in Javanese Gamelan Music, with Reference to the Gambang." *Asian Music* 11(1):59–79.

———. 1982. "Variation in Javanese Gamelan Music: Dynamics of a Steady State." Ph.D. dissertation, University of Michigan.

———. 1985. "Commercial Cassette Recordings of Traditional Music in Java." *World of Music* 27(3):23–45.

———. 1986. "New Theory for Traditional Music in Banyumas, West Central Java." *Pacific Review of Ethnomusicology* 3:79–101.

———. 1991. *Traditions of Gamelan Music in Java*. Cambridge: Cambridge University Press.

———. 1993. *Variation in Central Javanese Gamelan Music: Dynamics of a Steady State*. Monograph Series on Southeast Asia, Special Report no. 28. [Dekalb:] Center for Southeast Asian Studies, Northern Illinois University.

———. 1998. "Do Javanese Gamelan Musicians Really Improvise?" Pp. 69–92 in Bruno Nettl and Melinda Russell, eds., *In the Course of Performance*. Chicago: University of Chicago Press.

Suyenaga, Joan. 1984. "Patterns in Process: Java through Gamelan." In S. Morgan and L. Sears, eds., *Aesthetic Tradition and Cultural Transition in Java and Bali*. Madison: Center for Southeast Asian Studies, University of Wisconsin.

Sweetser, Eve. 1987. "The Definition of *Lie*: An Examination of the Folk Models Underlying a Semantic Prototype." Pp. 43–66 in Holland and Quinn 1987.

Tannen, Deborah. 1993. "What's in a Frame?" Pp. 14–56 in *Framing in Discourse*. New York: Oxford University Press.

Taylor, Charles. 1985. "Understanding and Ethnocentricity." Pp. 116–33 in *Philosophy and the Human Sciences. Philosophical Papers*. Vol. 2. Cambridge: Cambridge University Press.

Tirro, Frank. 1967. "The Silent Theme Tradition in Jazz." *Musical Quarterly* 53:313–34.

Tjokro Adi Koesoemo, R. M. T. 1907. "Pengatoeran boeat menambahi kemadjoean bagei orang Djawa." *Tijdschrift voor het Binnenlandsch Bestuur* 33: 454–64.

Turino, Thomas. 1993. *Moving Away from Silence*. Chicago: University of Chicago Press.

Tyler, Stephen. 1969. "Introduction." In S. Tyler, ed., *Cognitive Anthropology*. New York: Holt, Rinehart, and Winston.

Vosniadou, Stella. 1989. "Analogical Reasoning as a Mechanism in Knowledge Acquisition." Pp. 413–37 in S. Vosniadou and A. Ortony, eds., *Similarity and Analogical Reasoning*. Cambridge: Cambridge University Press.

Walser, Robert. 1991. "The Body in the Music: Epistemology and Musical Semiotics." *College Music Symposium* 31:117–26.

Walther, Johann Gottfried. 1732 [1953]. *Musikalisches Lexicon*. Kassel: Bärenreiter.

Walton, Susan. 1987. *Mode in Javanese Music*. Athens, Ohio: Ohio University Center for International Studies.

———. 1996. "Heavenly Nymphs and Earthly Delights: Javanese Female Singers, Their Music and Their Lives." Ph.D. dissertation, University of Michigan.

Ward, Thomas B. 1995. "What's Old about New Ideas?" Pp. 157–78 in S. M. Smith, T. B. Ward, and R. A. Finke, eds., *The Creative Cognition Approach.* Cambridge, Mass.: MIT Press.

Ward, Thomas B., Steven M. Smith, and Jyotsna Vaid. 1997. "Conceptual Structures and Processes in Creative Thought." Pp. 1–27 in T. B. Ward, S. M. Smith, and J. Vaid, eds., *Creative Thought.* Washington, D.C.: American Psychological Association.

Waridi. 1997. "R. L. Martopangrawit, Empu Karawitan Gaya Surakarta: Sebuah Biografi." Thesis (S-2), Graduate School, Gadjah Mada University, Yogyakarta.

Warsodiningrat, R. T. (R. Ng. Prajapangrawit). 1944 [1972]. *Serat Sujarah utawi Riwayating Gamelan (Wéddha Pradongga).* Surakarta: Konservatori Karawitan Indonesia.

———. 1987. "Wédha Pradangga." Translated by Susan P. Walton. In Judith Becker and Alan Feinstein, eds., *Karawitan: Source Readings in Javanese Gamelan and Vocal Music,* vol. 2. Ann Arbor: University of Michigan Center for South and Southeast Asian Studies. Michigan Papers on South and Southeast Asia, no. 30.

Weber, Gottfried. 1817. *Versuch einer geordneten Theorie der Tonsezkunst.* Vol. 1: Grammatik der Tonsezkunst. Mainz: B. Schott.

Weiss, Sarah. 1998. "Paradigms and Anomalies: Female-Style *Gendèran* and the Aesthetics of Central Javanese *Wayang.*" Ph.D. dissertation, New York University.

Werckmeister, Andreas. 1687 [1972]. *Musicae Mathematicae Hodegus Curiosus.* Hildesheim: G. Olms.

———. 1698 [1985]. *Die Nothwendigsten Anmerckungen und Regeln wie der Bassus continuus oder General-Bass wol könne tractiret werden.* Aschersleben: G. E. Struntze.

———. 1702 [1970]. *Harmonologia Musica.* In *Hypomnemata Musica zusammen mit Erweiterte und verbesserte Orgel-Probe, Cribrum Musicum, Harmonologia Musica, Musicalische Paradoxal-Discourse.* Hildesheim: G. Olms.

Whitney, Paul, Desiree Budd, Robert Bramucci, and Robert Crane. 1995. "On Babies, Bath Water, and Schemata." *Discourse Processes* 20:135–66.

Wirawiyaga, M. Ng. 1935–37. *Serat Lagu Jawi.* 3 vols. Surakarta: Sie Dhiam Ho.

Wiser, Marianne, and Susan Carey. 1983. "When Heat and Temperature Were One." Pp. 267–97 in D. Gentner and A. L. Stevens, eds., *Mental Models.* Hillsdale, N.J.: Erlbaum.

Wittgenstein, Ludwig. 1958. *Philosophical Investigations.* Translated by G. E. M. Anscombe. 3rd edition. New York: Macmillan.

Wong, Deborah, and René T. A. Lysloff. 1991. "Threshold to the Sacred: The Overture in Thai and Javanese Ritual Performance." *Ethnomusicology* 35: 315–48.

Wright, Owen. 1978. *The Modal System of Arab and Persian Music, A.D. 1250–1300.* Oxford: Oxford University Press.

Yampolsky, Philip. 1987. *Lokananta: A Discography of the National Recording Company of Indonesia: 1957–1985.* Bibliography Series no. 10. Madison: University of Wisconsin, Center for Southeast Asian Studies.

Zarlino, Gioseffo. 1558 [1968]. *The Art of Counterpoint.* Translated by Guy A. Marco and Claude V. Palisca. New Haven: Yale University Press.

———. 1561 [1999]. *Le Institutioni harmoniche.* Bologna: Arnaldo Forni.

Zbikowski, Lawrence. 2002. *Conceptualizing Music.* Oxford University Press.

Zemp, Hugo. 1978. "'Are'are Classification of Musical Types and Instruments." *Ethnomusicology* 22:37–67.

———. 1979. "Aspects of 'Are'are Musical Theory." *Ethnomusicology* 23:5–48.

Index

Page numbers in italics indicate music examples.

unpredictable divergence and, 65, 69, 72
Sindoesawarno, R. M., 122
singers, 38–39, 209n2, 210n4. *See also* "elaborating" parts; *gérong; pesindhèn*
sitār, 28
siter (zither), 39
sléndro tuning, xv, *xvi*, 40–41, 42; compared with *pélog* tuning, 41–42; conceptual range and, *51*; melodic location of instruments in, *50*; tone measurements for, 41; Western equivalents and, *xviii*, 40, *41*
slenthem (instrument), 38, 212n4. See also *saron* family
"slipping" *(plèsèdan)* motion, 54, 55, 56, 59, 91, 96, 152
Soelardi, R., 122
"soft-sounding" parts, 39, 44, 45, 56–57, *144, 145,* 146. See also *céngkok*
Solie, Ruth, 34
Solonese tradition, and melodic divergence, 64–65, 98
spirituality. *See* mysticism
stereotypes of Orientals, 165
Stockhausen, Karlheinz, 176
structured imagination, 208n14
stylization, 162–63
Suhardi, 9, 127–28; divergence and, 147–48, 167; historical context and, 168, 169–70; interpart relations and, 62, 63, 81–82, 114, 167; *lagu* concept and, 103–4, 111–12, 128–32, *129,* 140–42, 146, 150–52, *151–52,* 154, 156–57, 170, 191, 216n11; memorization and, 103–4
suling (flute), 39
Sumarsam, 8–9, 123, 128, 214n3, 216n10; divergence and, 146–47, 167; *gendèr* technique and, 23; historical context and, 168–69; idea of *balungan* guidance and, 109–10, 124–26; "inner melody" and, 126,

132–37, *135,* 138, 146, 149–50, 154–56, 166, 170; multi-octave *balungan* and, 81; "nuclear theme" idea and, 123–26, 214–15n8; Western theory and, 24, 124–26, 167, 196, 197–98
Sumodarmoko, Bambang, 168
Supanggah, 11, 90, 91, 123, 128, 214n3, 215n7; divergence and, 147–48, 167; "essential *balungan*" and, 137–42, *140–42,* 146–47, 154–56, 170; historical context and, 168, 169
Sutton, Andy, 131–32, 159
symbolism, 162–63, 165–66. *See also* allusiveness in Javanese culture; analogical thinking

tatakrama (etiquette), 160
taxonomy, 202
Taylor, Charles, 199
teaching process: *gendèr* damping technique and, 23–24; learning of nonclassical categories and, 25–28; Suhardi's approach to, 167; Suhardi's *lagu* and, 156–57, 191; Western musical ideas and, 189–90. *See also* musical learning; Suhardi
tembang melodies, 37, 112
thuthukan ("strokes"), 111
timbre, 45
Tjokro Adi Koesoemo, R. M. T., 121
tonic, and chord root idea, 183–86
transcription conventions, xv–xvii
transposition between tuning systems, 40
triad, notion of, 178. *See also* chord root, notion of
trias harmonica, notion of, 179–80, 191
tuning systems. See *laras*
Turahjo Hardjomartono, 10

unplayed melody. *See* implicit-melody concepts

vocal parts. See *gérong; pesindhèn*
vocal texts, 164–65

Text:	10/13 Aldus
Display:	Aldus
Compositor:	Integrated Composition Systems
Printer and Binder:	IBT Global